"Not many people would even think of including the book of Job in a biblical theology of mission. Tim Davy shows how much poorer we have been for that neglect. His wide-ranging and insightful survey illuminates rich biblical themes that undergird missional theology and praxis and shows how mission—the mission of God and the mission of the church—is far more extensive than the traditional and honorable calling of cross-cultural missionaries. This is a major and welcome contribution to both a biblical theology of mission and a missional hermeneutic of Scripture."

—Christopher J. H. Wright, Langham Partnership, author of *The Mission of God: Unlocking the Bible's Grand Narrative*

"In an age of growing chronic illnesses, pandemics, and global austerity, the ancient voice of Job calls out anew to the people of God painting a picture of a just society with YHWH as its good God who cares rightly for all people, even the least and most vulnerable. Tim Davy's brilliant book takes the reader on a life-or-death journey through the land of Uz. As Davy explains, it is indeed that dramatic because if we cannot answer the fundamental questions raised in the book of Job, then the very mission and character of God are at stake. This text is a must-read in the growing field of missional hermeneutics and biblical studies as it creatively and thoroughly bridges the gaps between theology, Bible, and missiology. Even as it builds these bridges, it calls God's people 'back' to a vision and formation of a just society where the poor and the vulnerable are not only cared for but are themselves key participants in God's mission of reconciling the world."

—C. Rosalee Velloso Ewell, Redcliffe College, and the Theological Commission of the World Evangelical Alliance

"This is a carefully researched and accessible book on why and how we can read Job with a missional lens. Tim Davy offers us a fresh approach with his missional reflection on Job. He also aligns it with our universal human experience as he explores questions of unjust suffering, lament, social justice, the nature of who God is, and the issue of poverty. This makes it a book for our times and will challenge some of our assumptions about both God and mission."

—Cathy Ross, Church Mission Society, Oxford, United Kingdom

"At the close of Luke's Gospel Jesus made it clear that the hermeneutical lens through which to read the Old Testament is both christocentric and missional. It is wonderful to see a missional hermeneutic developing among both biblical and mission scholars in the last three or four decades. Tim Davy has played a role in this development and now to see him push this into the wisdom literature and particularly the neglected book of Job is particularly gratifying. This book is a great example of how a missional hermeneutic can open up new insights into Scripture."

—Michael W. Goheen, Missional Training Center, Phoenix, AZ, and Covenant Theological Seminary, St. Louis, MO

"The book of Job is a key resource for thinking about how God acts in ways which we could not expect, and in contexts outside his special covenants. I am delighted that Tim Davy's work is being published, and trust that it will stimulate many more readings in places where people are agonizing like Job or providing unsatisfactory answers like the 'comforters.'"

—Ida Glaser, Centre for Muslim-Christian Studies

"With lucidity and insight, Tim Davy offers something lacking in the scholarship until now: the missional significance of the book of Job within the grand narrative of the Bible. Readers will find here how missional hermeneutics facilitates a fruitful reading of the book of Job. This is an enlightening book—academically substantial, exegetically rigorous, theologically robust, hermeneutically sound, and spiritually enriching."

—Alison Lo, Associate Professor of Old Testament, Bethel Seminary, Arden Hills, MN

"A wonderfully fresh approach to mission which takes seriously the pain of the world and our responsibility to bring this to God. At a time when other, very powerful theologies are promising untold prosperity, *The Book of Job and the Mission of God* provides us with an alternative narrative, a way of asking the big questions, and ultimately a plea to advocate for the poor. By looking at the world through tears, Tim Davy has taken Nicholas Wolterstorff's advice to heart, and in the process has offered us perspectives from the biblical text we could not otherwise see. A fascinating read."

—Ian Stackhouse, Guildford Baptist Church, United Kingdom, author of *Praying Psalms* and *Letters to a Young Pastor*

"What has the book of Job to do with the mission of God? Not very much, it would seem, given the frequent neglect of it in missionary literature, both at a popular level and, more surprisingly, in mission studies scholarship. The profound questions raised by Job do not appear to fit comfortably within hermeneutical approaches to the Bible stressing the progress and triumph of God's mission. Which is one reason why Job's name dare not be spoken in mission studies—until now! Tim Davy not only believes that the bypassing of Job is a mistake, but that in a broken world in which the very questions asked by Job resonate more clearly than ever, it constitutes an indispensable dimension of missionary theology, which in fact lacks authenticity without it. Davy's splendid book, which tackles this subject from many different angles, will make a unique contribution to both missiology and biblical studies, enriching both disciplines and enlarging and deepening the theological foundations of mission in the twenty-first century. It is warmly commended."

—David W. Smith, University of Aberdeen, author of *Mission After Christendom* and *Seeking A City With Foundations*

The Book of Job and the Mission of God

The Book of Job and the Mission of God

A Missional Reading

Tim J. Davy

FOREWORD BY
J. Gordon McConville

PICKWICK *Publications* • Eugene, Oregon

THE BOOK OF JOB AND THE MISSION OF GOD
A Missional Reading

Copyright © 2020 Tim J. Davy. All rights reserved. Except for brief quotations in critical publications or reviews, no part of this book may be reproduced in any manner without prior written permission from the publisher. Write: Permissions, Wipf and Stock Publishers, 199 W. 8th Ave., Suite 3, Eugene, OR 97401.

Pickwick Publications
An Imprint of Wipf and Stock Publishers
199 W. 8th Ave., Suite 3
Eugene, OR 97401

www.wipfandstock.com

PAPERBACK ISBN: 978-1-4982-9739-4
HARDCOVER ISBN: 978-1-4982-9741-7
EBOOK ISBN: 978-1-4982-9740-0

Cataloguing-in-Publication data:

Names: Davy, Tim J., author | McConville, J. G. (J. Gordon), foreword writer
Title: The book of Job and the mission of God : a missional reading / Tim J. Davy, with a foreword by J. Gordon McConville.
Description: Eugene, OR: Pickwick Publications, 2020 | Includes bibliographical references.
Identifiers: ISBN 978-1-4982-9739-4 (paperback) | ISBN 978-1-4982-9741-7 (hardcover) | ISBN 978-1-4982-9740-0 (ebook)
Subjects: LCSH: Bible.—Job—Criticism, interpretations, etc. | Missions—Biblical teaching. | Bible—Hermeneutics.
Classification: BS1415.3 D38 2020 (print) | BS1415 (ebook)

Manufactured in the U.S.A.   OCTOBER 13, 2020

For Joel

Table of Contents

List of Tables xii
Foreword by J. Gordon McConville xiii
Acknowledgements xv
Abbreviations xvii

1. An Introduction to the Book 1
2. The Use of Job in Bible and Mission Scholarship 22
3. Developing a Missional Approach to the Book of Job 61
4. The Universalizing Impulse in the Book of Job 94
5. A Missional Encounter with Cultures in Job 130
6. The Treatment of the Poor in Job 170
7. Summary and Conclusions 219

Bibliography 227

List of tables

Table 1: Frequency and distribution of key poverty terms in Job 175

Foreword

Tim Davy's venture into a "missional" interpretation of the Book of Job puts in focus the question of the place of the Bible in the life of the church. Biblical study long lay in thrall, at least in scholarly circles, to matters of history, philology and literature. Its relation to Theology and church has, as a consequence, been somewhat contested and undefined.

Recent developments in approaches to the use of the Bible, however, have opened up the possibility of various kinds of dialog between Bible, Theology and the church. In interpretation, the accent has shifted markedly towards the subject, that is, the reader or community using the text, as a locus of its meaning. This has allowed the interests of reading communities to flourish within the now generous boundaries of hermeneutics, while opening up new horizons (to use Anthony Thiselton's term) for all who have an interest in reading the Bible. Readers are discovering in fresh ways that the Bible can afford unexpectedly acute commentary on modern issues in politics, gender and the natural world, among others. This is true for readers within the church as well as outside it.

At the same time, Theology, always necessarily responsive to the changing world, is adapting to the special challenges of modern globalization. A prominent dimension of this is the church's understanding of its mission in a world that is acutely aware of diversity and difference and their claims, and it can be perplexed as to how to engage with them.

Missional interpretation, in this context, is a timely development. A relatively "new kid on the block" in hermeneutical terms, it operates precisely in this interface between modern interpretation and the new challenges to the church. In the theological curriculum, an argument can be made that mission is the uniting and compelling point of its separate strands, since mission is the defining purpose of the church. Missional interpretation asks how our reading of the Bible can serve that purpose.

It understands mission in the broadest sense, as proclaiming that all creation and all truth belong to God, and takes it as a mandate to explore fully what this might mean. The whole Bible is its subject matter, and its premise is not only that mission informs our reading of the Bible, but that the Bible in its full scope informs our concept of mission.

To address the Book of Job in this connection is an astute move. The Old Testament's Wisdom literature in general turns out to be particularly hospitable to the method and fruitful in its results. In Wisdom, as is well known, the story and destiny of Israel moves aside, and space is created for a kind of grappling with the conundrums of life that is international in scope. Solomon, it will be recalled, was wiser than all the sages of the East (1 King 4:29–34), yet in that affirmation the reality of their wisdom is acknowledged. Proverbs famously has strong affinities with the work of the Egyptian sage Amenemope. Wisdom exists, therefore, in the borderlands between the biblical witness to the God of Israel and other ancient attempts to apprehend truth. It is thus potentially a model and rich resource for the modern endeavor to testify to God who, in Christ, "was reconciling the world to himself" (2 Corinthians 5:19), while understanding and hearing the testimonies of others.

Tim Davy has turned the searchlight on the Book of Job in particular, whose action and central character are pointedly located, not in Israel, but in the land of Uz, that is, broadly within that eastern region known for its wisdom. Job only thinly veils a distinctively Israelite theological world, yet gives voice to deep and troubling questions about reality that were felt much more widely. Its agonized refusal of set answers makes it extremely compelling for both theology and mission. Davy has not only enriched our understanding of this great book, but also enhanced the young enterprise of "missional hermeneutics" in the most illuminating way.

J. Gordon McConville
Professor of Old Testament Theology
University of Gloucestershire

Acknowledgements

THIS BOOK IS A revised version of my PhD thesis, completed at the University of Gloucestershire under the supervision of Prof. Gordon McConville, a constant model of wisdom, insight, grace and patience throughout my postgraduate studies. Similarly, Dr. Alison Lo, my second supervisor, consistently offered dedication, enthusiasm and attention to detail. I hope that I will be able to emulate the excellence and integrity they have both modelled to me. I am also grateful to my two examiners, Dr. Ida Glaser and Dr. John Bimson, for their probing questions and encouraging feedback.

Thanks are due to Bible Society and the Tyndale Fellowship for providing financially toward my studies.

It is my privilege to teach at Redcliffe College. Both staff and students, current and former, have journeyed with me through this research and it is all the stronger for their fellowship. I am especially grateful for those who took on extra loads to enable me to take sabbaticals in early 2013 and late 2019. In particular, it has been wonderful to explore missional readings of Scripture with students and colleagues involved in the MA module *Reading the Bible Missionally*, and also through the wider work of the Centre for the Study of Bible and Mission initiative, a collaboration between Redcliffe and Trinity College, Bristol.

Throughout my life my parents have provided a constant example and source of support, for which I will always be grateful.

To Hannah, my wife, words cannot express how grateful I am for your love, patience and support over these years: may we enjoy many more. And to Zoe and Luke, I am so very proud of you both and love you to bits.

This book is dedicated to the memory of Joel Samuel Davy, our stillborn son, who came into the world on July 31, 2010. Though he never knew life outside of the womb, he above all people has shaped this work.

Soli Deo gloria

Abbreviations

ABD	*Anchor Bible Dictionary*. 6 vols. Edited by David Noel Freedman. New York: Doubleday, 1992.
ANET	*Ancient Near Eastern Texts Relating to the Old Testament*. 3rd ed. Edited by James B. Pritchard. Princeton: Princeton University Press, 1969.
BDB	Francis Brown, S. R. Driver, and Charles A. Briggs. *Hebrew and English Lexicon of the Old Testament*. Oxford: Clarendon, 1907.
BHS	*Biblica Hebraica Stuttgartensia*. 5th ed. Stuttgart: Deutsche Bibelgesellschaft, 1997.
BSac	*Bibliotheca Sacra*
CBQ	*Catholic Biblical Quarterly*
COS	*The Context of Scripture*. 3 vols. Edited by William W. Hallo and K. Lawson Younger. Leiden: Brill, 1997–2003.
DMT	*Dictionary of Mission Theology: Evangelical Foundations*. Edited by John Corrie. Nottingham: InterVarsity, 2007.
DOTWPW	*Dictionary of the Old Testament: Wisdom, Poetry & Writings*. Edited by Tremper Longman and Peter Enns. Nottingham: InterVarsity, 2008.
ERT	*Evangelical Review of Theology*
ESV	*The Holy Bible: English Standard Version*. Wheaton: Crossway, 2001.
GOCN	*Gospel and Our Culture Network*

IBMR	*International Bulletin of Missionary Research*
IJFM	*International Journal of Frontier Missions*
IRM	*International Review of Mission*
JBL	*Journal of Biblical Literature*
JETS	*Journal of the Evangelical Theological Society*
JSOT	*Journal for the Study of the Old Testament*
JTI	*Journal of Theological Interpretation*
MS	*Mission Studies*
NIDOTTE	*New International Dictionary of Old Testament Theology and Exegesis.* 5 vols. Edited by Willem A. VanGemeren. Carlisle: Paternoster, 1996.
NIV	*The Holy Bible: New International Version: Popular Cross Reference Edition.* London: Hodder & Stoughton, 1992.
NRSV	*The Holy Bible: New Revised Standard Version, Anglicized Edition with Apocrypha.* Oxford: Oxford University Press, 1995.
TB	*Tyndale Bulletin*
TDOT	*Theological Dictionary of the Old Testament.* 14 vols. Edited by G. Johannes Botterweck and Helmer Ringgren. Translated by Geoffrey W. Bromiley et al. Grand Rapids: Eerdmans, 1974–2004.
TLOT	*Theological Lexicon of the Old Testament.* 3 vols. Edited by Ernst Jenni and Claus Westermann. Translated by Mark Biddle. Peabody: Hendrickson, 1997.
ZAW	*Zeitschrift für die Alttestamentliche Wissenschaft.*

1

An Introduction to the Book

"I shall look at the world through tears. Perhaps I shall see things that dry-eyed I could not see." – Nicholas Wolterstorff[1]

IN THIS BOOK I develop and apply a missional hermeneutic to the book of Job; that is, I offer a reading of Job in the light of the missional nature of the Bible. Such a study can be located at the intersection of three scholarly trends that have been evident in recent decades. First, the Christian church's understanding of "mission" developed considerably through the course of the twentieth century with the concepts of *missio Dei* and holistic mission being of particular relevance for this book. Also during the twentieth century and into the twenty-first is the well-documented rise, or resurgence, in scholarly interest in the Wisdom Literature.[2] Finally, and most recently, the last two decades have witnessed the emergence of "missional hermeneutics," an approach to biblical interpretation that seeks to read texts in the light of the missional nature of the Bible.

I will outline the first and third trends in more detail below. Regarding the resurgence of interest in wisdom, it is sufficient to say that this volume contributes to this welcome and sustained re-engagement with biblical wisdom with a particular study on the book of Job and mission. As I will demonstrate, particularly in my review in chapter 2 of the use of

1. Wolterstorff, *Lament for a Son*, 26.

2. See, for example, Crenshaw, *Old Testament Wisdom*, xi, xiii, 1–4; Perdue, *Wisdom Literature*, chapter 1.

Job in Bible and mission scholarship, biblical theologies of mission and related works have tended to neglect the book of Job, and the Wisdom Literature more broadly. In this regard writing on the Bible and mission seems to be lagging behind more general biblical scholarship and so I hope that this book will contribute to a reimagining of how an understanding of the Wisdom Literature may be informed by, and contribute to the church's missional thinking and practice.

I should explain at this stage what I mean by the term "mission." Later in this chapter I will outline my understanding of mission as it relates to the concepts of *missio Dei* and holistic mission. Through this it will become clear that I consider "mission" to be, primarily, an act of God to restore creation to himself. Moreover, it is an activity in which the people of God (whether in the days of the Old or New Testaments or in our own day) are invited, indeed required, to participate. This participation is, I believe, a holistic endeavor, which addresses every aspect of human life in transformational ways. Therefore, while it certainly includes, for example, the traditional notion of "saving souls," mission is not restricted to this.

By "missional" I follow Christopher Wright's use of the term as "simply an adjective denoting something that is related to or characterized by mission, or has the qualities, attributes or dynamics of mission."[3] Apart from the fact that this term reflects current scholarly usage, an advantage of "missional," as opposed to the more traditional adjective "missionary," is that it allows me to speak, for example, of the missional relevance of aspects of Israel's life or theology without necessarily implying that they had the same mandate to "evangelize" that is evident in the New Testament (NT) church.[4] It therefore contributes towards a more nuanced understanding of how mission features in the Old Testament (OT), avoiding reductionist approaches that either dismiss prematurely the existence of mission in the OT or define it in anachronistic ways.[5]

In this introductory chapter I lay the groundwork for the book in several ways. First, I give a rationale for choosing the book of Job. After all, what has Job got to do with mission? In this section I aim to show why Job is not only legitimate as a subject of missional reflection, but

---

3. Wright, *Mission of God*, 24; cf. Kelly, "Biblical Theology and Missional Hermeneutics," 68.

4. This important distinction is helpfully articulated by Wright, *Mission of God*, 25.

5. For an example of a helpful and nuanced approach, see, Okoye, *Israel and the Nations*, 10–12.

compelling, urgent and necessary. I then address some important issues of context for subsequent discussions. In particular I clarify the notions of *missio Dei* and holistic mission, both of which contribute in significant ways to my understanding of mission, and therefore how texts might be read missionally. Finally, I provide a brief, initial orientation to missional hermeneutics, which points to a fuller treatment in chapter 3.

Why Job?

I am convinced that the book of Job is a rich and compelling source of material for biblical reflection on the mission of God, making an important and distinct contribution to missionally relevant questions. My aim in writing this book is, therefore, to demonstrate that by including the book of Job more intentionally and more substantially in our biblical reflection on mission, our appreciation of and engagement with the mission of God can be more enriched.

I will also show how a greater sensitivity to missional questions will lead to an enriched understanding of the biblical text. However, not all scholars connecting the Bible and mission appear to share this optimism concerning Job. In chapter 2 I examine the limited ways in which the book of Job has been referred to by writers working on the relationship between the Bible and mission. On the one hand perhaps this relative lack of engagement is not all that surprising. The particularities and ambiguities of the figure of Job and the book more broadly do present questions which make associating Job with mission a potentially more complex task than some other parts of the Bible. For example, placing Job on the chronological storyline of the Bible, an important step for many writers who see the biblical story as recounting God's redemptive actions in history, is not straightforward. The book does not "progress" the storyline of Israel and makes no explicit mention of covenant, law, monarchy or exodus. It appears to be set (although not written) in patriarchal times yet, more important than this, there is a prominent non-Israelite motif with the action being set in the mysterious land of Uz, and the characters being portrayed as non-Israelites. Put simply, how can events occurring outside Israel to non-Israelites connect to Israel's participation in God's mission? Perhaps, too, Job's anger and claims of righteousness, as well as the somewhat ambiguous portrayal of Yahweh in the Prologue and his speeches, dampen missional interest.

On the other hand, some of these ambiguities are, I would argue, precisely why the book of Job should be considered as such a compelling subject for missional reflection. Job addresses some of the most profound dilemmas faced by humanity, concerning the universal and vexing question of unattributed suffering, and the nature of true piety. As I will argue, the book presents Job as a universalized figure who embodies and expresses the reality of unattributed suffering. He faces the vexing ambiguities of human experience and processes them before God and, in doing so, "speaks to and for all humanity."[6] In him we also see played out an examination of a question that is absolutely critical to the mission of God. When the accuser asks whether Job fears God for no reason in Job 1:9b, he is in effect putting into doubt the validity and meaning of God's mission. If the divine-human relationship is merely one of purchased loyalty is it really a genuine relationship? To what, therefore, is God restoring creation? Is the divine-human relationship "a sham"?[7] Is the mission of God, therefore, a sham? Nowhere else in the Bible is such an acute question asked of God's purposes in the world. In the book of Job, I will argue, the very mission of God is at stake.

As with the Wisdom Literature more generally, a more "international" perspective is evident in Job, not least through the non-Israelite motif and other universalizing themes. In addition, the book of Job exhibits resonances with other explorations of suffering in the Ancient Near East (ANE), while still making a distinct, Israelite contribution to the international conversation. I will go on to show how the existence of intercultural encounters in biblical texts can be suggestive of a missional encounter between competing renderings of reality, and that such encounters are apparent and important in the book of Job.

Finally, in the light of a conceptualisation of mission that encompasses issues of social justice, important missional connections can be made with Job, which includes the treatment of the poor as a significant theme.

In summary, I would articulate four principal reasons why Job is an appropriate and, indeed, compelling subject of study for a missional reading of Scripture. First, as I will demonstrate in chapter 2, Bible and

6. "The author of the Book of Job cannot be precisely placed temporally or geographically, but this is of no great consequence for he speaks to and for all humanity about a problem that has perplexed thinking and feeling men in all times and places" (Pope, *Job*, xxxviii).

7. Brown, *Character in Crisis*, 52.

mission scholarship has not on the whole paid sufficient attention to Job. Many important works on the biblical theology of mission, for example, either do not engage with Job, or do so in relatively peripheral or underdeveloped ways. While there have been a small number of specific examinations of Job and mission, these are carried out with varying degrees of success, and on the whole I suggest that the time is ripe for a more intentional, substantial, sustained and nuanced treatment of the book of Job in the light of the mission of God.

However, this volume is more than an exercise in filling a perceived gap in the literature. Secondly, it seems evident that there are a number of important themes addressed in Job, which connect very clearly with missional concerns, especially when mission is framed holistically and in terms of the *missio Dei*. Themes such as the universal experience of unattributed suffering, questions of social justice, and the articulation of truth about God in the midst of alternative articulations are each missional in their own way. In Pope's phrasing, the book of Job "speaks to and for" the world, which seems to me to be a profoundly missional statement.[8] But how does the book do this and what does it say? These questions should be of the utmost interest to those thinking through and participating in the mission of God. The book of Job, therefore, has much missional potential.

Thirdly, the book of Job makes for a compelling subject of missional study because of its complexity. Many Bible and mission scholars focus their attention on how a particular text functions within the "salvation-history" narrative of the Bible. The book of Job presents challenges to this way of approaching the Bible missionally. How can a book like Job be said to "fit into" the grand narrative of the Bible? What are we to make of the non-Israelite motif evident in the book, with the events occurring outside of Israel to non-Israelites, Job included? What are we to make of the ambiguity of certain characters in the book and of the climax of the book in the speeches of Yahweh, for example? That the book of Job provokes endless fascination and says something compelling about human experience is evident from the voluminous literature on the book, as well as its reception in art, literature, and film.[9] It is my view that Job can also make a fascinating contribution to the study of the Bible and mission. Not least,

---

8. Although he does not use mission terminology in his own discussion; Pope, *Job*, xxxviii.

9. See, for example, Clines, *Job 38–42*, 1377–464; Seow, *Job 1–21*, 110–247; Balentine, *Job*.

as we enter into the grief of the world through Job's experience, perhaps, to appropriate Wolterstorff's language, in looking at the world through Job's tears (and even, perhaps, through our own) we will see things about mission that dry-eyed we could not see.[10]

Finally, the book of Job makes for an important case study in the developing conversation around missional hermeneutics. Although with notable antecedents, the explicit methodology of missional hermeneutics is still relatively new. Advocates for the approach assume, it seems to me, that a missional hermeneutic may be applied to any text of the Bible. While it may be more obvious how to read some texts than others, this book is in part a case study in reading what many would consider to be a less obvious candidate. It is, therefore, something of a test case in this emerging field of study.

It should now be clear what I consider the contribution of this book to be, but it is worth stating explicitly nonetheless. In setting out a missional reading of the book of Job I am contributing to scholarship by: first, addressing the relative weakness of Bible and mission scholarship's engagement with Job by offering a more intentional, substantial, sustained and nuanced treatment of the book in the light of the mission of God; secondly, bringing out more clearly the missional aspects of the book of Job, which will contribute to a furthering of knowledge concerning the book; and thirdly, contributing to the developing conversation around missional hermeneutics by applying it to an untried book, thereby providing, in part, a test case for this emerging method. It is also my hope that the volume will encourage greater and deeper reflection by the church on the book of Job that will inform our thinking and practice concerning the mission of God.

I now need to explain more about this emerging method of missional hermeneutics. However, before I do this two concepts that are essential to my understanding of mission should be explored further: *missio Dei* and holistic mission.

Missio Dei and Holistic Mission

Until near the midpoint of the last century the church's mission was often understood rather narrowly, being interpreted in terms such as

---

10. Wolterstorff, *Lament for a Son*, 26.

individual salvation, and cultural, or ecclesiastical expansion.[11] Through theologians such as Barth and Hartenstein this understanding of mission began to be challenged, however, when a shift occurred from conceptualizing mission as a human activity to viewing it primarily as an activity of the triune God:

> The classical doctrine of the *missio Dei* as God the Father sending the Son, and God the Father and the Son sending the Spirit was expanded to include yet another "movement": Father, Son, and Holy Spirit sending the church into the world.[12]

A defining moment in this seismic shift in mission thinking occurred in 1952 when the concept (though not the term) of *missio Dei* was clearly articulated at the Willingen Conference of the International Missionary Council, with the popularization of the term being established through the publication of Vicedom's 1958 work *The Mission of God: An Introduction to the Theology of Mission*.[13]

With reference to Bible and mission scholarship, and at the request of the World Council of Churches, Blauw produced a survey and assessment of biblical scholarship in the light of this new conceptualizing of the nature and mission of the church, entitled *The Missionary Nature of the Church: A Survey of the Biblical Theology of Mission*.[14] This became "the major work for Bible and mission until the mid-1970s" with perhaps Senior and Stuhlmueller's *The Biblical Foundations for Mission* being the next significant publication on the biblical theology of mission.[15]

The concept of *missio Dei* became broadly accepted across different Christian traditions and became a key way of understanding mission in subsequent decades.[16] Perhaps its appeal lay in part in the breadth of its

---

11. Bosch, *Transforming Mission*, 389. See Goheen, "Continuing Steps," 57.

12. Bosch, *Transforming Mission*, 390. Cf. Pachau, "*Missio Dei*," 233; Bevans and Schroeder, *Constants in Context*, 290.

13. Bosch, *Transforming Mission*, 390; Wright, *Mission of God*, 63. See Vicedom, *Mission of God*. For a critique of some of the ways the development of *missio Dei* has been accounted for, see Flett, *Witness of God*. See also Michael Stroope's critique of the language of mission more generally in Stroope, *Transcending Mission*.

14. Goheen, "Critical Examination," 254. See Blauw, *Missionary Nature*.

15. Goheen, "Critical Examination," 254. See Senior and Stuhlmueller, *Biblical Foundations*.

16. Bosch and Bevans and Schroeder, for example, note its adoption in Protestant, Catholic, and Orthodox circles. See Bosch, *Transforming Mission*, 390–91; Bevans and Schroeder, *Constants in Context*, chapter 9.

scope, having "the divine mystery at its center . . . an open-endedness, leaving room for creative theological exploration of the divine purpose in the world."[17] This certainly seems to be the case in the way it has been adopted in Bible and mission scholarship, opening up more of the Bible for missiological reflection.

However, its breadth has also led to *missio Dei* being taken in different, even contradictory directions, with one school of thought focusing on God's mission as being expressed through the church, while the other prefers to see God's mission as occurring independently of, and even against the church.[18] Despite these developments it seems unnecessary to give up on the notion, as long as it is clear which view of *missio Dei* is intended. I am in agreement with Bosch who still saw the concept as useful, caveats notwithstanding:

> *Missio Dei* has helped to articulate the conviction that neither the church nor any other human agent can ever be considered the author or bearer of mission. Mission is, primarily and ultimately, the work of the Triune God, Creator, Redeemer, and Sanctifier, for the sake of the world, a ministry in which the church is privileged to participate. . . . It is inconceivable that we could again revert to a narrow, ecclesiocentric view of mission.[19]

Also referred to as "integral mission" or "mission as transformation," holistic mission is an understanding of the mission of the church that seeks to hold together (indeed, to integrate) the need to proclaim the message of the gospel and demonstrate it as well, for example, through acts of compassion and social engagement.[20] The relationship between these two activities has been much debated but recent decades have seen a growing (although not wholesale) acceptance that they belong together as an expression of the church's mandate in the world.[21]

---

17. Pachuau, "*Missio Dei*," 233.

18. Pachuau, "*Missio Dei*," 234; Bosch, *Transforming Mission*, 391–92; Skreslet, *Comprehending Mission*, 31–33.

19. Bosch, *Transforming Mission*, 392–93.

20. Although the different terms can emphasize different aspects of the concept, it is sufficient for my purposes to view them as interchangeable. See Tizon, *Transformation After Lausanne*, 93; Woolnough, "Good News for the Poor," 4–6.

21. It is not my intention to go over the history of the debate here. See, for example, Tizon, *Transformation after Lausanne*, chapters 1–4; Sugden, "Mission as Transformation," 31–36; Padilla, "Holistic Mission," 157–58.

In an influential statement on the subject the Micah Network offered the following definition, which has been cited or adopted by related works:

> Integral mission or holistic transformation is the proclamation and demonstration of the gospel. It is not simply that evangelism and social involvement are to be done alongside each other. Rather, in integral mission our proclamation has social consequences as we call people to love and repentance in all areas of life. And our social involvement has evangelistic consequences as we bear witness to the transforming grace of Jesus Christ.[22]

Following the broadening of an understanding of mission achieved through the notion of *missio Dei*, the concept of holistic mission seems an appropriate recognition of a more holistic view of God's work in the world and of human experience.[23] Such a view of mission also widens the range of biblical texts that may be perceived as relating to mission, implying that the whole Bible may be relevant to some degree.

Certain biblical themes are highlighted to explain holistic mission, a crucial one being the idea of the kingdom of God.[24] Woolnough, however, focuses on the Hebrew concept of *shalom* שָׁלוֹם, which he suggests

> is at the heart of [sic] holistic gospel. Thus not only does it propose a way of restoring our relationship with God, but also to mend individual psyches, to bring justice and peace to the political systems between peoples, and to heal our relationship with God's created environment.[25]

This, it seems to me, is a helpful way of framing what God's mission is working to restore. Relating to well-being, health, prosperity, fulfilment, peace and a wholeness of relationships between individuals, communities and nations, the broad connotations of *shalom* שָׁלוֹם address that which is so often lacking in human experience.[26] In this light mission may be understood as God carrying out his restoring purposes

---

22. Micah Network, "*Micah Declaration*," 19.

23. Indeed, it could be argued that the notion of *missio Dei* paved the way—partly, at least—for holistic mission. See, for example, Claydon, "Holistic Mission," 403.

24. See, for example, Tizon, *Transformation after Lausanne*, chapters 5–6.

25. Woolnough, "Good News," 7. His categories of relationships are taken from Myers, *Walking With the Poor*.

26. Nel, "שלם," 130–35.

in creation, a process which, from a human perspective, works towards *shalom* in all areas of life.

The book of Job tells the story of a man (as I will go on to show, an "everyman" figure) who experiences a lack of *shalom*, and does so *in extremis*. To paraphrase the insightful work of Seitz, the book of Job embodies the results of the "something awry" in the world to which mission is God's address.[27]

One further issue needs to be clarified concerning holistic mission as it is of considerable interest to this book. Without wanting to undermine the interconnectedness of many important themes and issues, writing on integral or holistic mission makes particular and consistent reference to the issue of poverty.[28] Indeed, it was on account of a desire to have an understanding of mission theory and practice that better represented the challenges of poverty, injustice, and other social issues that the move towards holistic mission occurred.[29] Representative of this body of literature is Sugden, who summarizes:

> Those proposing the theology and mission of transformation were recovering themes in the bible which had been neglected by the whole evangelical family, themselves included.
> These themes were the place of the poor in the proclamation and demonstration of the good news: what did good news to the poor really mean, the definition of the good news as the good news of the kingdom of God, and that the good news had to do with redeeming and reconciling the whole of the world.[30]

I highlight the issue of poverty here in anticipation of work later in the book. In chapter 6 I devote considerable attention to the function of the treatment of the poor in the book of Job. In highlighting poverty as a key concern of holistic mission I demonstrate that my choice of that particular theme has not been arbitrary but derives from the very heartbeat of my conception of mission. It is also worth noting that, as part of the

---

27. Seitz, *Figured Out*, 147, 157.

28. See, for example, Wright, *Cape Town Commitment*, 21, 27–29, 42–44; Tizon, *Transformation after Lausanne*, 94, 141–45; Padilla, "Holistic Mission," 159, 161; Claydon, "Holistic Mission," 402–4; Sugden, "What is Good about Good News," 236–60; Woolnough, "Good News," 3–14.

29. See Tizon, *Transformation after Lausanne*, chapters 1–4; Padilla, "Holistic Mission," 157–58.

30. Sugden, "Mission as Transformation," 32.

increasing interest in the Wisdom Literature noted above, scholars have paid greater attention to issues of wealth and poverty in these texts.[31]

Missional Hermeneutics

As I will demonstrate the term "missional hermeneutics" covers a variety of approaches but it can be broadly defined as an approach to biblical interpretation that seeks to read texts in the light of the missional nature of the Bible. In chapter 3 I provide a more developed treatment of the different ways in which the concept of missional hermeneutics has been understood, and how these may relate to a reading of the book of Job. However, at this stage, a brief orientation to what I mean by the missional nature of the Bible would be useful.[32]

The Missional Nature of the Bible

"Missional," it has been argued, characterizes the emergence, content, and purpose of the biblical writings.[33] These ideas require some unpacking. In so doing I provide a context from which to understand further discussion of the missional hermeneutics approach. I also use these categories in the book's conclusion to demonstrate how my work has brought into sharper focus the missional nature of the book of Job.

---

31. There has been a particular interest in the topic as it occurs in the book of Proverbs. See, for example, Sandoval, *Discourse of Wealth and Poverty*, 2: "Only recently, however, has intensive and extensive work having to do with matters of wealth and poverty in specifically wisdom texts begun"; Whybray, *Wealth and Poverty in the Book of Proverbs*; Pleins, "Poverty in the Social World of the Wise," 61–78; Washington, *Wealth and Poverty*; Leeuwen, "Wealth and Poverty," 25–36; Wittenberg, "Terminology for 'Poor' in the Book of Proverbs," 40–85. See also, Míguez-Bonino, "Poverty as Curse, Blessing, and Challenge," 3–13; Gutiérrez, *On Job*; Ruíz Pesce, "Dios del Pobre," 207–20; Ceresko, *Psalmists and Sages*, 180–94; Susaimanickam, "Dalit Reading of the Book of Job," 181–200; Grenzer, "Armenthematik," 229–78.

32. It is beyond the scope of this book to account for the historical development of the approach of missional hermeneutics, and it has been covered helpfully elsewhere. See, for example, Goheen, "History and Introduction to a Missional Reading"; Hunsberger, "Mapping the Missional Hermeneutics Conversation." See also my "Missional Hermeneutics Bibliography," co-written with Michael Goheen.

33. Following the language of Wright, Goheen, and others.

The Emergence of Biblical Texts as "Missional": The Bible as a "Product" of Mission

By "emergence" I am referring to both the very existence of the biblical writings, and also the conditions and processes by which they originated and were gathered together.

Assuming a certain theological commitment and perspective on the nature of the Bible and divine inspiration, the Bible could be described as saying something about God's mission simply by its existence.[34] The Bible can be understood as a "product" of God's mission partly because its existence is evidence of a God who desires to be known and takes the necessary initiative to enable that to happen.[35] Although this depends on at least some confessional commitment to the divine inspiration of the Bible, it is nevertheless entirely consistent within that understanding and, in my view, provides a helpful context for understanding other aspects of the missional nature of the Bible. This also relates to the function of the Bible as a means by which God's mission is carried out, which I address below.

A second aspect of the missional nature of the emergence of the biblical writings concerns the origins of particular texts. The Bible is also a "product" of mission in that many of the circumstances out of which the biblical writings emerged could be termed as "missional":

> Events or struggles or crises or conflicts in which the people of God engaged with the constantly changing and challenging task of articulating and living out their understanding of God's revelation and redemptive action in the world. Sometimes these were struggles internal to the people of God themselves; sometimes they were highly polemical struggles with competing religious claims and worldviews that surrounded them.... The text itself is a product of mission in action.[36]

This understanding of the origins of the biblical texts seems helpful, acknowledging as it does the intercultural dynamic of the biblical writers' environments, the theme of conflict as a context for emerging texts, and the struggles within the community of the people of God, as well as from

---

34. Wright, *Mission of God*, 48. See also Taber, "Missiology and the Bible," 231–33; Wright, *Scripture and the Authority of God*, 23.

35. Taber, "Missiology and the Bible," 232; cf. Kelly, "Biblical Theology and Missional Hermeneutics," 68.

36. Wright, *Mission of God*, 49.

external pressures, though of course the two may overlap (for example, with the temptation to syncretism).

Marshall's description of the NT as "the documents of mission" seems apposite here.[37] The writings of the NT were the result of the mission of Jesus and his followers, proclaiming and explaining the gospel, seeking to shape the church and address issues that may be hindering the progress of the gospel:

> In short, people who are called by God to be missionaries are carrying out their calling by the writing of Gospels, letters and related material. They are concerned to make converts and then to provide for their nurture, to bring new believers to birth and nourish them to maturity. . . . They are at one and the same time the product of a dynamic process of evangelism and nurture, and the tools for accomplishing that process.[38]

To give some examples, the Gospels were written to explain the "good news" of the death and resurrection of Jesus, and Luke-Acts even has a missional shape about it with "witness to the nations" being a key theme at the end of Luke and the beginning of Acts.[39] In his letters the apostle Paul seeks to shape the communities of the early church for their participation in God's mission by dealing with discussions of the Gentile mission, Greek-influenced polytheism, internal theological disputes, and so on.[40] Finally, the book of Revelation sought to shape church communities as they struggled in the face of external pressures and internal disputes.[41]

It seems reasonable, therefore, to suggest that the writings of the NT reflect missional contexts. But could the same be said of the OT? The accounts in Genesis 1–11, for example, are often considered to have, in part at least, a polemical function against (especially) Babylonian origin stories and, therefore, religious beliefs.[42] The events of the exodus may be seen as a confrontation between Yahweh and Pharaoh's false claims

---

37. Marshall, *New Testament Theology*, 34.
38. Marshall, *New Testament Theology*, 35–36.
39. Wright, *Mission of God*, 49.
40. Wright, *Mission of God*, 49.
41. Senior and Stuhlmueller, *Biblical Foundations*, 302–5; Flemming, "Revelation and the *Missio Dei*."
42. Wright, *Mission of God*, 50; Wenham, *Genesis 1–15*, xlvi–l; Walton, *Genesis*, 27–35; McConville, *God and Earthly Power*, 23.

to deity and ownership of Israel.[43] Moreover, drawing on conceptions of mission by Seitz ("Getting at the something awry") and Bauckham (as being closely associated with the movement between the particular and the universal), Blackburn has demonstrated that the book of Exodus can be understood to have a "missionary heart" in that it accounts for a part of the story in which God attempts "to make himself known among the nations" and that Israel's election had a universal goal.[44]

An important theme running through particularly the historical and prophetic books is the struggle of Israel to resist the temptations and threats of the Canaanite Baal religion.[45] While some may interpret the Baal imagery applied to Yahweh as an instance of demythologizing, texts such as 1 Kings 17–19 or the book of Hosea are suggestive of a clear polemic against Baalism and so it seems reasonable to discern this tendency more broadly in the OT.[46]

The shattering experience of the exile and Israel's subsequent return to the land produced biblical writings that sought to articulate Israel's identity and role as God's people in new and uncertain times and "under the shadow of foreign empires."[47] Isaiah's strong polemic against the idols of Babylon (Isa 40–48) and vision concerning God's purposes for the world mediated through his servant (Isa 49:1–7; 52:13–53:12) are two examples in that particular book.[48]

Clearly the Wisdom Literature is of particular interest in this study and will be dealt with in much more detail below. It will suffice, however, at this stage to note that the wisdom writers engaged with wisdom

---

43. Wright, *Mission of God*, 50; Enns, *Exodus*, 196, 200, 205, 228–229, 245, 299.

44. Blackburn, *God Who Makes Himself Known*, 16–18. See also Wright, *Mission of God*, chapter 3; Seitz, *Figured Out*, 147, 157; Bauckham, *Bible and Mission*, 11.

45. See, for example, Chisholm, "Polemic Against Baalism"; Day, "Baal (Deity)"; Endris, "Yahweh versus Baal"; Wright, *Mission of God*, 50.

46. Chisholm, "Polemic Against Baalism," 268; cf. Day, "Baal (Deity)," 547–48; Preuss, *Old Testament Theology*, 72; McConville, *God and Earthly Power*, 158–59. Indeed, as is so clearly evidenced—for example, in the book of Hosea—the application of Baal language to Yahweh is carried out in the context of a polemic against the Baal cult so that the very borrowing of a competing rendering's language functions as a way of critiquing it. See Day, "Baal (Deity)," 549. See also Macintosh, *Hosea*, 219, although he speaks more of an "appropriating to Yahwism elements of Canaanite religion which, properly understood, belong to it."

47. Wright, *Mission of God*, 50.

48. See, for example, Wright, *Mission of God*, 140, 237–38; Schultz, "Nationalism and Universalism in Isaiah," 135–37.

traditions of other cultures, employing both acceptance and critique.[49] This raises an important element of this dimension which is the need to recognize that the intercultural engagement by the biblical writers was not always negative. As I will demonstrate, particularly in chapter 3, while the rendering of reality articulated in the Bible is ultimately being told over and against alternative renderings, the biblical writers were still at liberty to affirm (either implicitly or explicitly) elements of other belief systems that were in line with their own experience and beliefs.

The point is not that a missionary intention should be articulated in every book in the OT or NT. Rather, that the biblical writings evidence an engagement by their authors and editors with issues and circumstances that could be understood in missional terms. Clearly some elements of this argument are based on a certain way of defining Israel's "missional" function. Viewed in this way, however, the biblical writings can be understood, among other things, as responding to missional circumstances, or as the results or "products" of mission.

To speak about the circumstances or events that prompted the emergence of biblical writings may, in my view, refer to various stages in the development of a text. For example, it could be applicable to the circumstances that prompted its original teaching (perhaps in oral form); its being written down; its editorial shaping; and its inclusion in the canon.[50] While the precise details of the stages of emergence of biblical writings may be unclear at times, what does seem evident is that the texts of the Bible emerged out of the context of struggle; a struggle to articulate the truth about Yahweh and his ways with the world, and the place of Israel within those purposes. This process, it seems to me, can be understood as missional.

As part of this book I will seek to probe the missional nature of the emergence of the book of Job. While there is much ambiguity surrounding its origins, particularly in relation to its dating and literary unity, my main focus in this regard will be to investigate the nature of the intercultural encounter in the book, including how it relates to similar texts and beliefs within the international conversation on the subject of suffering. I will also reflect on the significance of there being a book of Job; that is, the significance of such a sustained, probing examination of suffering being included in the canon.

49. Wright, *Mission of God*, 50.
50. See Beeby, *Canon and Mission*.

The Content of the Biblical Texts as "Missional": The Bible as a Record of Mission

As well as the missional nature of the contexts and processes of the emergence of biblical writings, the content of the Bible may also be understood as missional. By this I mean that the Bible may be understood to render to the reader a complex-yet-coherent overarching narrative that describes, records, or witnesses to the mission of God.[51]

The idea of the Bible telling the story of God's mission is particularly important to advocates of missional hermeneutics, and usually centers on the concept of the *missio Dei*.[52] It is this broad definition of mission that enables Wright, for example, to state boldly that the content of the Bible revolves around mission, which becomes the foundational assumption of missional hermeneutics.[53] The *missio Dei*, therefore, is the driving force behind the biblical story, the focal point of coherence for the biblical story, and the chief purpose of the biblical story. The Bible, then, tells the story of God's actions in the world.[54]

Put very briefly, in a narrative approach the Bible tells the story of God, who creates the universe, including humanity, sees humanity rebel against his rule and seeks to set this rebellion right by calling a man, Abram, as a means of blessing to the nations. Abram's descendants become a people, Israel, who enjoy the privileges and responsibilities of covenant life under Yahweh, lived out in the midst of the nations. Yet they too are rebellious and do not live up to their high calling, ultimately being exiled to Babylon and, though they are brought back to the land, are left waiting for a deliverer from Yahweh who would free them from the powers that hold them captive.

As the story progresses to the NT we read about Jesus Christ, God's anticipated deliverer, yet the means by which he would bring deliverance unexpectedly involves sacrifice and suffering, death and resurrection. His followers form the early church and begin to proclaim the good news of

---

51. The language of rendering, describing, recording, or witnessing tend to be used interchangeably to make similar points. See Beeby, "Missional Approach," 272; Goheen, "Continuing Steps," 61; Wright, *Mission of God*, 48; Kelly, "Biblical Theology and Missional Hermeneutics," 68.

52. This broad acceptance of *missio Dei* in missional hermeneutics is correctly observed, for example, by Hunsberger, "Proposals for a Missional Hermeneutic," 312.

53. Wright, *Mission of God*, 29, 51.

54. Cf. Brueggemann, *Theology of the OT*, 33.

God's kingdom. The biblical story ends with a vision of the end of history itself in which the purposes of God are finally and fully carried out.

In chapter 3 I deal with important issues connected with considering the Bible as a narrative, including the nature and validity of treating the biblical canon as a narrative, and the possibility and importance of a biblical "metanarrative" and its relationship to other metanarratives. I also bring out certain characteristics of that narrative such as the particular-universal dynamic; the nature and desirability of ambiguity; and the theme of social justice, all of which have important functions within the book of Job.

As I have already indicated, it will be of crucial importance in this volume to examine the relationship between the book of Job and the grand narrative of the Bible. How does Job function in relation to the *missio Dei*? In particular I will suggest that the importance of Job in this regard is not primarily in how Job fits into the storyline but in how the book stands apart from, and speaks into it. I will show that the crucial issue of genuine piety, expressed most succinctly in Job 1:9b, functions as a way of holding to account the entire project of the *missio Dei*.

The Purposes of Biblical Texts as "Missional": The Bible as the Means by which Mission Is Carried Out

As well as being a product and record of mission the Bible has been understood to function, in part, as a means by which God's mission is carried out.[55] There does not seem to be a single satisfactory term that encapsulates all of the nuances of this idea. Nevertheless, words such as tool, agent or instrument are useful.

One way in which the biblical writings function as an instrument of mission is closely related to the above discussions concerning the missional contexts and processes which led to the emergence of those writings, and the function of the *missio Dei* in Scripture. The biblical texts addressed the people of God in response to circumstances (internal and external) that challenged their identity and role as God's people, called to participate in the mission of God. They shaped the people of God, aligning them to the biblical story, giving order to life and worship, offering rebuke and promise, and enabling them to bring to God the entirety of

---

55. Wright, *Scripture and the Authority of God*, 22, 37–38, 44; Goheen, "Continuing Steps," 90.

their experiences.[56] Understood in the light of the *missio Dei* this process can be framed in terms of shaping God's people for God's mission.[57]

The scriptures, then, were an important means by which God shaped and equipped his people in order to achieve his purposes in and through them. This significant function of the biblical writings, present in the time of Ancient Israel and the early church, is also relevant to the contemporary church as it seeks to be shaped by and for the purposes of God in today's world: "the Bible must continue to confront, to convert, and to transform the community for faithful witness."[58] They place the lives and communities of the people of God, then and now, within the *missio Dei*, demonstrate their role within that overarching narrative, and shape and equip them for those purposes.[59] In this sense we might also describe a function of the Bible as being "generative of mission" in the sense that it spurs on the people of God to realize an active participation in the mission of God.[60] This highlights an important assumption across the literature, that the biblical writings have a compelling, contemporary relevance for the people of God today as they participate in the mission of God. A missional reading of the Bible must therefore lead to action.[61]

A further dimension of the Bible as a means of mission is the sense in which the Bible may exhibit ways in which the people of God's participation in God's mission might be carried out. Traditionally this has been seen, for example, in examining the methods and strategies of the Apostle Paul and determining how these might be normative in contemporary mission contexts.[62]

Given the contextual nature of the biblical events and writings, Bosch seems justified in cautioning against too direct or simplistic an application of "missionary principles or models . . . from isolated texts or passages."[63] Nevertheless, the Bible does contain many instances of

---

56. Wright, *Scripture and the Authority of God*, 22, 27, 29–30. See also Goheen, "Continuing Steps," 91.

57. Goheen, "Continuing Steps," 91.

58. Guder, "Biblical Formation," 62. See also Hunsberger, "Proposals for a Missional Hermeneutic," 313.

59. Bauckham, *Bible and Mission*, 12; Barram, "Social Location," 49.

60. Kelly, "Biblical Theology and Missional Hermeneutics," 71.

61. Bauckham, *Mission as Hermeneutic*, 14.

62. See, for example, Allen, *Missionary Methods*; Plummer and Terry, *Paul's Missionary Methods*.

63. Bosch, "Biblical Models," 188.

God's mission being worked out in the particularities of the biblical writings, which can be reflected upon as the contemporary church seeks to refine its understanding and practice of mission, which will change from generation to generation, and from context to context. Examples of such biblical material could include the ways in which the apostles went about starting and nurturing new congregations in the NT or the intercultural engagement evident in the OT.[64]

In line with these missional dimensions of the purposes of the Bible I must ask, then, how the book of Job sought to shape and equip the people of God for their participation in God's mission. Such a broad theme must be more clearly defined in terms of this book. Within the current scope of this volume I intend to pursue these issues by addressing the significance of the intercultural engagement in the book. I will also examine how the book attempted to shape the ethics of its readers, with specific reference to responding to unattributed suffering and the treatment of the poor.

This brief outline of some of the missional dimensions of the Bible illustrates the complexity of thinking of the Bible as "missional" and goes some way to accounting for the variety of emphases and approaches evident in missional hermeneutics scholarship, as noted above. However, I would suggest that a fuller engagement with the breadth of missional dimensions of the Bible will enable a greater capacity for innovative and fruitful missional reflection on biblical texts, and especially for texts, like the book of Job, that have hitherto been neglected.

An Outline of the Book

Having set out a number of important background issues and given an explanation and rationale for this study I conclude this introductory chapter with an outline of the rest of the book.

Chapters 2 and 3 continue the theme of approaching a missional hermeneutic for the book of Job. In chapter 2 I examine the extent to which and the ways in which Job has been engaged with in Bible and

---

64. As examples of the latter, see Glaser, *Bible and Other Faiths*, 59–66; Ruiter, *Single Hand*. It is worth, too, acknowledging the significant role the Bible has played in the history of Christian mission—for example, relating to the work of Bible translation. See Skreslet, *Comprehending Mission*, 36–37. In this sense we might also describe the Bible's missional instrumentality in terms of how it is used as an "artifact" of mission activity in that it is used by the Church as one of the ways of communicating the Christian gospel.

mission scholarship up to this point. This will show that a significant proportion of writing on the Bible and mission either omits Job entirely or cites texts from Job in a rather peripheral way to illustrate points in much broader discussions. Secondly, when writers do pay more attention to Job their treatment is often rather brief and could not be said to be engaging in a thorough and sustained way with the book on its own terms. Of particular significance, in my view, is where this occurs in work that aims to present a biblical theology of mission; that is, to articulate an understanding of mission that represents the canon of Scripture as a whole, or at least either the OT or NT. Thirdly, while there are some scholars who attempt to engage with the book of Job in a more intentional, specific and substantial way, they still leave significant room for considering how the book of Job might be read missionally. Throughout chapter 2 I connect the survey with my own reading of Job, showing how I will build on the strengths I see in the literature and how I will address perceived gaps, weaknesses and underdeveloped themes.

Chapter 3 then builds on this survey by showing how a missional framework for reading the book of Job can be developed. I do this by focusing on the missional hermeneutics scholarship introduced in the current chapter, working through different facets of the emerging conversation in order to isolate particularly useful lines of inquiry for my own work. Select aspects of missional hermeneutics highlighted by the GOCN Forum on Missional Hermeneutics are instructive here, although I move beyond them in places, seeking to engage with them critically, while also assessing their potential and problems as I seek to relate them to the book of Job. I conclude chapter 3 with some clear lines of inquiry for a missional reading of Job, which I then pursue in the remaining chapters of the study.

Chapters 2 and 3 therefore set up my missional reading of Job but in doing so they also begin that reading. These initial connections with Job then pave the way for the second half of the volume, applying a missional hermeneutic to the book of Job. Here I focus three substantial chapters on the pursuit of particular lines of inquiry for a missional reading of Job. In chapter 4 I examine what I term the "universalizing impulse" in the book, focusing on the Prologue with its prominent non-Israelite motif and the crucial, universally important question posed by the accuser, "Is it for nothing חִנָּם that Job fears God?" (Job 1:9b). In chapter 5 I discuss the intercultural engagement of the book as it relates to similar texts and ideas of the ANE. As such I aim to show evidence of a missional encounter between Job and alternative renderings of reality.

Chapter 6 then develops my missional reading of Job by examining a particular theme that, as I have shown, is a particular concern in a holistic understanding of mission: the treatment of the poor. Here I examine how poverty functions in Job, with a special treatment of three texts which each exhibit a concentration of poverty language: Job 24:1–17; 29:11–17; and 31:13–23. I also take to the text the themes of chapters 4 and 5 and show how the missional understanding of Job plays out through a concrete theme.

In the final chapter I offer a summary and conclusion to the study in which I draw together the principal findings of my missional reading of Job. This is done, in part, by returning to the idea of the missional nature of the Bible outlined in this introductory chapter and considering, in the light of my work, the ways in which the book of Job may be considered "missional." I will also offer suggestions for further research.

2

The Use of Job in Bible and Mission Scholarship

THIS CHAPTER MOVES TOWARDS my own missional reading of Job, by examining in more detail the extent to which and the ways in which relevant scholarship has engaged with the book in the light of God's mission. Such a survey enables me to consider previous thinking, highlight recurring themes, and identify strengths, weaknesses, gaps and underdeveloped areas. It will also inform the discussion in chapter 3, in which I look specifically at the lines of inquiry pursued by missional hermeneutics scholars in order to develop my own missional approach to Job.

Initially I consider the relative neglect of Job in Bible and mission scholarship, while also recognizing that there are legitimate reasons why a study may not turn to that particular book.[1] Noting some prominent examples, I show that a significant proportion of BMS either does not mention Job, or does so in rather peripheral and underdeveloped ways. Of particular significance, in my view, is the book's omission or neglect among scholars who aim to convey a whole-Bible foundation for mission.

I then turn to instances where Job receives more attention and identify a number of recurring themes, and consider how these topics may feature in my own treatment of Job, thereby illustrating both the continuity and distinctiveness of my reading of the book.

Overall the chapter demonstrates that, while there is precedent for missional reflection on Job, often this has been carried out in rather

---

1. Henceforth, "Bible and Mission Scholarship" will be referred to as BMS.

limited and underdeveloped ways. The book of Job, I conclude, remains a relatively untapped resource for missional reflection.

I should clarify the criteria I use in my survey to identify and examine appropriate literature. I have taken BMS to refer to scholarly works that attempt to discuss the Bible in relation to the mission of God. Of particular significance is the extent to which and the ways in which "biblical theologies of mission" engage with Job. To pursue this I have given special attention to articles or books that aim to present an outline, foundation or basis of Christian mission (however the author defines it) from the OT or Bible as a whole.

What is presented here is selective and representative of the field.[2] I begin the survey with works that have little or no reference to the book of Job.

The Relative Neglect of Job in BMS

A low level of engagement with Job can be observed in BMS throughout the twentieth century and into the twenty-first. An initial observation is that the choice of OT texts examined tends to focus on the Pentateuch, Psalms and Prophets, thereby sidelining books like Job.[3]

For example, despite claiming to have traced the idea of mission through "every part" of the OT, Glover makes no mention of Job or the Wisdom Literature more broadly in the chapter "The Bible and Missions: The Missionary Character of the Scriptures."[4] Elsewhere Glover cites Job as an example of a biblical character who received an "exalted vision of [God], with profound spiritual results," although little is made of this connection.[5]

Wright's 1961 essay on the OT and mission found no place for Job in its three "perspectives" on the subject, which dealt with texts concerning

---

2. For valuable—if much briefer—attempts to do this, see Wilson, *Job*, 379–82; Wilson, "Job as a Problematic Book," location 1417–39.

3. See, for example, Bashford, *God's Missionary Plan*, 43–57; Carver, *Missions*; Carver, *Missionary Message*; Rowley, *Missionary Message*; Bavinck, *Science of Missions*, chapter 2; Peters, *Biblical Theology*; Kane, *Christian Missions*; Kaiser, *Mission in the OT*; Seitz, *Figured Out*, chapter 11.

4. Glover, *Bible Basis*, 21.

5. Glover, *Bible Basis*, 188.

the redemption of the world, God's actions, and OT themes that may be problematic for mission.[6]

Blauw's *The Missionary Nature of the Church* contains no references to Job or Ecclesiastes, instead focusing on a nuanced discussion concerning the relationship between universalism and mission, followed by an examination of eschatological and messianic texts, particularly in the Prophets and Psalms.[7] While Blauw does engage with Proverbs and wisdom more generally, his conclusion seems particularly apposite in the context of this survey: "It seems to me that so far the wisdom literature has not received the attention it deserves, particularly in missionary science."[8]

Bosch's landmark *Transforming Mission* contains under four pages on mission in the OT and so his discussion is very limited, concentrating especially on Isaiah and themes such as the legitimacy of speaking of mission in the OT, Israel's God acting in history, covenant and election, the role of the nations, and eschatology.[9]

Köstenberger and O'Brien focus on texts that relate "in a significant way to the proclamation of God's name and of his saving purposes in Christ to the unbelieving world."[10] As such, in their single chapter on the OT they pay particular attention to texts and themes relating to the promises to Abraham and, as a consequence, the book contains no references to Job.[11]

Okoye's conception of the four aspects or "faces" of mission in the OT leads him to consider a range of texts: Yahweh's universality (focusing on Gen 1, 12 and Ps 8); Israel as a community-in-mission (Exod. 19; Amos and Jonah); centripetal mission (Ps 96; Isa 2); and centrifugal

---

6. Wright, "OT Basis," 17–30.

7. Blauw, *Missionary Nature*, chapters 1–3.

8. Blauw, *Missionary Nature*, 62.

9. Bosch, *Transforming Mission*, 16–20. Bosch's lack of attention to the OT in *Transforming Mission* is often noted. See, for example, Wright, "OT and Christian Mission," 37; Bekele, "Biblical Narrative of the *Missio Dei*," 155. For Bosch's works that do engage more with the OT, see, for example, Bosch, *Witness to the World*; "Why and the How," 33–45; "Scope of Mission," 17–32; "Biblical Perspective"; "Towards a Hermeneutic," 65–79; "Scope of the 'BISAM' Project," 61–68; "Biblical Models." On Bosch's use of the book of Job, see Bosch, "Vulnerability of Mission," 351–63, which is dealt with below.

10. Köstenberger and O'Brien, *Salvation to the Ends of the Earth*, 21–22.

11. Köstenberger and O'Brien, *Salvation to the Ends of the Earth*, 22.

mission (further texts from Isaiah and Zechariah).[12] As such Okoye does not refer to Job or Ecclesiastes, although he does mention the book of Proverbs in relation to a broader point about the Wisdom Literature, which he sees as "international and universal" in that they omit key Israelite themes such as covenant, election and the law, placing "Israel and the nations on the same footing with respect to the experience of God and the practice of true religion."[13]

Given the context of my study it is also worth highlighting the general lack of engagement with Job in the material usually associated with the developing conversation on missional hermeneutics. However, this is perhaps not surprising, given the approach is still relatively new and has tended until recently to focus on methodological issues and more typical texts.

Concerning the representative works surveyed up to this point, it is clear that much BMS does not engage significantly with the book of Job. While scholars may differ over the extent to which they explore OT texts, and their approaches for doing so, certain texts such as Genesis, Exodus, the Psalms and the Prophets (notably Isaiah) receive considerably more attention than other books. While the importance of these texts makes such a trend understandable, the effect of such a concentration is that less obvious texts often fall by the wayside or are treated rather sporadically.

Although I note, above, certain factors for the omission or underdeveloped treatment of Job in BMS, this overall trend seems significant and concerning, especially where an author is aiming to set out a case for showing how mission is a characteristic or theme of the whole Bible. If a framework for understanding biblical mission does not (or possibly cannot) accommodate texts such as the Wisdom Literature in a meaningful way, such an approach would seem to be undermined and open to the questioning of its rigor and adaptability.

However, despite the trend noted above, there remain a significant number of studies that do engage to a greater degree with the book, including some treatments specifically focused on Job.[14] Such discussions tend to revolve around a number of particular themes, which provide a structure for the next section.

---

12. Okoye, *Israel and the Nations*, 11–12.

13. Okoye, *Israel and the Nations*, 4.

14. For example, Van Zyl, "Missiological Dimensions," 24–30; Allen, "Missionary Message," 18–31; Waters, "*Missio Dei*," 19–34; Hesselgrave, *My Redeemer Lives*.

Themes in the Use of Job in BMS

In this section I isolate the key themes with which BMS concerns itself when dealing with Job. In each case I summarize and evaluate the ways in which scholars engage with the theme. I also show how my study relates to these discussions, thereby illustrating both the continuity and distinctiveness of my treatment of Job.

Job's International Outlook

A common observation in BMS and more general scholarship is the lack of references in Job, and the Wisdom Literature more generally, to particular Israelite features such as the law, the temple, covenant, the exodus and so on.[15] In BMS this is often taken to be an indication of a more international outlook. Senior and Stuhlmueller, for example, mention Job alongside Jonah and Ruth as possible "scattered attempts" to offer prophetic, "more universal outreach" critique in the post-exilic period.[16] While this may be one particular way of understanding the book of Job it is not developed sufficiently by Senior and Stuhlmueller to provide a strong reading of Job.

In a similar vein, Horton's 1908 study of mission as "the bearing and trend of [the Bible]" viewed the Wisdom Literature as "remarkable" in its detachment from Israel's history and Law.[17] For Horton this frees the texts from "national bias" making them suitable for all humanity, and allowing them to subvert orthodox assumptions about sin and suffering.[18] He also considered whether Job has something to say as a symbol of Israel in exile, giving a word of hope that Israel's suffering (in line with the Prophets) would be a means of "service to the world."[19]

Horton's points are valid to an extent. While the omission in Job of certain Israelite institutions and terms does suggest a form of distancing from OT thinking connected more overtly with Israel's story, this does

---

15. For this observation in more general Biblical scholarship, see, for example, Dell, *Get Wisdom*, 2; Clements, *Wisdom in Theology*, 20–26.

16. Thereby assuming a later dating for the book. See Senior and Stuhlmueller, *Biblical Foundations*, 40. The only other reference to Job in Senior and Stuhlmueller is to Job 16:14, as part of a discussion of God as divine warrior (53).

17. Horton, *Bible*, 28, 161.

18. Horton, *Bible*, 161–62.

19. Horton, *Bible*, 162.

not necessarily mean that Job therefore is not a thoroughly Israelite book. I see no contradiction between Job (and the Wisdom Literature more generally) having "a meaning and a message for all the world," while also retaining its distinctively Israelite perspective.[20] Indeed, I will argue that it is precisely this distinctive characteristic that is Job's most meaningful contribution to the world. The book of Job certainly does have a universal theme and interest, yet it engages with them in particularly Israelite ways. This is seen both in the universally relevant themes explored in the book, and also in the ways in which the book engages with how other ANE belief systems explored them.

In *Unity and Plurality: Mission in the Bible* Legrand ties Job very closely to the universalism he detects throughout the Bible.[21] For Legrand, the meaning of the book of Job reflects a "frequent theme" to be found in the Bible: "The Universality of God's love, in the face of the universality of human misery, abides. Nothing else."[22] Despite all he experiences and the failure of all human attempts to comfort him, "Job has met God. 'My eye has seen you' (Job 42:5), he says, and that is enough."[23]

Widbin also notes the universal involvement of God with humanity, likening the Wisdom Literature to that of the early part of Genesis, concluding: "God is involved in the lives of all people simply because they *are* people."[24]

Building on his prior discussion on mission, creation, and humanity in God's image, Wright sees the Wisdom Literature as "a broad tradition of faith and ethics built on a worldview that employs the wide-angle lens of precisely this whole-creation and whole-humanity perspective."[25] Wright sees the Wisdom writings of the OT as part of an international body of literature produced by the class of wisdom writers who could be found throughout the ANE even centuries before the books of Job, Proverbs and Ecclesiastes were written.[26] The Israelite writers were clearly aware of this in relation to individuals (see, for example, the indirectly

---

20. Horton, *Bible*, 157.
21. Legrand, *Unity and Plurality*.
22. Legrand, *Unity and Plurality*, 25.
23. Legrand, *Unity and Plurality*, 25.
24. Widbin, "Salvation for People," 74.
25. Wright, *Mission of God*, 441.
26. Wright, *Mission of God*, 442.

positive assessment of the wisdom of non-Israelite individuals in 1 Kings 4:30–31) and nations as a whole.[27]

Wright also points to associations between ANE and OT wisdom texts, which evidence "a lot of contact between Israel's wisdom thinkers and writers and those of surrounding nations," thus making Israel's Wisdom Literature "undoubtedly the most overtly international of all the materials in the Bible."[28] Indeed, it seems strange that so few writers on Bible and mission make this connection, or develop it in substantial ways. There is a sense in which the international nature of Israel's wisdom texts would suggest that it could be one of the first groupings of texts to be considered, not the last. As already suggested, perhaps it is the (in many ways very helpful) focus of many scholars on the salvation-historical narrative that steers them away from the Wisdom Literature.

For Wright it is not just the perspective of the wisdom writers that is international but the content of their writings in the sense that they engage with many issues that are also found in the Wisdom Literature of the wider ANE, such as living and relating well, power and politics, the moral order, divine justice and suffering, and life's "absurdities."[29]

A missional approach to Job will, therefore, seek to draw out the significance of the book's treatment of these issues and consider them in relation to the mission of God. In my study I attempt to do this both in my examination of the theme of poverty but, more fundamentally, in my discussion of the universalizing impulse in the book of Job.

Job as a Non-Israelite

One particularly striking feature of the book of Job is the way in which it intensifies the international tenor or outlook of the Wisdom Literature, discussed above, by having a non-Israelite as its central human character and setting the events of the book outside of Israel (Job 1:1).

Rétif and Lamarche's study of the theme of universalism throughout the Bible offers some, albeit limited, reflection on the figure of Job and the book that bears his name.[30] They describe as "both strange and

---

27. Wright, *Mission of God*, 442.
28. Wright, *Mission of God*, 443.
29. Wright, *Mission of God*, 443, 445.
30. Rétif and Lamarche, *Salvation of the Gentiles*.

interesting" Ezekiel's choice of the non-Israelites Noah, Dan'el, and Job as examples of righteous men in Ezekiel 14:14.[31] The book of Job itself

> marks a reaction against the claims of human wisdom. A man who lives on the borders of Arabia and Edom, who does not belong to the race of Israel, is nevertheless engaged in a dramatic argument with God. It is such a gentile whom God puts to the test and who bows down in worship of him without wanting to find a human explanation of the problem of suffering.[32]

For Legrand, Job is "a saintly pagan.... Job's problem is a universal problem, and the divine response, as well, has universal validity. Here indeed is a decentralized universalism, in the sapiential tradition."[33] This is illustrative of a number of scholars who discuss the non-Israelite status of Job, although they claim different types and degrees of significance from this. Horton, for example, suggests that the author's choice of a non-Israelite "to portray a character of lofty excellence and faultless piety" is an example of an international outlook.[34] Similarly, Montgomery cites Job as an example of the less nationalistic attitudes of some within Israel, being written by a "great thinker [who] was going to the Land of Uz to find an example of a true servant of Jehovah in the person of Job."[35] However, it is unclear whether she means this journey to be metaphorical or, more intriguingly, whether she envisages an Israelite sage as bringing back the story from the land of Uz.

Job is seen as an example of a godly non-Israelite who worships and pleases God without explaining how he knows God.[36] Verkuyl notes this theme and considers the accounts of non-Israelites such as Melchizedek, Job and Ruth as a means of considering "the vast expanse of people outside the nation of Israel and hear the faint strains of the missionary call to all people already sounding forth."[37]

---

31. Rétif and Lamarche, *Salvation of the Gentiles*, 64.
32. Rétif and Lamarche, *Salvation of the Gentiles*, 96.
33. Legrand, *Unity and Plurality*, 25.
34. Horton, *Bible*, 159.
35. Montgomery, *Bible and Missions*, 27.
36. See, for example, Schultz, "Mission im AT," 41; Schnabel, *Jesus and the Twelve*, 58; Glaser, *Bible and Other Faiths*, 39.
37. Verkuyl, *Missiology*, 95.

Beeby sees great missiological significance in the non-Israelite identity of Job.[38] He notes the "missionary potential" given by the international links shared between Proverbs, Job and Ecclesiastes and the surrounding cultures of Israel.[39] However, it is Job that Beeby highlights as being the book in which "the missionary motive is explicitly seen."[40] He justifies this by suggesting that the non-Israelite setting allows the writer to address "the missionary problem of how a non-Israelite is to stand before Israel's God."[41] Elsewhere Beeby cites Job as an example of OT "missionary literature" stating that "in it a theophany produces repentance and restoration to a non-Israelite."[42] Unfortunately Beeby does not provide adequately developed support for these bold claims.

Hedlund's biblical theology of mission notes a Genesis connection when discussing Job.[43] Given its patriarchal setting, he sees the book as supplementing the universality of early parts of Genesis, dealing in a non-Israelite setting with concerns other than the covenant.[44] Indeed, he sees Job as "a meaningful indication of Yahweh's gracious intervention and intention. Job represents the universality of God's concern."[45]

In a discussion on God's choice of Abraham, Hedlund emphasizes this as "an act of pure grace"; after all, there were other (perhaps more righteous) candidates like Melchizedek and Job.[46] He also notes the acceptance of God of people outside Israel, citing Job as a particularly impressive example as he has an entire book devoted to his story.[47] His book reveals God's righteousness and justice, witnesses to a knowledge of God in the ancient world, seems based on a universal covenant, and shows that God brought salvation "within paganism."[48]

The greatest concentration of Hedlund's material on Job is as part of a chapter on "Light-shedding Wisdom."[49] He highlights the book of Job

38. Beeby, *Mission and Missions*.
39. Beeby, *Mission and Missions*, 32.
40. Beeby, *Mission and Missions*, 32.
41. Beeby, *Mission and Missions*, 32.
42. Beeby, *Canon and Mission*, 89.
43. Hedlund, *Mission of the Church*.
44. Hedlund, *Mission of the Church*, 26.
45. Hedlund, *Mission of the Church*, 26.
46. Hedlund, *Mission of the Church*, 37.
47. Hedlund, *Mission of the Church*, 66.
48. Hedlund, *Mission of the Church*, 26.
49. Hedlund, *Mission of the Church*, 134–40.

as being, "of particular missionary interest" due to its representation of a non-Israelite tradition, thereby reflecting, "God's universal covenant."[50] Job is therefore, "a representative of the nations . . . [who] has the knowledge of the true God" which is evidenced in his awareness of God as "Creator and Sustainer and as the source of wisdom."[51]

Hedlund sees Job as offering a confession of faith in God as "the Almighty, the Redeemer" (Job 14:14, 16–17; 19:25–26) and becoming personally aware

> of God's grace and mercy in the forgiveness of sins and catch a glimpse of belief in the resurrection that is rare in the Old Testament. The missionary significance of Job is that he, a representative of the Gentile world, was a recipient not only of God's general revelation but also of redemption. Job was a representative of those who seek and find for he had come to hope in the living God.[52]

As is evident, the nature and significance of Job's non-Israelite provenance is presented in a variety of ways, including it being a challenge to nationalistic attitudes (Montgomery); an example of a Gentile being saved (Widbin); and an instance of a missionary movement from God to an outsider (Beeby).

More compelling, in my view, is the idea that Job's non-Israelite provenance is a means by which to universalize the book. That said, I would understand the nature of Job's provenance as being a complex portrait in that it is not as simple as depicting him "just" as a Gentile. In chapter 4 I set the discussion of Job's provenance within the broader context of the non-Israelite motif, seen particularly in the book's Prologue. In so doing I bring out the nuances of the discussion in more depth, and show how it fulfils an important function in the missional relevance of the book.

The Relationship between Job and the ANE

Although dealing with the Wisdom Literature and OT more generally, Goheen describes the engagement between the biblical story (which articulates the Israelite rendering of reality) and alternative stories as

---

50. Hedlund, *Mission of the Church*, 134.
51. Hedlund, *Mission of the Church*, 134–35.
52. Hedlund, *Mission of the Church*, 135.

"missional encounter with culture which both embraces the treasures and opposes the idolatry of all cultures."[53] The same point is made in more detail by Wright: Israelite wisdom writers, he notes, felt at liberty to incorporate the work of non-Israelites into their own, seen most explicitly in the inclusion in the book of Proverbs of sayings by Agur (Prov 30) and King Lemuel (Prov 31), as well as the implicit use of the Wisdom of Amenemope in Proverbs 22:17–24:22.[54]

Wright adds an important caveat at this point which is that these borrowings from non-Israelite sources are not carried out uncritically. Israel's distinctive faith (especially its understanding of Yahweh's uniqueness, and Israel's covenant relationship with him) shaped this process of contextualisation in two different ways.[55] First, certain aspects common in ANE sources such as mentions of gods and goddesses, or the validity of magic or divination are absent in the biblical texts.[56] Secondly, the biblical Wisdom writers offer a critique of some of the tenets of non-Israelite wisdom themes. As an example Wright suggests that the personification of Wisdom and Folly in Proverbs 1–9 represents Yahweh, "the source of all true wisdom," and other albeit seductive "gods."[57] Further, the Israelite writers sought to critique the consequences of a non-Israelite polytheism, such as potential cynicism about morality and a general fatalism about life.[58]

This caveat is an important element in Wright's thinking. While other scholars, such as Beeby and Goheen, mention this phenomenon using language such as "cultural borrowing," "transformed borrowing," "embrace," and "engagement" they do not explain in any depth how this relationship functions.[59] Wright's discussion suggests some of the nuanced ways in which it occurs, yet even here his argument is relatively limited to a few remarks, and mainly focused on the book of Proverbs. This dynamic of openness and critique in the Wisdom Literature has not, I would suggest, been adequately explored in BMS.

53. Goheen, "Notes Toward a Framework," 5. Goheen also understands wisdom to be helping to shape Israel's daily life "in conformity to God's creational order" (Goheen, "Continuing Steps," 92).
54. Wright, *Mission of God*, 442.
55. Wright, *Mission of God*, 444.
56. Wright, *Mission of God*, 444.
57. Wright, *Mission of God*, 444.
58. Wright, *Mission of God*, 444.
59. Cf. Beeby, *Canon and Mission*, 87.

Wright's choice of the Proverbs and Amenemope example is a useful one in that it is one of the clearest examples of a possible direct relationship between ANE wisdom texts and the Bible.[60] However, his treatment is brief and requires considerable development in order to make the case more thoroughly. Moreover, he focuses his point on direct borrowing, which lends itself well to that well-known case in Proverbs, yet not enough is said about the possibility of less direct interaction between texts. Perhaps because of this focus Wright does not deal in great depth with Job, which relates to ANE texts in important but less direct ways. It would seem appropriate, then, that my treatment of Job should address the extent to which, and the ways in which, Job exhibits a "missionary encounter" with ANE texts and ideas. However, it is important to note that it is not necessary to demonstrate a direct relationship between specific texts in order to prove such an engagement exists. As I will show later in this volume, the relationship between Job and other ANE texts is not a direct one but it certainly does seem to show elements of affirmation and critique with the belief systems of Israel's neighboring cultures.

For Wright, Israelite wisdom's motto, "the fear of YHWH is the beginning of knowledge/wisdom" (Prov 1:7a) is foundational in that "the beginning" refers to "a first principle that governs everything else."[61] This means that, although the Wisdom Literature does not make explicit references to Israel's "salvation history" or covenant, these concepts are "embodied in the name of YHWH himself, that underlies all the reflection, teaching and wrestling that goes on in these pages."[62]

Because it affirms many aspects of thought in the wisdom writings of "noncovenant nations," Wright views Israel's Wisdom Literature as "an important counterbalance to the more familiar rejection of the gods and religious practices of other nations that we find in the law and the prophets. Wisdom is remarkably open and affirming."[63]

What accounts for this openness as distinct from other parts of the OT canon? Wright suggests this is due in part to "the strong creational assumption that Israel made about the whole earth and all humanity. The Wisdom of the Creator is to be found in all the earth, and all human

---

60. Though the degree of directness in the relationship between these texts is not without its doubters. See, for example, Kitchen, "Proverbs 2," 562–66.

61. Wright, *Mission of God*, 444.

62. Wright, *Mission of God*, 444–45.

63. Wright, *Mission of God*, 445.

beings are made in his image."⁶⁴ Indeed, "Israel had no monopoly on all things wise and good and true."⁶⁵

Wright also sees in this welcoming of foreign wisdom a subtle dimension of the strand of eschatological thought that anticipates the nations bringing tribute and worship to Yahweh, although this is perhaps a little speculative.⁶⁶ Nevertheless, I would draw on Wright's main point of "welcoming" to suggest that part of my examination of the relationship between the book of Job and other ANE texts and ideas should look to what it affirmed, either implicitly or explicitly, both in content and form. This will be examined in more depth in chapter 5. There is, then, significant heuristic value in understanding the existence and process of agreement, as well as its content.⁶⁷

However, Wright offers a balancing argument that Israel's openness to the wisdom of other cultures was tempered by its use of "the religious and moral disinfectant provided by Yahwistic monotheism."⁶⁸ This meant Israel's sages felt at liberty to ignore or change elements of the "borrowed" wisdom writings in order to fit them within their distinctive theological framework.⁶⁹ This relates to Israel's unique gift of the *torah*, which was Israel's means of discerning what was and was not appropriate, and as such was their unique gift of wisdom to the world.⁷⁰ Wright suggests that this exercise of discernment was and is for the people of God an ongoing "missiological task": "If Israel sought to do this through the revelation contained in the Torah, how much more is it incumbent on us to make use of the whole Bible in this mission task of cultural discernment and critique?"⁷¹

---

64. Wright, *Mission of God*, 445.

65. Wright, *Mission of God*, 446.

66. Wright, *Mission of God*, 446. He cites Isa 60–66; Rev 21:24–27 as examples.

67. See also Rétif and Lamarche, *Salvation of the Gentiles*, 95; Glaser, *Bible and Other Faiths*, 120–22.

68. Wright, *Mission of God*, 446. The rather strong term, "disinfectant," is problematic. While I agree with Wright's assessment of the process of Israel's discriminating adaptation of others' wisdom, I would prefer to use a less loaded metaphor such as a filter.

69. Wright, *Mission of God*, 446.

70. Wright, *Mission of God*, 446–47, citing Eakin, "Wisdom, Creation, and Covenant," 237.

71. Wright, *Mission of God*, 447.

This seems to me to be a very important point and will feature significantly in my treatment of Job. Despite looking for elements of affirmation or commonality, it will be the distinctive features of Job that will demonstrate most clearly how the book contributes to an articulation of a Yahweh-shaped rendering of reality in contrast to alternative renderings. It is this aspect of the dual dynamic of affirmation and critique that allows the process to be understood as missional. Therefore, when examining Job in the light of similar ANE texts I will need to establish the extent to which, and the ways in which, the book of Job presents a distinctively Israelite approach to the issues in the book.[72] Given the lack of a direct literary relationship between Job and similar ANE texts, my purpose will be to examine how Job engaged with ANE beliefs which may be exhibited in certain texts. This is most fully carried out in chapter 5.

Job as Illustrative of Suffering and Weakness as the Context of Mission

Bosch brings in the book of Job to a discussion on unattributed suffering, one response to which is that of "acceptance and faith, as in Job."[73] Bosch later likens the weakness and seeming failure exhibited at Jesus' crucifixion, with its denial of human success and triumph, to the probing question of the accuser in Job 1:9–10, which is based on an assumption that religious devotion is motivated by reward.[74]

The significance of Job's immediate response to his suffering is also of interest to Waters, who makes it a central part of an essay that seeks to read the book in the light of the *missio Dei*.[75] Waters understands Job to be "part of the progressive revelation of God's purpose and mission, so that the book is, in a sense, missional and evangelistic."[76] Specifically, Waters defines the missionary purpose of the book as showing that "a believer's suffering should be viewed, as seen in Job's experience, as a witness not only to God's sovereignty but also as a witness to His goodness,

---

72. Furthermore, in the light of these distinctives, to what extent and in what ways might the book of Job be understood as a "gift" to the world? See Glaser, *Bible and Other Faiths*, 119, who notes how Solomon's encounter with the Queen of Sheba could be seen as exhibiting God's blessing both for Israel and the nations.

73. Bosch, "Vulnerability of Mission," 353.

74. Bosch, "Vulnerability of Mission," 355.

75. Waters, "*Missio Dei*."

76. Waters, "*Missio Dei*," 19.

justice, grace, and love to the nonbelieving world."[77] For Waters, the book, therefore, provides a model for how a believer's suffering may function in relation to the *missio Dei*, providing a corrective to so-called prosperity teaching and demonstrating an emphasis on grace, which acts "as a catalyst for this message throughout the region and beyond."[78]

While (with Bosch) Waters is right to highlight "acceptance and faith" as one response to suffering, I would suggest that a central theme of this book is that there is room for other responses.

Suffering as the context of mission is also a theme touched on by Burnett, who relates the supremacy of God to the realities of living in a suffering world, and concludes that

> the most important thing to understand in the midst of suffering is that God knows our plight and is all powerful. What he allows is ultimately for our good. When God restores Job's fortunes, this demonstrates not only God's power, but also His justice and His love. God blesses not just with material things, but with intangible things such as love, joy and peace.[79]

Burnett's points focus on developing religious principles from the plot of Job. To some extent they seem to use Job illustratively rather than dealing in a substantial way with the ambiguities of the book on its own terms.[80] A more nuanced, if brief, treatment is offered by Glaser: "The missionary is called to minister to the traumatized, but our shared humanity means that she is also in danger of trauma, and the missionary calling increases the danger."[81] The church, she suggests, should recognize that traumatic events are the norm in human experience, yet can ultimately become, "the place of mission."[82] It is in an encounter with God that such experiences can be both transformed and used to equip the church for mission.[83] These themes of vulnerability and encounter with God will be returned to as part of my reading of Job.

---

77. Waters, "*Missio Dei*," 19.

78. Waters, "*Missio Dei*," 31; cf. 29–33.

79. Burnett, *Healing of the Nations*, 96.

80. He also notes, "Not only must the people of God recognize that mission will be carried out within a suffering world, but also appreciate that mission itself will involve suffering" (Burnett, *Healing of the Nations*, 92).

81. Glaser, *Trauma, Migration, and Mission*, 4.

82. Glaser, *Trauma, Migration, and Mission*, 14–15.

83. Glaser, *Trauma, Migration, and Mission*, 14, 22.

Also touching on general or unattributed suffering, Goheen (drawing on Goppelt) describes the suffering of the NT church as reflecting a "Daniel" model of suffering (that is, persecution), rather than a "Job" model, which articulates "the pain that comes from living in a fallen world."[84] This seems like a missed opportunity. While it is true that persecution or external pressure were often the immediate contexts of the emergence of biblical writings, I would argue that the Job model (to use the concept) is always relevant. While I do not think either Goheen or Goppelt would deny this, in practice attributed suffering such as persecution seems to be the usual way of reflecting on suffering and mission.[85] While this is understandable I would argue that more attention should be given to missional reflection on unattributed suffering. As indicated in chapter 1, this volume is an attempt to do just that, with chapters 4 to 6 seeking to engage specifically with how the universalizing impulse and the poverty theme may inform missional reflection on unattributed suffering and mission.

In a whole-Bible outline of the "good news" of the Gospel, Wright includes a section discussing the Wisdom Literature's contribution.[86] For Wright, Job contains good news because it declares, "*that God can be known and trusted, against all that points in the opposite direction.*"[87] Furthermore Job exhibits good news in the way that it confronts, "some of the desperate contradictions of life in this fallen world . . . [while continuing] to affirm the goodness and sovereignty of the one true living God and to hope in him."[88] Its very existence demonstrates

> how seriously God himself takes these issues that trouble us so deeply, and thereby enables us not only to rejoice in the hope that the gospel provides, but to continue to wrestle with these things on the foundation of that faith and hope.[89]

Given the particular angle Wright uses to approach these texts he highlights a degree of connection between Job and mission, yet there is much scope for development. His main point seems to be focused on the heuristic value of the inclusion of books like Job and Ecclesiastes in the

---

84. Goheen, *Light to the Nations*, 187; cf. Goppelt, *Variety and Unity*, 174.
85. For a recent example of this tendency, see Taylor et al., *Sorrow and Blood*.
86. Wright, "Whole Gospel," 4–18.
87. Wright, "Whole Gospel," 15.
88. Wright, "Whole Gospel," 15.
89. Wright, "Whole Gospel," 15.

biblical canon. Seen within the context of Christian theology, Job asks questions that resonated deeply and painfully with human experience, while also offering hope, seen ultimately in the work of Jesus Christ.[90] In my view this combination of allowing pain to "breathe" while seeing it in the context of hope and the mission of God is important, and I will address this further in chapters 4, 5, and 6.

As part of Wright's more substantial treatment of the Wisdom Literature in *The Mission of God*, he considers the honesty with which these books address the ambiguities of life. For Wright, the most striking contrast between the Wisdom Literature and the rest of the Hebrew canon is the way in which the former expresses doubts about "the universal applicability" of some of the main affirmations offered by the latter, as illustrated by texts like Job 24:1–12 and Ecclesiastes 8:14–9:4.[91] Indeed, it is as if Israel's sages held up orthodox beliefs, "and then throw out the challenge: 'How can this belief be squared with the real world we live in? Life often simply doesn't follow these rules.'"[92] Moreover, Wright suggests:

> It is part of the strength and convincing power of the biblical case that it contains *within itself* precisely this degree of internal debate and wrestling with the core affirmations of a worldview that was explicitly founded on God's revelation and redemption.[93]

Wright considers this dynamic of the biblical material to have profoundly missional implications. Following Brueggemann, he describes Israel's self-understanding:

> It held its own faith *in trust for the world*. Israel's very existence was for the sake of the nations. Israel's God was God of all the earth. Whatever was true for Israel was true for all. Whatever Israel struggled with would be a problem for all.[94]

For Wright, the uncomfortable questioning of the Wisdom Literature must be taken seriously as "part of our missional responsibility" for the world's sake.[95] Such attentiveness, he suggests, helps to avoid "the

---

90. He is, of course, making certain positive assumptions about the portrayal of God in Job and how it relates to the NT.

91. Wright, *Mission of God*, 450.

92. Wright, *Mission of God*, 451. He is correct to point out that "language of complaint, protest and baffled questioning" also features, for example, in the Psalms.

93. Wright, *Mission of God*, 451.

94. Wright, *Mission of God*, 451. See Brueggemann, *Theology of the OT*, 324.

95. Wright, *Mission of God*, 451.

folly and lies of the so-called prosperity gospel, on the one hand, and the problem-denying triumphalism of the worst kinds of arrogant fundamentalism of the other."[96]

If Israel's faith is being held "in trust for the world," are there ways in which the Wisdom Literature exhibits this in differing or deeper ways than other parts of the canon? Wright concludes his reflections on the Wisdom Literature with the following statement:

> For the sake of the world, then, we must take this tone of voice in the Wisdom Literature seriously, with its awkward questions, its probing observations, its acceptance of the limitations of our finitude. It is part of our missional responsibility to do so. . . .
>
> The fact is that the world poses some very hard questions for those who, in line with the whole Bible testimony, believe in one, good, personal, sovereign God. Wisdom provides a licence to think, to wrestle, to struggle, to protest and to argue. All it asks is that we do so with the undergirding faith and humble commitment encapsulated in its own core testimony that "the fear of the Lord—that is wisdom, / and to shun evil is understanding" (Job 28:28).[97]

This perspective of Wright's seems very important for a potential missional reading of a text like Job. He takes as positive and constructive the inherent tensions between Job and other parts of the canon and casts them in a missional light. Rather than ignoring or explaining away the deep questioning of elements of Israelite faith in Job, Wright frames this in the context of Israel's role in the world. This seems to be a more satisfactory way of approaching the ambiguities of Job. Not only does Wright's approach refrain from shying away from the book's difficulties; it actually champions them as a vital missional endeavor.

Perhaps more striking still is Van Zyl who considers the book of Job as exemplifying a way of doing "Mission in bold humility."[98] The church, he contends, should carry out its witness from a place of weakness, which

---

96. Wright, *Mission of God*, 452.

97. Wright, *Mission of God*, 452. See also Yong's treatment of Job, which focuses on the role of wind/spirit in the book. For Yong, a spirit-informed framing of mission "invites coming alongside others in prolonged solidarity (like Elihu, unlike Job's 'friends') amid whatever grief and tragedy. No human distress is thereby untouched by the *missio Spiritus*" (Yong, *Mission After Pentecost*, 101).

98. Van Zyl, "Missiological Dimensions," 29. "Bold humility" is a phrase attributed to Bosch. See Bosch, *Transforming Mission*, 489; Saayman and Kritzinger, *Mission in Bold Humility*.

would demonstrate the true power of the gospel.[99] In this, Van Zyl suggests the book of Job could be seen as paradigmatic because it subverts wisely and ingeniously: it does not attempt to "uproot systems" but rather "bears witness to alternatives, liberating people, and liberating God from being taken captive, enslaved by human systems!"[100]

In my view this theme is a promising area of exploration as it opens up the potential for Job to contribute to missional reflection in a distinctive way, accounting for the ambiguities and hard questions of the book and relating them to God's purposes in the world. In particular, this theme connects closely with elements of the universalizing impulse in the book explored in chapter 4, and examined in relation to poverty in chapter 6.

Job and Social Justice

The Lausanne Movement's Manila Manifesto cites Job 24:1–12 to illustrate the importance of "The Gospel and Social Responsibility."[101] The more recent *Cape Town Commitment* (a successor document to the Lausanne Covenant and Manila Manifesto) has several references to Job, illustrating their commitment to working on behalf of the world's poor, suffering and immigrants (Job 29:7–17; 31:13–23; 29:16).[102]

In a 2011 article Jesurathnam reflects on holistic concerns by seeking to apply a discussion of the theme of social justice in the Wisdom Literature to contemporary mission activities "with, from and also for" Dalit communities in India.[103] Jesurathnam's understanding of mission, as identified in the context of this discussion, focuses less on "conversion" and more on the restoration of the downtrodden and marginalized to wholeness, dignity, and empowerment.[104] This chimes closely with holistic concerns although Jesurathnam does not address in detail how these aspects relate to, for example, confessions of faith.

---

99. Van Zyl, "Missiological Dimensions," 29.

100. Van Zyl, "Missiological Dimensions," 29. Thus, "The epilogue of the book suggests that the system in itself may not be only bad. What is bad is that it is used to crush down people, especially suffering people, and to legitimize the positions of the powerful."

101. Lausanne, "Manila Manifesto."

102. Wright, *Cape Town Commitment*, 21, 27–99, 42–44.

103. Jesurathnam, "Dalit Interpretation," 347.

104. Jesurathnam, "Dalit Interpretation," 347–48.

Jesurathnam's treatment of Job focuses on the book's use of three terms for the poor (דַּל, אֶבְיוֹן, and עָנִי) and, like the Lausanne documents, draws upon passages such as Job 24:1–17 and chapters 29–31 to bring out Job's teaching on the poor and marginalized.[105] Job is "the representative of the oppressed and the powerless [who] laments bitterly for his pathetic condition"; God is "directly involved in executing his justice as the creator of the earth on behalf of the poor and the powerless in the society"; "the underprivileged and marginalized of his society . . . are the victims of economic and political injustice," systems against which Job fought to advocate on behalf of the poor, the ignored, and the helpless.[106]

In a rather cryptic conclusion to the Joban material, Jesurathnam states that Job argues both that Yahweh is in control of creation yet (quoting Gottwald), "Job is also of the view that 'God does not have evil and suffering totally under control, and thus God also suffers.'"[107]

Relating his material to mission, Jesurathnam notes how the Wisdom Literature teaches God's people to work towards helping the oppressed and marginalized to retrieve their God-ordained identity, dignity and value that is the mark of all people, regardless of "class or caste"; that "God has special concern for these marginalized communities and the Church should take this Mission of God seriously in word and deed"; and that the challenge to the mechanical application of the doctrine of retribution, seen especially in Job, should be articulated against systems and beliefs that continue to disempower and oppress groups such as Dalit communities.[108] In sum,

> Mission to the marginalized and the underprivileged communities was at the heart of the biblical wisdom writers, and the same is at the core of Dalit theological discourse too. The Hebrew sages present the underprivileged of their society as active subjects of God's emancipative action, not simply the passive objects. . . .
>
> Hebrew sages not only recorded their reflections but wanted their learning communities to practice God's mission to the most vulnerable and those in the margins of the society.[109]

---

105. Jesurathnam, "Dalit Interpretation," 342–44.

106. Jesurathnam, "Dalit Interpretation," 342–43.

107. Jesurathnam, "Dalit Interpretation," 344, quoting Gottwald, *Hebrew Bible*, 578.

108. Jesurathnam, "Dalit Interpretation," 347–55.

109. Jesurathnam, "Dalit Interpretation," 353–55.

For Van Zyl, the book of Job addresses the retribution model of sin and suffering which, in effect, "legitimized the position of the prosperous and powerful, and 'demonized' the sick, the have-not's, the working class."[110] Such a critique, therefore, "brings hope to the poor and suffering that they may understand more of God than the wise do. . . . It critiques theology which has become ideology."[111]

Concerning mission in contemporary, Western contexts (which he relates to concerns of the "Gospel and Our Culture" network) Van Zyl considers Job to have an important contribution. In the West, he suggests, Christians accept the culture because they assume (after centuries of Christianity) that it is in some sense acceptable and "Christian." But the socio-political and economic systems mean "good news (gospel) to those who are advantaged by it. In fact these are those in positions of power, mostly economic power."[112] For Van Zyl, Job models an approach to tackling issues of poverty and injustice that are achieved only when the church

> becomes part of the other side, comes to experience something of the suffering of those who are disadvantaged by the systems and ideologies of society, that its eyes are opened and it can become a voice for the voiceless. It needs to experience how the system, in the name of God, dehumanizes and even demonizes people, people who have real pain, physical and mental.[113]

It is the Church's missional responsibility to challenge unjust systems, especially the "prosperity syndrome" that

> leaves suffering people feeling left behind, useless and Godforsaken. The system may even create guilt pathology with those suffering, as those friends of Job tried to do. It leaves no room for the possibility of the meaningfulness of suffering. The physically disabled, AIDS sufferers, displaced people, refugees, orphans, minorities, and victims of the "system" need the church not only to minister to their needs, but to address the macro systems and ideologies which create and sustain these systems.[114]

---

110. Van Zyl, "Missiological Dimensions," 28.
111. Van Zyl, "Missiological Dimensions," 28.
112. Van Zyl, "Missiological Dimensions," 29.
113. Van Zyl, "Missiological Dimensions," 29.
114. Van Zyl, "Missiological Dimensions," 29.

Although the Lausanne documents only have the scope to mention Job briefly, they do (along with Jesurathnam and Van Zyl's reflections) illustrate something of the potential of the book of Job to connect with themes of poverty and justice.[115] As I indicated in chapter 1, my holistic understanding of mission allows me (indeed, requires me) to probe such issues and see them as missionally relevant. In chapter 6, therefore, I will do this by engaging in a substantial discussion on the theme of the treatment of the poor in Job. Unlike Jesurathnam I do not tie this to a particular context. Nevertheless, I show how the book of Job has a unique contribution to make to the OT's treatment of the issue of poverty. As such, this also demonstrates a further aspect of Job's unique contribution to a biblical understanding of mission.[116]

Correcting False Teaching

A further aspect of the interaction with Job in BMS is how the book aims to correct false teaching. Glasser et al. view the book of Job as challenging conventional wisdom's assumption that those suffering deserved what they were experiencing, a view espoused by Job's friends.[117] Even Elihu's claim that there was "disciplinary value" in Job's suffering (Job 33:14–30) is "brushed aside" by God's speeches which champion the mystery of Yahweh's wisdom and actions.[118]

Arguing against contemporary "prosperity" teaching, Wright cites the book of Job as an example of when loss and suffering are not explained by disobedience.[119]

The extent to which this process is missional is worth considering. Van Zyl, for example, understands this corrective aim as being part of a

---

115. See also Sunquist's brief mention of Job in his *Understanding Christian Mission*, 346.

116. I should acknowledge Hesselgrave's inclusion of the themes of justice and poverty in his *My Redeemer Lives*. See, for example, 27–28, where, among other sources, he quotes from the original form of my thesis.

117. Glasser et al., *Announcing the Kingdom*, 159.

118. Glasser et al., *Announcing the Kingdom*, 159–60. Also writing on the theme of corrective teaching, Waters is more charitable towards Elihu: "Job's struggle with suffering and a false theology contrary to grace, Elihu's corrective measures guiding Job into God's presence, and God's remarkable and unusual speeches are all a part of the *missio Dei* in communicating His loving concern for humanity" (Waters, "*Missio Dei*," 20).

119. Wright, *Salvation*, 80.

"critique-of-culture" dynamic of mission. As well as exploring the question of suffering Van Zyl asserts that Job "should be read as a critique of the prevailing views of standard wisdom of its time."[120] Opting for a post-exilic dating, he sees the book's attack on retribution as a condemnation of the ways in which the powerful at that time were legitimizing their positions in society by appealing to the theology of the Deuteronomist and the sages of Israel and elsewhere.[121]

Van Zyl notes that Job does not exactly abandon the notion of causality but that "he draws other conclusions"; that is, the world should run in the prescribed way but "God does not respond to this wisdom paradigm."[122] He views Job's relationship with God as complex, in that he both accuses and seeks God, suggesting the existence of "an alternative to the one-dimensional relationship with God, which the book aims to unmask."[123] Similarly, he detects an alternative to conventional wisdom in the fact that Job spoke *to* God rather than simply *about* God.[124]

Correcting false ideas may also be understood in relation to the discussion concerning the missional purposes of the biblical writings articulated in the previous chapter. By contributing to an articulation of a rendering of reality shaped by faith in Yahweh, biblical texts will, deliberately or implicitly, function as correctives to renderings of reality that are shaped by other beliefs. This contending for truth about Yahweh may be an internal process, challenging false assumptions (in this case) concerning the application of the retribution principle within the community of Israel. As such it may be understood as missional (as I have framed it) by shaping the people of Israel for their participation in God's purposes. However, it may also be an outward facing process that seeks to correct the beliefs of Israel's neighbors.[125]

In the book of Job both aspects seem to be at work. In chapter 3 I address the question of how the book of Job seeks to correct faulty assumptions concerning the relationship between suffering and piety. I then tackle the intercultural engagement and critique in more detail in chapters 4 and 5.

120. Van Zyl, "Missiological Dimensions," 27.
121. Van Zyl, "Missiological Dimensions," 27.
122. Van Zyl, "Missiological Dimensions," 27–28.
123. Van Zyl, "Missiological Dimensions," 28.
124. Van Zyl, "Missiological Dimensions," 28. See also the work of Gutiérrez, discussed below, especially in chapters 4–6.
125. See also Hesselgrave, *My Redeemer Lives*, 24–26.

The Accuser (הַשָּׂטָן) in Job

At several points the use of Job in BMS focuses on הַשָּׂטָן, the accuser figure of the book's Prologue. Although to varying degrees of nuance, in most cases the assumption is made that הַשָּׂטָן equates, in some way, to the personal being, "Satan." Filbeck, for example, cites Job 1:6–12 as an example of Yahweh's uniqueness: "It is he alone who allows and restrains Satan."[126] Likewise, הַשָּׂטָן is a connecting point to Job for Glasser et al., Perriman, Piper, and Burnett, by illustrating the reality of the unseen supernatural in the world.[127]

For Allen, "The Enemy" in Job is a figure that exploits humanity's ignorance of the true nature of God (as exemplified by Job) by providing alternative ways of understanding, leading to the development of other religious systems.[128]

Considering the phenomenon of "The Evil One" in Job, Burnett deduces from the Prologue that, first, "the evil intruder is a person, and secondly, that person is limited in his influence, by the constraints of God himself."[129]

Waters's discussion of the accuser is instructive, though in my view limited. In line with BMS, Waters addresses the question of the accuser, seeing as crucial the exchange in 1:8–10.[130] In asking whether the accuser had considered his servant Job,

> God took the initiative for the purpose of advancing His redemptive purpose. In a missiological sense God used Job's experience to reveal Himself to Job's world. . . . *Missio Dei* in Job therefore began with suffering and God's initiative.[131]

The accuser's response in 1:9–10 evokes important issues because it questions the nature of the relationship between God and his worshippers,

---

126. Note the lack of definite article and capitalization here and with others. For example, Filbeck, *God of the Gentiles*, 72.

127. Glasser et al., *Announcing the Kingdom*, 330; Perriman, *Re: Mission*, 58; Piper, *Let the Nations be Glad!*, 84n8; Burnett, *Healing of the Nations*, 96–97, 199.

128. Allen, "Missionary Message," 26.

129. Burnett, *Healing of the Nations*, 96. A more ambiguous position is implied by Wright, who, in the context of a chapter on idolatry, notes that "Israel was also aware . . . of agencies within that exalted company that *questioned* God," although he does not expand on this carefully chosen language (Wright, *Mission of God*, 144).

130. Waters also uses the name "Satan" when discussing the accuser.

131. Waters, "*Missio Dei*," 23.

suggesting "a *quid pro quo* system of theology" akin to other ANE beliefs, rather than "Job's personal intimate relationship with God based on love, trust, and faith in Him (1:8–10; 2:3; cf. 1:21–22; 2:10)."[132]

For Waters, the breadth and severity of Job's suffering plays an important function in God's "conflict" with the accuser.[133] Job demonstrates "the proper response to suffering" in Job 1:21–22 and 2:10 which "would then lead to triumph over the enemy's accusations and would help reach the world with God's message of grace."[134] Job's response in 2:10 is particularly important for Waters as it "reveals a clear understanding of God's grace and the importance of handling suffering in light of that grace."[135] Job is, therefore, a demonstration that

> in a believer's suffering God communicates His purpose to others through conversation, pain management, and attitude. Even though Job did not epitomize or demonstrate this witness consistently, he never let go of his belief that all things come from God and that ultimately it was to God alone that he could turn.[136]

Waters is right to give attention to the crucial question of the accuser in Job 1:9b, which is also a key text I identify in my own reading. However, in my view his treatment of the Prologue does not account sufficiently for the ambiguities of the text. For example, although Yahweh initiates the conversation concerning Job, and therefore appears to invite the accuser's challenge, to apply the language of "redemption" at this stage seems inappropriate.[137]

Waters's understanding of the accuser is crucial to his reading of the book. Although he acknowledges some of the subtleties of the accuser's identity and role in a footnote, Waters seems to identify the accuser with the Devil and sets up the story as a conflict between him and God. By framing it in this way Waters's approach dictates his conclusions about

---

132. Waters, "*Missio Dei*," 23. Waters's language should be noted here. He seems to describe Job's relationship with God in modern Christian terms ("personal intimate relationship"; "love, trust, and faith in Him"; "grace"; and so on). This gives his discussion, in my view, an anachronistic feel. For example, more could have been made of other elements of OT Wisdom spirituality, such as the fear of God.

133. Waters, "*Missio Dei*," 25. See my discussion in chapter 4, where I note how the breadth and extent of Job's suffering helps to universalize the book.

134. Waters, "*Missio Dei*," 25.

135. Waters, "*Missio Dei*," 25.

136. Waters, "*Missio Dei*," 25.

137. Waters, "*Missio Dei*," 23; cf. Pope, *Job*, 11–12; Clines, *Job 1–20*, 24–25.

"the proper response to suffering," in which a faithful believer must now "triumph" over the lies of the evil one by responding in acceptance and trust.

Waters makes a strong case for the missional significance of a submissive response to suffering that exhibits trust in God, regardless of circumstances. While I would agree that trusting submission is one element of the missional potential of the book's teaching, I have serious misgivings about his description of Job's submission in the Prologue as being "the proper response to suffering."[138] This seems too simplistic a view of the nature of Job and also what the book might be teaching about how a suffering believer "should" respond to their circumstances.[139] Waters's statement that "Job did not epitomize or demonstrate this witness consistently" is illuminating.[140] Because of his view of the "correct" response to suffering there seems to be little room in Waters's analysis for the possibility that Job's struggling and protest throughout most of the book was legitimate and may function missionally.

In my view the complaints of Job are more than just an aberration in the book. As such, a missional reading must give them due attention and ask whether the protests of Job can be a catalyst for mission, as well as his submission. In chapters 4, 5, and 6 I examine this theme in more depth, both in relation to the universalizing impulse of the book, and concerning the treatment of the poor.

It is not my intention here to detail the lengthy discussion on the precise identity of this figure or the divine assembly more broadly. My view is that הַשָּׂטָן is an ambiguous figure who has the particular responsibility among the angelic beings of bringing to light human failings.[141] To personify this figure as "Satan" or "evil" seems to misread the characterisation and function of הַשָּׂטָן, thereby making too simple a connection between הַשָּׂטָן and issues of the presence of evil and spiritual warfare in the world.[142] Importantly for my study, such an approach to הַשָּׂטָן also distracts the scholarly discussion away from his true missional relevance.

---

138. Waters, "*Missio Dei*," 25.

139. See, for example, Clines, *Job 1–20*, xxxviii–xxxix.

140. Waters, "*Missio Dei*," 25.

141. See Clines, *Job 1–20*, 19–23; Weiss, *Job's Beginning*, 31–46; Balentine, *Job*, 48–53; Walton, *Job*, 63–67.

142. My intention here is not to deny the presence of evil in the world; rather, I am cautious in applying to this particular biblical text more than is appropriate.

My reading of Job will not, therefore, address the identity of הַשָּׂטָן in any great depth. In my view the key issue of missional importance concerning this figure is the question he asks in 1:9b: הַחִנָּם יָרֵא אִיּוֹב אֱלֹהִים "Is it for nothing that Job fears God?" As I indicated in chapter 1 I consider this questioning of the possibility of a genuine relationship between God and humanity to be of the utmost importance to the *missio Dei*. As such, this will be the focus of my treatment of הַשָּׂטָן. Beyond this it is difficult to draw any firm conclusions concerning this rather enigmatic character, but I intend to show that a more cautious approach to his identity will be more helpful in refocusing to a more useful discussion of the missional relevance of him, and the book in which he plays a role.

Job as a "Tool" of Mission

Several writers discuss what might be termed the "instrumentality" of Job in mission, which relates in my terms to an understanding of the Bible as one of the means by which mission is carried out, as outlined in chapter 1.

Discussing the Wisdom Literature in general, Wright, for example, suggests that because Israel's Wisdom writers dealt with the universal concerns of the Wisdom Literature throughout the ANE (namely, the meaning of life and how to negotiate it successfully), these texts might be used profitably in missionary activity.[143] Insights into a culture can be gained by paying attention to its wisdom sayings and, "some missiologists and crosscultural practitioners suggest that the Wisdom Literature provides one of the best bridges for biblical faith to establish meaningful contact and engagement with widely different human cultures around the world."[144]

With more specificity Lapham suggests ways in which certain biblical texts might be relevant to missionary activity amongst particular groups. The Wisdom Literature, he suggests, might be especially helpful in working with humanists as it seems to present itself as "the Wisdom of the Wise," without much recourse to inspiration.[145] He suggests that the Wisdom teachers know the limits of wisdom, and that they keep the

---

143. Wright, *Mission of God*, 445.

144. Wright, *Mission of God*, 445; "OT Theology of Mission," 708. See also Glasser et al., *Announcing the Kingdom*, 161.

145. Lapham, *Missionary Handbook*, 93.

suffering of the righteous in the foreground.[146] This introduces his discussion on the book of Job. Job has a "greatness of soul" as illustrated in numerous places (1:1, 8; 2:3, 10; 9:32–35; 13:3; 23:3–12; 19:25–27).[147] It contends with the oversimplified belief in action and consequence, punishment and reward, which "belittle" both God and religion.[148]

Rather, when interacting with those of other faiths, a fruitful course of action might be, "to encourage them to think about and discuss what we call 'painful mysteries of Providence,' the many happenings in the world that are not on the lines of poetic justice."[149] He also thinks that "religious progressiveness" on a national level could be attained through Ecclesiastes or Job-like experiences that bring "enlightenment" through pain.[150]

According to Van Zyl, in certain African congregations the instance of Job's neighbors and friends bringing him gifts in the book's Epilogue has become a model for contemporary care for those in or recovering from difficulty, which suggests to him an assumption by those readers at least that the book does have "missionary dimensions."[151]

A further dimension is offered by Allen, who applies his insights (particularly concerning the ignorance of humanity concerning what God is like) to the motivation for missionary activity: "There are billions in the world today like Job. They want to hear a true word from God, but they do not know where to find it."[152] Just as God sent Abraham and, ultimately, Jesus to address that ignorance, now he sends the contemporary church.[153]

Russell's short introduction to a missional hermeneutic gives some mention of Job in the context of a wider coverage on the Wisdom Literature, which he thinks relates to the biblical story by reflecting on life and creation, engaging in universal questions yet in distinctive ways:

> Israel's unique contribution to the lore of the ancients is profoundly missional: "The fear of the LORD is the beginning of

---

146. Lapham, *Missionary Handbook*, 100–101.
147. Lapham, *Missionary Handbook*, 102.
148. Lapham, *Missionary Handbook*, 102.
149. Lapham, *Missionary Handbook*, 103–4.
150. Lapham, *Missionary Handbook*, 104–5.
151. Van Zyl, "Missiological Dimensions," 26.
152. Allen, "Missionary Message," 29.
153. Allen, "Missionary Message," 29.

knowledge" (Prov 1:7). The implication is this: *careful attention to the human condition may prepare persons for the truth about God* (cf. Eccl 12:12–14).[154]

Hedlund goes on to suggest that the universalism of the Wisdom Literature made it useful in the "missionary application" of later Judaism, claiming that sections from Proverbs and Job may have been "used as missionary tracts," a practice that could also be adopted today.[155]

Certain assumptions are evident in this angle on Job. While the "openness" of Job is acknowledged, these scholars seem to frame this in the light of a traditional, "conversionist" model of mission which ultimately seeks the acceptance of the proclaimed Gospel message. In each case the book of Job is envisaged as a means through which greater engagement can occur, leading to a more helpful reception of the Gospel message. As such it may have a preparatory function as part of a process of evangelism. The assumption is, therefore, that Job is not enough in itself to bring about "conversion," which is a necessary result of this form of mission.[156] Although without much support, Hedland's suggestion about how Job may have been used is suggestive. As I explain further in chapters 4 and 5, it seems reasonable that the book of Job had the potential to engage non-Israelites with recognisable issues while still contributing to an articulation of faith in Yahweh. Thus, in itself it embodies a testimony of Yahweh faith which had the potential to be used in commending Israel's faith.

The approach taken in the literature concerning the contemporary instrumentality of Job seems reasonable as a description of one of the ways the book of Job may provide a means by which mission is carried out. It is not within the scope of this volume to examine the use of Job in contemporary praxis, although I do refer to it at points. For example, in my examination of Job's intercultural engagement in the context of the ANE I make some suggestions concerning how this may be seen in the context of contemporary mission.

It is also worth considering the limitations of this approach. Is the real missional value of Job only in its capacity to move people to a more

---

154. Russell, "What Is a Missional Hermeneutic?"

155. Hedlund, *Mission of the Church*, 140, 144–45. However, he is not able to provide much support for these intriguing statements.

156. Sharing similar assumptions, Wright, for example, speaks of the Wisdom Literature as a "bridge" that "does not in itself contain the saving message of the whole biblical gospel" (Wright, *Mission of God*, 447). See the discussion on Wright below.

receptive hearing of the Gospel? As well as contributing to the process of proclamation and conversion it would seem worthwhile to look at how Job may be instrumental in carrying out other elements of holistic mission. I will return to this in more detail in chapter 6 when dealing with the issue of poverty.

Job and the Rest of the Biblical Narrative

Long-established discussions concerning the complex relationship between a book like Job and the rest of the OT are also reflected in BMS. As I noted in chapter 1, and will develop in more detail in chapter 3, there is a strong theme in BMS of the missional nature of the "grand narrative" of the Bible. It is of significant interest, therefore, to understand how this theme may have been perceived as connecting to Job. The complexity of this question is well illustrated, for example, by Glasser et al. in their *Announcing the Kingdom*, which includes a section entitled, "Wisdom Literature and God's Kingdom Mission."[157] Here, they describe Job (and Ecclesiastes) as akin to "antiwisdom" in that they "encourage faith when bad things happen to good people . . . there are times when revision and addition are necessary. While it is then that such changes become invaluable to us, making them is always traumatic."[158]

Glasser et al. point to the importance of the fear of the Lord (citing Job 28:28) as a distinguishing feature of Israel's wisdom, and for Israel's claim that "Wisdom is derived from God and should be attributed to God alone (Job 12:13; Prov 3:19–20; 8:22–31; Isa 31:2; etc.)," which was especially important given the generally universal tenor of the wisdom material.[159]

In my view Glasser et al. reflect the difficulties of many others who attempt to connect Job (and wisdom more broadly) with the mission of God. This is exemplified in a statement in the concluding section of their discussion of the Wisdom Literature:

> We grant that the wisdom literature does not directly concern itself with the ongoing redemptive purposes of God, even though some might argue that Job intimated otherwise when he said:

---

157. Glasser et al., *Announcing the Kingdom*, 157–61.
158. Glasser et al., *Announcing the Kingdom*, 158.
159. Glasser et al., *Announcing the Kingdom*, 158.

"The fear of the Lord—that is wisdom and to shun evil is understanding" (28:28).[160]

When starting from a framework that privileges the "storyline" of the Bible, it is not always straightforward to slot in books that do not "progress" this story on a temporal plane. Waters, for example, explores the idea of *missio Dei* but does not focus on how Job fits into the chronological storyline of the Bible, but rather how faithful people's experiences of unattributed suffering, as seen in Job, may be an example of, and serve to advance the *missio Dei*.[161]

Waters believes Job was a historical person, albeit a prepatriarchal, heroic figure.[162] In line with a number of BMS writers he discusses Job's provenance, although acknowledging the ambiguity surrounding Job's cultural or ethnic background, concluding that:

> The missiological importance of this is that God was "on mission" through an individual whose life would impact people around him, as well as generations of readers after his death. Job "serves ideally as a setting for the *universal spirit* and character of the message conveyed by the book of Job."[163]

One attempt to place Job into the plotline of the biblical narrative is offered by Allen, who suggests that Job's "unique contribution" is that the book "presents the cry of the human heart at the time of the Patriarchs for more knowledge of God, for a better revelation of God."[164] This is especially important for Allen as Job becomes representative of humanity's ignorance of God to which God responds in Genesis 12, by calling Abraham "so that he and his descendants would become the means by which humanity would be able to know exactly what God demands of humanity. This is the missionary message of Job."[165] Allen then ties this calling to the contemporary church: "It is vital . . . because this message

---

160. Glasser et al., *Announcing the Kingdom*, 161. Perhaps because of its organizing principle of "The Kingdom of God," the treatment of Wisdom in this work is fairly brief.

161. Waters, "*Missio Dei*," 21.

162. Waters, "*Missio Dei*," 21–22.

163. Waters, "*Missio Dei*," 22, quoting Carter, "Book of Job," 14.

164. Allen, "Missionary Message," 18.

165. Allen, "Missionary Message," 19.

calls the church . . . to be God's means of healing a diseased and suffering world."[166]

Concerning the variety and complexity of the biblical narrative (and Job's place within it) Beeby argues for an approach to the Bible that detects "a unified missional whole," seen in its consistent "witness to the mystery of God Almighty and the mysterious *missio Dei*," while also acknowledging the differing perspectives offered, for example by the Wisdom Literature and the prophets.[167]

Similarly, noting the diversity and richness of the biblical canon, Bauckham mentions Job as "confronting a perplexity at the heart of biblical faith but virtually without reference to the Old Testament story of God and his people," and Ecclesiastes as "almost postmodern in its inability to make sense of the story."[168] Yet, he suggests, this should not mean that these books are marginalized or assimilated too simplistically into the rest of the biblical story, concluding: "Actually in their problematic and marginal character they too may be resources for a missionary church."[169] Frustratingly Bauckham does not elaborate on this final point, although I would understand this to mean that the Bible's inclusion of difficult and marginal texts reflects and speaks into the ambiguities of human experience in the world.[170]

Also addressing the relationship between the Wisdom Literature and the overall biblical story Wright notes the limitations of the Wisdom Literature in that it does not account for the whole, redemptive message of the Bible.[171] He detects a "self-critiquing" strand of thought within the Wisdom Literature "that questions its own adequacy to solve the problems it addresses"; hence setting Job and Ecclesiastes alongside the book of Proverbs.[172] Job and Ecclesiastes deal especially with the ambiguities

---

166. Allen, "Missionary Message," 19.

167. Beeby, "Missional Approach," 279. Moreover, "Within wisdom Job does not agree with Proverbs, and Ecclesiastes is out of tune with almost everybody" (Beeby, "Missional Approach," 279).

168. Bauckham, *Mission as Hermeneutic*, 13.

169. Bauckham, *Mission as Hermeneutic*, 13.

170. On suffering as the context of mission, see above. I also address questions concerning the complexity and legitimacy of conceiving of the Bible as a canonical unity in chapter 3.

171. Wright, *Mission of God*, 447. See also "OT Theology of Mission," 708.

172. Wright, *Mission of God*, 447. Though the contrast between Proverbs' "naivety" and Job and Ecclesiastes' critique can be overplayed. See, for example, Leeuwen, "Wealth and Poverty."

and troubling aspects of life in the world since humanity's rebellion in Genesis 3.[173] For Wright, the Wisdom Literature cannot on its own answer the questions of "satanic malice, suffering, frustration, meaningless toil, unpredictable consequences, uncertain futures, the twistedness of life and the final mockery of death," but it can act as a signpost to where "the answer" might lie: in the fear of Yahweh himself, who is the one known to Israel in "their historical experience of election, redemption and covenant."[174]

Wright's points are clearly based on his assumptions about the canonical nature of the Bible and should also be understood with reference to his Christian reading of Scripture. I address these in more detail in chapter 3 when considering the validity and potential of canon and narrative in a missional reading of the Bible.

A further aspect of the relationship between the Wisdom Literature and the more explicitly "redemptive" narrative of the Bible can be seen, for Wright, in the connection made between Solomon and the extent of the Davidic covenant: "the historical narrative binds Wisdom into that tradition through its association with Solomon. Any wisdom that is associated with Solomon must be connected with the Solomonic tradition that God should bless the nations in their interaction with Israel."[175]

Similarly, Schultz sees in the Wisdom Literature a degree of movement out to the nations through its associations with Solomon (cf. 1 Kgs 5:9–14) and, given its universal nature and themes and encouragement to embrace the fear of Yahweh, suggests that these books may have been written with a "limited missionary intention."[176] While attractive it is difficult to assess Schultz's suggestion, or the significance of the Solomon link to Job more broadly. Unlike Proverbs and Ecclesiastes, the book of Job is not normally associated with Solomon. It seems then that the Solomon question is less relevant to Job but the attempts of Wright and others to relate Job (and the Wisdom Literature more broadly) to the overarching biblical story in terms of a salvation-historical narrative are important. Clearly this will be something I engage with as part of my missional reading of Job. My main focus in this regard is to ask a different type of question concerning the relationship between Job and the

---

173. Wright, *Mission of God*, 447.
174. Wright, *Mission of God*, 447. See also Hesselgrave, *My Redeemer Lives*, 18–20.
175. Wright, *Mission of God*, 448.
176. My translation. Schultz, "Mission im AT," 44.

biblical narrative. Rather than seeking simply to place the book within the chronological storyline of the Bible, I seek instead to examine how the book of Job functions in relation to it by speaking into it. This will be developed considerably in chapters 3 and 4.

Job and Creation

Glasser et al. suggest that the book of Job illustrates the importance "of the doctrine of Creation" in that "Job never had an adequate conception of God until confronted by the marvels of God's creative work and his providential care over all he had made (38:1–4; 42:5–6)."[177] The degree to which Job's understanding of God at the end of the book is "adequate" is debatable. It could be argued that while Job's overwhelming encounter with God was sufficient for him to know his place and live accordingly, much of his circumstances and his understanding of God remained a mystery. Perhaps too it was the encounter itself with God that was sufficient, rather than the details of the speeches. I will address the function of Yahweh's speeches and Job's responses in more detail in chapters 4 and 5.

In *Let the Nations be Glad!*, Piper cites Job when discussing the wonder of creation and the majesty (Job 26:14) and sovereignty (Job 42:1) of God.[178] Burnett makes a similar point, following a general summary of the contents of Job, with a mention of Job 38 in relation to God's pleasure in Creation, and that, due to God being "Creator and sustainer of the universe, his power is supreme over all things."[179]

Peskett and Ramachandra also reference Job (38–41; 12:10) in relation to discussions on creation.[180] Notably, they pick up on themes of God's delight in creation and the way that creation reflects God's glory. The latter forms part of a discussion on "Mission as earth-keeping," which examines the church's responsibility to care for creation.[181]

For Hedlund the theme of creation in Job is missiologically significant in that "God himself describes his creation as a universal witness

---

177. Glasser et al., *Announcing the Kingdom*, 34.
178. Piper, *Let the Nations Be Glad!*, 19, 65.
179. Burnett, *Healing the Nations*, 95–96.
180. Peskett and Ramachandra, *Message of Mission*, 34, 48, respectively.
181. Peskett and Ramachandra, *Message of Mission*, 48–52. See also Campbell, *Holistic Mission*, who makes two brief references to Job 38–42 in the context of its section on the care for creation.

to the presence and power of God (Job 38–41)" and that "there is also a witness in human wisdom and conscience . . . [that] point to the wisdom of God."[182]

Wright's discussion on the creation theme in the Wisdom Literature focuses on its ethical implications.[183] He contrasts the "motivational appeal" found in Wisdom writings, which is broadly based on Israel's beliefs about the creation (illustrated by, among other texts, Job 31:13–15), and that of the Law and the Prophets, which tend to refer to the "redemptive history" of Israel.[184] For Wright, this distinct, though complementary stress of the Wisdom Literature is missiologically significant in that it emphasizes that, regardless of a person's ethnic, social, or religious distinctives, "we share a common humanity and (whether they acknowledge the fact or not) a common Creator God."[185] Indeed, this commonality should therefore provide fruitful starting points for the communication of "the biblical story of redemption."[186]

Wright connects this sense of universality to the area of ethics as well in that all people are made in the image of God and live in God's creation, and so at some level biblical ethical values will resonate with them.[187] Although the issue of ethics is complex and nuanced, Wright's point does seem plausible, although how it worked or works out in practice is another matter. This discussion relates closely with the theme of Job and social justice, which is discussed above.

Elsewhere, Wright draws on illustrative texts from Job when arguing for the sanctity (but not divinity) of creation (Job 31:26–28); that everything (including creation) belongs to God (Job 4:11); and to support his statement that, "Part of the meaning of the goodness of creation in the Bible is that it testifies to the God who made it, reflecting something of his good character" (Job 12:7–9).[188]

Given the prominence of the theme in Job, and the Wisdom Literature more broadly, it is natural that BMS would mention the book when discussing creation. Often a connection is made between Yahweh's

---

182. Hedlund, *Mission of the Church*, 135.
183. Wright, *Mission of God*, 448–50.
184. Wright, *Mission of God*, 449.
185. Wright, *Mission of God*, 450.
186. Wright, *Mission of God*, 450.
187. Wright, *Mission of God*, 450.
188. Wright, *Mission of God*, 402, 397, 398, respectively.

speeches and his attributes, or affections towards creation. As such these observations seem reasonable up to a point, but they tend not to probe the complex contexts of such references. For example, while the Yahweh speeches do illustrate the power of God, this is often taken in isolation without a discussion of the ambiguities of the tone of the speeches.

A helpful angle explored, for example, by Hedlund and Wright is that of the universal implications of the creation theme in Job. This will be something I will return to in my approach to Job when discussing the universalizing impulse of the book and the treatment of the poor in Job.[189] I will also discuss these themes in relation to a more nuanced treatment of the Yahweh speeches than has been offered by BMS.

Job as an Example of Dialogue

Both the content and form of Job make the book an example that is sometimes drawn upon when scholars discuss the biblical grounding for religious dialogue. As part of a discussion on dialogue in contemporary mission Stott, for example, uses Job as one of several examples from the Bible of God entering into "dialogue" with humanity, citing God's words in Job 38:3; 40:7.[190]

Beeby also draws on Job when discussing contemporary religious dialogue.[191] He considers reflection on dialogue to have been inadequate in how it has appealed to biblical studies.[192] Having reiterated his commitment to the whole canon of Scripture as the source for understanding what may be termed "biblical," Beeby suggests that, outside the book of Job, the Bible evidences little knowledge of dialogue between or within faiths.[193] Frustratingly he does not expand on this assertion about Job.

On a different aspect of "dialogue," Thampu draws on Job to commend the importance of dialogue as a model for relating to God. "The Book of Job," he contends, "is as much on theology, as it is of theology.... What helps, in the end, is that the voice of God is heard."[194]

---

189. Also of note is Hesselgrave's discussion of Job's suffering in relation to creation: "Job shares in the disorder of a creation which is in anguish and longs for transforming (Rom 8:19–22)" (Hesselgrave, *My Redeemer Lives*, 62).

190. Stott, *Christian Mission in the Modern World*, location 726–27.

191. Beeby, *Canon and Mission*, chapter 4.

192. Beeby, *Canon and Mission*, 58.

193. Beeby, *Canon and Mission*, 61.

194. Thampu, *Rediscovering Mission*, 128.

While the book of Job is indeed a particularly sustained example from within the Bible of alternating speech concerning religious beliefs, the extent to which it could or should be a model of contemporary interreligious dialogue is not clear. I would argue that while the dialogue is effective in airing the different views, it cannot be seen as a discussion that builds to mutual understanding in a constructive way. Rather, the parties are silenced by the authoritative word of Yahweh.[195]

Perhaps Job is better understood as a tool rather than a model of interreligious dialogue; that is, a text that can be discussed, for example, by adherents of Judaism, Christianity and Islam, whose sacred texts all include the character of Job. One such example is the practice of Scriptural Reasoning, whereby adherents to (usually) Judaism, Christianity and Islam read together from their sacred texts for mutual appreciation and understanding.[196] However, this may be carried out without any missional intention.[197]

In chapters 4 and 5 I develop the idea of the book of Job as joining an international conversation on the theme of unattributed suffering. In this sense it could be described as entering into dialogue with other beliefs. As already indicated, perhaps Job was even used in this way in its original context, although there is no way of knowing.

Conclusions

The purpose of this chapter was to evaluate the extent to which and the ways in which BMS has engaged with Job in order to give a context for my own missional reading of Job and to highlight promising lines of discussion that I can develop as part of my approach.

As I have demonstrated, the majority of BMS does not engage in significant depth with Job, with many works either failing to mention the book, or doing so in relatively peripheral and underdeveloped ways. While I sought to explain why this inattention to Job might be understandable, given the subject, scope and approach of many of the publications, I concluded that for certain studies this tendency is both significant

---

195. The tone of the debate is also at odds with that envisaged by contemporary adherents to dialogue. See Matthey, "Serving God's Mission," esp. 33–34, who connects the openness of the broader Wisdom Literature to the idea of dialogue.

196. See, for example, Ticciati's issue of *The Journal of Scriptural Reasoning*, focused on the theme of the "Wisdom of Job."

197. See, for example, Scriptural Reasoning, "FAQs."

and concerning. For example, where a study aims at presenting an understanding of mission from across the OT or Bible as a whole, to neglect the book of Job or the Wisdom Literature more generally may suggest that the adopted framework is insufficient.

Following this discussion on the relative neglect of Job I then isolated a number of themes around which BMS did engage with the book of Job. It seems clear that, despite engaging with Job in a variety of ways, the literature examined in this chapter allows considerable room for further missional consideration of the book. My study builds on what has gone before by developing certain themes in a more intentional, substantial, sustained and nuanced manner.

For example, I give considerable attention to the international or universal outlook of Job, seen especially through the non-Israelite setting of the book. In chapter 4 I deal with issues such as the absence of explicit Israelite elements such as the temple, the *torah*, or the exodus, and the universal relevance of the book's themes. Following an in-depth examination of the non-Israelite setting of the book I explore the missional significance of Job's non-Israelite provenance. I read this not primarily as a statement about the status of non-Israelites in relation to God, but more as a means of universalizing the book's message. However, by highlighting the universalizing impulse in Job, I show that this was not achieved at the expense of a unique presentation of Israelite faith. Indeed, where I engage with the relationship between Job and similar ANE texts in chapter 5, I develop the characterisation of Job's universalism by showing that it is founded on a belief in the uniqueness of Yahweh, and therefore the inadequacy of other explorations of the problem of unattributed suffering. Nevertheless, this encounter with ANE ideas should be understood in terms of both affirmation and critique.

As such this relates also to the discussion in BMS on the way in which Job corrects false teaching, particularly the misapplication of a belief in retribution, either within Israel, in the ANE more broadly, or even in contemporary contexts. Closely connected to this theme is the way in which the issues of poverty and social justice are engaged with in Job. In line with my holistic understanding of mission, I focus chapter 6 on an extended study of the treatment of the poor in Job. Here I show how poverty functions within the book and how Job has a unique contribution to make to this important missional issue.

As has been clear in the current chapter, the question of how Job relates to the "story of redemption" is one that has not been easily resolved in BMS. I address this by examining issues of canon and story in relation to competing renderings of reality. Instead of asking how Job fits into and progresses the *missio Dei* I conclude that a more useful and distinctive question for Job is to ask how the book stands apart from and speaks into the *missio Dei*. The focus of this argument is the question posed by the accuser in Job 1:9b: "Is it for nothing that Job fears God?" Therefore, while much BMS discussing the accuser focuses on his identity and God's power over him, I take the accuser theme in a different direction by seeing his question as being of primary importance. If his accusation is true, the whole project of the *missio Dei* is thrown into question. In Job, therefore, the very mission of God is at stake. In contrast with the majority of BMS, by framing Job in this way I locate the book more centrally into discussions on mission.

The BMS theme of Job as illustrative of suffering and weakness as the context of mission also features in my study. In chapters 4 and 5 I show how the universalizing impulse in Job relates to the ambiguities of human experience and how this may be understood missionally. In chapter 6 this is addressed with specific reference to the issue of poverty.

Although important for mission, the themes of creation care, interfaith dialogue, and Job as an instrument of contemporary mission activity do not feature significantly in the study, largely for reasons of scope. Nevertheless, these are highlighted as examples of possible future research in my concluding chapter.

This chapter has shown that my study stands in a tradition of missional reflection on Job. However, it has also demonstrated that this tradition seems rather marginal to most BMS and remains significantly underdeveloped. As such it seems clear that this volume has the potential to make what I hope will be a significant contribution to BMS, and move the conversation forward in helpful ways. In so doing it will also provide an innovative way of approaching the biblical text of Job.

But how can such an approach be framed? The next step is to build on the material in this chapter by developing a framework for approaching the book of Job using a missional hermeneutic. In the following chapter I will set out an understanding of missional hermeneutics, and show how its diverse lines of inquiry can enable me to build on the work noted in this chapter, and provide rich possibilities for a missional reading of Job.

3

Developing a Missional Approach to the Book of Job

IT IS CLEAR FROM the preceding chapter that the book of Job has not received sustained or, in my view, adequate attention from BMS. The majority of scholars have either ignored Job or used it in rather peripheral or underdeveloped ways, and although the literature does include a variety of attempts to relate the book of Job to mission, in general these are limited in scope and mixed in their success. However, while chapter two highlighted a number of potential themes that might be addressed in a missional reading of Job, it did not address the method or framework for doing so. The present chapter addresses this by setting my reading of Job in the context of the approach to biblical interpretation known as missional hermeneutics.

Still relatively early in its development, writing on missional hermeneutics has not yet produced an explicit and substantial treatment of Job of the scale I am attempting. One prominent feature of the missional hermeneutics conversation is the variety of ways in which it has been conceptualized and implemented. Seen positively this affords the interpreter a striking array of choices concerning how to read the biblical text missionally. More negatively, the sheer variety of options presents a challenge: which one or ones should be employed and which should be sidelined? By what criteria should these decisions be made? Are particular lines of inquiry more suitable for some texts than others?[1]

---

1. See Barram, "Response."

In the present chapter I examine the principal ways in which missional hermeneutics has been understood in order to move towards my own treatment of Job. I do this by examining two of the main lines of inquiry proposed by advocates of missional hermeneutics. In each case I assess its validity and applicability to Job, and discuss the extent to which and the ways in which my own reading of Job will engage with it. Such an approach thereby acts as an initial foray into my missional reading of Job.

In the final part of the chapter I draw together the discussion and set out my own lines of inquiry, which I apply to Job in the rest of the volume. I conclude that, while there are a number of different and important questions that could be asked of the book, my focus will be on the relationship between the particular and the universal, the book's missional encounter with culture, and the theme of the treatment of the poor in Job. I will also show in the later part of this book how the *missio Dei* brings together these different elements.

Lines of Inquiry for a Missional Hermeneutic

In the introductory chapter I explained that missional hermeneutics is an approach to biblical interpretation that seeks to read texts in the light of the missional nature of the Bible. I then outlined some of the missional dimensions of the Bible, with some initial comments as to how these function in relation to the book of Job. One outcome of that review was to demonstrate something of the breadth and complexity of thinking of the Bible as missional, which goes some way to accounting for the variety of emphases and approaches evident in missional hermeneutics scholarship, while also showing its potential for beneficial missional reflection on biblical texts.

With this in mind I now discuss two of the main lines of inquiry pursued by missional hermeneutics scholars.[2] As will become clear,

---

2. These are the first two of the taxonomy offered by the SBL/AAR Gospel and Our Culture Forum on Missional Hermeneutics, which proposes that those engaged in missional readings of biblical texts will "pay attention to a number of interlocking realities in the text: (1) the ways in which the biblical text renders the identity of the missio Dei, the God who is engaged in mission to the whole creation; (2) the ways in which the biblical text is shaped for the purpose of forming a people of God who are called to participate in God's mission to the creation; (3) the ways in which the biblical text evokes and challenges a missionally located community's interpretive readings and questions; (4) the ways in which the biblical text relates the received tradition to a particular context in light of the good news of the reign of God in Jesus Christ;

although this categorization is useful up to a point, I do find it somewhat uneven in places. The approaches themselves provide useful material for consideration but some are rather limited when it comes to my particular approach to Job.

The Missional Direction of the Story

> The *framework* for biblical interpretation is the story it tells of the mission of God and the formation of a community sent to participate in it.[3]

> The ways in which the biblical text renders the identity of the missio Dei, the God who is engaged in mission to the whole creation.[4]

The line of inquiry that has received the most attention from scholars is the notion that the Bible as a whole renders a coherent narrative that describes the mission of God. Indeed, this may even be considered as foundational for all other approaches.[5]

The Bible as a Whole: Canon, Story, and the Story

A missional hermeneutic is based, in part, on the assumption that the Bible *as a whole* is relevant to mission, and not just a few isolated texts. Bauckham, for example, sees this as essential: "What sort of hermeneutic will enable us to enter into the Bible's own missionary direction from the particular to the universal? It must be, in the first place, a canonical hermeneutic, that is, a way of reading the Bible as a whole."[6]

This commitment to approaching the whole of the Bible as a resource and context for missional reflection is contrary to the so-called

---

and (5) the ways in which the biblical text discloses its fullest meaning only when read together with the culturally and socially 'other'" (GOCN, "Forum on Missional Hermeneutics"). The first four categories are straight from Hunsberger, "Proposals." The fifth category, focusing on the "other," is still closely related, the roots of which can be discerned from both responses to his 2008 paper. See Barram, "Response"; Brownson, "Response." The headings I employ below reflect Hunsberger's phrasing.

3. Hunsberger, "Proposals," 310.
4. GOCN, "Forum on Missional Hermeneutics."
5. An observation made by Hunsberger, "Proposals," 312.
6. Bauckham, *Bible and Mission*, 11–12; similarly, Wright, *Mission of God*, 17.

"text-assembly" approach which seems to have characterized a significant amount of writing on the Bible and mission in the past.[7] An advantage of this approach is that it has the potential to give greater biblical weight to missional discussions, helping to guard against the biases that may arise through inappropriate selectivity of particular texts or images for mission.[8] It also opens up the way for reflecting on less obvious texts, which may yield different insights. On the other hand, an attempt to see texts within the context of the whole Bible will at times be challenging, given the tensions evident within the canon.[9]

The notion of the Bible as canon brings to the fore the processes by which the texts in their final form and position came into being. On the whole I consider this an aspect of canon that has not been explored in great detail thus far in missional hermeneutics scholarship, with the notable exception of Beeby, for whom it plays an important role and relates closely to the discussion on the missional origins of texts noted in chapter 1. The canon, Beeby suggests, was formed in crisis and met a missional need. The *torah*, for example, was collated in the exile when Israel were asking of themselves fundamental questions concerning their identity, role, worship and hope.[10] What the process of canonisation offered was both stability by telling the primal story, and flexibility through a measure of ambiguity, which made it possible for Israel to adapt its Scriptures to new challenges and contexts.[11]

Beeby then throws open the question:

> Is it possible in any sense to say that the canon exists for mission and that the *missio Dei*, the *missio Christi* and the *missio ecclesiae* are in great part the explanation for the existence of the canon? Dare we advance a step further as we query whether Christian mission can effectively exist without the canon and also whether we can effectively understand the canon unless we are constantly aware of its missionary roots, its growth in mission and its missionary imperative? Is mission hidden beneath the non-missionary language of the canonizing process?[12]

---

7. Wright, *Mission of God*, 36; Bosch, "Hermeneutical Principles," 439–40.
8. Beeby, *Canon and Mission*, 6.
9. Beeby, *Canon and Mission*, 4.
10. Beeby, "Missional Approach," 272.
11. Beeby, "Missional Approach," 273.
12. Beeby, "Missional Approach," 274.

I will return to the theme of canon in more depth when addressing the question of the missional encounter with cultures evident in the biblical story. In particular I will draw on the work of Sanders, who speaks about the process by which texts emerged and were used and re-used enabling the reader to detect, "the struggle of Israel and the early churches to respond by monotheizing over against the several forms of polytheism in the five culture eras through and out of which the Bible was formed and shaped."[13]

Another central tenet of this line of inquiry is that the Bible functions as a narrative. The understanding here is that in its canonical wholeness the Bible tells a story, which will require "a narrative hermeneutic."[14] Such a hermeneutic will account for the overarching narrative that encompasses many smaller stories and non-narrative genres, while still "constituting in its overall direction a metanarrative, a narrative about the whole of reality that elucidates the meaning of the whole of reality."[15]

Bauckham's helpful statement touches on several important points. First, an approach to reading and interpreting the Bible must account for the narrative nature of much of its material. The OT, for example, is dominated by the narrative of the people of Israel and their dealings with Yahweh and it is through this story that we learn about who God is.[16]

One strength of this approach is its acknowledgment of the complexities inherent in understanding the Bible as an overarching story, which relates closely to the above discussion on canon. That this single story encompasses many other stories is an important point which guards against naive assumptions about the nature of the biblical story. Thus, the story the Bible renders is not a simplistic, "tightly woven story with no loose ends."[17] Rather, this "sprawling collection of narratives" includes stories told more than once and from differing perspectives (for example, Kings, Chronicles, the Gospels), "the profusion and sheer untidiness" of the numerous smaller stories within larger narratives, and many other features of ambiguity and incompleteness.[18] In sum, "the biblical story

---

13. Sanders, *Canon and Community*, 36. The five culture eras he refers to are the Bronze Age, the Iron Age, and the Persian, Hellenistic, and Roman eras.
14. Bauckham, *Bible and Mission*, 12.
15. Bauckham, *Bible and Mission*, 12.
16. Goldingay, *Israel's Gospel*, 30.
17. Goheen, "Urgency," 473.
18. Bauckham, *Bible and Mission*, 92. See also Goldingay, *Israel's Gospel*, 35–41.

refuses to be summed up in a finally adequate interpretation that would never need to be revised or replaced."[19]

The question of non-narrative material and texts that do not fit neatly into the chronological storyline of the Bible comes into play here as well. This also relates to well-established discussions concerning the ways in which writings such as the Wisdom Literature relate to other material within the canon.

Here it helps to consider "story" as a broader concept than purely narrative writing. The OT story includes much non-narrative material, which is either already located within a narrative context (for example, the legal materials within the Moses story), or other texts which may be connected in some way with the overall narrative framework of the OT.[20] In terms of the Wisdom Literature it seems helpful (albeit up to a point) to use the Solomon association as a means of locating it within that narrative.[21] However, this is less helpful for the book of Job which, unlike Proverbs and Ecclesiastes, tends not to be associated with Solomon. Locating Job in the chronological storyline of the OT is far from straightforward. Should the story of Job be placed before or around the time of Abraham, according to its archaic setting (as Allen does), or should we try to locate it at the point when it was written, or at least put together? If the latter, when should this be, in light of the lack of consensus about the book's dating?

In my view these complicating aspects to the biblical narrative do not negate attempts to work towards an account of the storyline of the Bible.[22] Although there are caveats to bear in mind, I would see them as indications of something profoundly important inherent in the canon. I mean by this that the ambiguities and tensions within the canon are indicative of the potential of the biblical narrative to speak for and speak into the complexities of human experience, with all the ambiguities and vexing questions that life entails.[23] The book of Job, I will argue, is an excellent example of this.

---

19. Bauckham, *Bible and Mission*, 93.

20. Barr, *Biblical Theology*, 356; Goheen, "Urgency," 472–73.

21. As do, for example, Barr, *Biblical Theology*, 356; Wright, *Mission of God*, 448. They both note the importance of "association," so they are not making any claims about Solomonic authorship.

22. Bauckham, *Bible and Mission*, 93.

23. See Goldingay, *Israel's Gospel*, 41; Beeby, "Missional Approach," 275.

"Narrative" is not just a description of a principal genre within the Bible. The Bible may be understood as rendering a "big story," an overall narrative which ultimately constitutes a metanarrative that purports to explain the nature of reality. A powerful aspect of the biblical narrative is, therefore, that it creates a world and invites us to locate ourselves within it, thereby shaping our identities.[24]

The biblical story is therefore not just presented as *a* story, but as *the* story, which functions as a means of transformation for its readers. The effect of this claim is profound as it is through the overarching narrative that we are able to discern the worldview of the one telling the story:

> In reading these texts we are invited to embrace a metanarrative, a grand narrative. And on this overarching story is based a worldview that, like all worldviews and metanarratives, claims to explain the way things are, how they have come to be so, and what they ultimately will be. . . . [It is] a *rendering of reality*—an account of the universe we inhabit and of the new creation we are destined for. We live in a storied universe.[25]

However, is not the very idea of a metanarrative arrogant, or even dangerous? In the current climate, it should be acknowledged that there exists a suspicion that a narrative that claims to tell *the* story of reality is suppressive and oppressive.[26] In response it can be argued that the biblical narrative is fundamentally different to modern, post-Enlightenment metanarratives that are built on the idea of progress and "human mastery."[27] God's purposes will be achieved but there remains considerable ambiguity as to the precise nature of this fulfilment.[28] The biblical metanarrative, as articulated in the text itself, is rarely depicted as the dominant worldview of its time.[29] Moreover, I would argue that the biblical story finds its focal point at a moment of ultimate weakness and

---

24. Bauckham, *Bible and Mission*, 12.

25. Wright, *Mission of God*, 55–56. The notion of a "big story" has, so far, been seen as essential to work on missional hermeneutics. See Hunsberger, "Proposals," 312. I take as synonyms various terms used by scholars, often interchangeably, including, "big story," "metanarrative," "grand narrative," "macronarrative," "overarching narrative," and so on.

26. A view articulated and argued against by Bauckham, *Bible and Mission*, 89.

27. Bauckham, *Bible and Mission*, 90–91; Bartholomew and Goheen, "Story and Biblical Theology," 166.

28. Bauckham, *Bible and Mission*, 92.

29. Bauckham, *Bible and Mission*, 103.

suffering, at the crucifixion of Jesus Christ.[30] Indeed, suffering and weakness as the context and means of its progression is an important feature of the whole narrative.[31]

The theme of diversity is also a crucial one in answering objections to the legitimacy of a grand narrative. As noted already, the biblical canon is not uniform but includes within it a mix of genres, multi-perspectival accounts, stories within stories, and ambiguity: "the particular has its own integrity that should not be suppressed for the sake of a too readily comprehensible universal."[32]

Indeed, it could be argued that the biblical metanarrative seeks to celebrate cultural diversity, rather than eradicate it. In Colossians 3:11, for example, Paul's denial of there being Greek, Jew, barbarian or Sythian refers to "cultural privilege, not cultural diversity."[33] But in a much broader sense it is the very nature of the Christian gospel, as depicted in the biblical narrative, to embrace cultural diversity; indeed, to be at home in it.[34]

Therefore, that the Bible presents a coherent narrative which makes universal claims does not need to equate to uniformity and suppression: "it is also a story that affirms humanity in all its particular cultural variety. This is the universal story that gives a place in the sun to all the little stories."[35]

However, despite the important dynamic of diversity and weakness evident in the biblical story, this should not undermine the radical claims that the biblical story makes in relation to other renderings of reality. I will return to the notion of the biblical story as an alternative or competing rendering of reality below. Before I do this, however, I need to explore why this grand narrative might be understood as missional.

---

30. Bartholomew and Goheen, "Story and Biblical Theology," 167.

31. See, for example, Bosch, *Vulnerability*; "Hermeneutical Principles," 444–45, 450. See also Bauckham's important discussion on "To all by way of the least" (*Bible and Mission*, 49–54), which I address below. See also McConville, *God and Earthly Power*, 29: "Yahwism never takes the form of the domination of the weak by the strong. On the contrary, it is advocated in political weakness, and in the face of such power."

32. Bauckham, *Bible and Mission*, 93. See also Senior and Stuhlmueller, *Biblical Foundations*, 344.

33. Bauckham, *Bible and Mission*, 110. See also Brownson, "Response."

34. See, for example, Senior and Stuhlmueller, *Biblical Foundations*, 344; Sanneh, *Whose Religion*, 97–98; Walls, *Missionary Movement*, chapter 1; Brownson, *Speaking*, chapter 2.

35. Wright, *Mission of God*, 47.

The Mission of God as Concept for Framing the Content of the Biblical Narrative's Rendering of Reality

As noted above, advocates of a missional hermeneutic tend to accept an understanding of mission and of the Bible that is framed by the *missio Dei*. Beeby illustrates this tendency well, his central argument being, "that the Bible read as scripture centers on the *missio Dei*. It is the record of the word and works of the loving, revealing God who created in love and redeems in love."[36]

Such a starting point means that the whole of the biblical narrative comes into view. Understood through the lens of the *missio Dei*, God's purposes, speech and actions and his relationship to humanity and the whole of creation can all be read as rendering an account of the mission of God. It is from this initial perspective that so many of the writers on missional hermeneutics begin.

The *missio Dei*, therefore, may be understood as the driving force behind the biblical story, the focal point of coherence for the biblical story, and the chief purpose of the biblical story, as the discussion on the missional dimensions of the Bible in chapter 1 illustrates.

Two important motifs running throughout the biblical story are the concepts of the universal and the particular. Indeed, the complex relationship between these is a long-established subject of discussion in BMS, as well as in more general works on the Bible.[37] Alluding to the call of Abram in Genesis 12:1–3, Wright frames the discussion helpfully by describing a "tension between the universality of the goal *(all nations)* and the particularity of the means *(through you)*," both of which he considers as "crucial in unlocking the Bible's grand narrative."[38]

In my view this is a significant aspect of a biblical understanding of mission. As such, it would be helpful to examine in more depth this relationship between the particular and the universal and how it functions within the biblical story and in relation to the book of Job. A particularly useful approach is proposed by Bauckham, who sets the story within the context of the language of the movement from the particular to the

---

36. Beeby, "Missional Approach," 272.

37. See, for example, discussions in Wright, *Mission of God*, chapter 7; Bauckham, *Bible and Mission*, 11–26; Legrand, *Unity and Plurality*, chapter 3; Martin-Achard, *Light to the Nations*, chapter 3; Rétif and Lamarche, *Salvation of the Gentiles*; Schultz, "Universalism."

38. Wright, *Mission of God*, 222.

universal.[39] This, I believe, provides a helpful way in to discussions on Job, because the biblical canon enables the Bible to speak into the specificity of human experience in relationship with God, while setting this in the context of God's universal purposes. As we read the "stories about people facing the challenges, potentials, questions, achievements, ambiguities, puzzles, disappointments, demands and failures that are intrinsic to life with God," we find ourselves invited, "to reflect on the equivalent specificities of [our] own lives in light of the stories' implicit convictions about who God is and what human life is. Such reflection needs the help of narrative with its concreteness and specificity."[40]

Yet the story does not remain in its specificity. Bauckham sees the Bible as "a kind of project aimed at the kingdom of God, that is, towards the achievement of God's purposes for good in the whole of God's creation."[41] A Christian community or individual reading the Bible is always on an outward journey from the particular (as defined by the Bible or their own situation) to the universal, which "is to be found not apart from but within other particulars. This is mission."[42]

The particular-universal movement is also a reflection of God himself as revealed in the Bible: he "is the God of the people Israel and the one human, Jesus Christ, and is also the Creator and Lord of all things."[43] The identity of the biblical God is a *narrative* identity, as is the identity of his people: "God identifies himself as the God of Abraham, Israel and Jesus *in order to be* the God of all people and the Lord of all things."[44]

Bauckham then portrays this particular-universal direction of the Bible in three ways (temporal, spatial and social) and considers their implications for mission. The *temporal* dynamic begins at creation and moves forward into "the eschatological future."[45] In this context, "mission is movement into the new future of God."[46] This movement is seen definitively in the person and work of Jesus: "Mission is the movement

---

39. Bauckham, *Bible and Mission*.
40. Goldingay, *Israel's Gospel*, 36–37.
41. Bauckham, *Bible and Mission*, 11.
42. Bauckham, *Bible and Mission*, 11.
43. Bauckham, *Bible and Mission*, 12.
44. Bauckham, *Bible and Mission*, 13.
45. Bauckham, *Bible and Mission*, 13.
46. Bauckham, *Bible and Mission*, 13.

that takes place between Jesus' own sending by his Father, and the future coming of Jesus in the kingdom of his Father."[47]

The *spatial* movement of the biblical story concerns geography, "from one place to every place, from the center to the periphery, from Jerusalem to the ends of the earth . . . *mission is movement towards ever-new horizons.*"[48]

Finally, the theme of social movement in the Bible accounts for the *numerical* movement, "from the one to the many, from Abraham to the nations, from Jesus to every creature in heaven, on earth and under the earth. Socially, then, *mission is a movement that is always being joined by others, the movement, therefore, of an ever-new people.*"[49]

It is worth pausing to reflect upon how these relate to the book of Job. I have already noted the difficulty in placing Job on the chronological storyline of the Bible. The early setting of the book may place the events around the time of Abraham, but little can be concluded from this. Perhaps, given the non-Israelite motif in Job, the notions of the spatial and social movements of the biblical story are more promising. Yet even here the book of Job seems to separate itself from the main storyline of the Bible. There has not been a movement, as such, from Israel to Uz. We are never told how Job came to know Israel's God; indeed it may be anachronistic to ask this question. It seems that the author of Job is not concerned with connecting his story to Israel's storyline. Or, rather, the author seems more concerned to create "a sense of narrative distance."[50] I will say more about this in chapter 4, which highlights the significance of the dynamic of the particular and the universal in Job, which I discuss in terms of the universalizing impulse of the book.

Having set out something of his approach, Bauckham illustrates how an awareness of the particular-universal movement might inform a reading of the biblical story. He concentrates on four "strands" in the grand story. The first three revolve around a "singular" choice of God which embody "thematic trajectories": Abraham (the trajectory of blessing), Israel (God reveals himself to the world) and David (God's rule).[51]

---

47. Bauckham, *Bible and Mission*, 13.
48. Bauckham, *Bible and Mission*, 14.
49. Bauckham, *Bible and Mission*, 15.
50. Newsom, "Job," 345.
51. Bauckham, *Bible and Mission*, 27.

The fourth strand characterizes all that has come before it and marks the church's mission as well; it is "the movement to all by way of the least."[52]

Having shown how each of the first three strands' trajectories can be discerned throughout the biblical metanarrative, Bauckham maintains that, "God's purpose in each of these singular choices was universal: that the blessing of Abraham might overflow to all the families of the earth, that God's self-revelation to Israel might make God known to all the nations, that from Zion his rule might extend to the ends of the earth."[53]

Although Bauckham does not consider these strands in themselves to constitute "mission," he does think that they, "make the church's mission intelligible as a necessary and coherent part of the whole biblical metanarrative. . . . They establish the purpose of God for the world that, again, the church is called to serve in mission to the world."[54]

He therefore contends that "mission" is very rare in the OT, but that the OT still has a vital contribution to make to a biblical understanding of mission.[55]

The universal purposes of God in his election of, and dealings with Israel is, in my view, of great importance for a missional reading, reflecting as it does Israel's participation in the *missio Dei*. While, as I have suggested, the relationship between the book of Job and the biblical storyline is not straightforward, the universal context of God's purposes does at least shed some light. In this sense we might ask, in what ways does the book of Job function in the service of God's universal purposes? Even if it does not fit naturally into Israel's storyline, it is still part of Israel's Scriptures, functioning as we have seen to shape their participation in God's mission. This is a theme to which I return below when discussing the missional purpose of the biblical writings, but also, more fully, in chapters 4, 5, and 6.

A further characteristic of the biblical story that Bauckham highlights well concerns God's tendency to use the weak and powerless to achieve his purposes.[56] This is seen ultimately in the crucifixion and exultation of Christ, as depicted in Phil 2:6–11, and so it becomes incumbent on those engaged in mission to heed this call to identify with "the least":

52. Bauckham, *Bible and Mission*, 49.
53. Bauckham, *Bible and Mission*, 46.
54. Bauckham, *Bible and Mission*, 47.
55. Bauckham, *Bible and Mission*, 47.
56. Bauckham, *Bible and Mission*, 49–54. As examples, he cites Deut 7:7; 1 Sam 2:3–8; 16:6–13; 1 Cor 1:26b–9.

The gospel does not come to each person only in terms of some abstracted generality of human nature, but in the realities and differences of their social and economic situations. It engages with the injustices of the world on its way to the kingdom of God. This means that as well as the outward movement of the church's mission in geographical extension and numerical increase, there must also be this (in the Bible's imagery) downward movement of solidarity with the people at the bottom of the social scale of importance and wealth. It is to these—the poorest, those with no power or influence, the wretched, the neglected—to whom God has given priority in the kingdom, not only for their own sake, but also for all the rest of us who can enter the kingdom only alongside *them*.[57]

Bauckham does not involve himself in technical discussions concerning the validity of holistic mission, but this acknowledgment of the importance of the poverty theme, particularly as it is integrated into his broader framework, seems significant. This interest in poverty and social justice is reflected in BMS to varying degrees, as outlined in my previous chapter.[58] In addition to Bauckham, for example, Wright and Barram have addressed the significance of poverty as part of their missional hermeneutic approaches. Wright devotes two chapters of his *The Mission of God* to material on the themes of redemption and restoration, and sees these texts as being closely related to a holistic view of mission and, as such, particularly relevant to issues of poverty and justice.[59] As with other chapters in his book, Wright then describes how these concerns play out in the unfolding narrative of the Bible. For Wright, then, poverty (alongside other social, economic and political concerns) is a most appropriate (indeed, necessary) topic of interest for a missional reading.

Like Wright, Barram's approach to poverty issues reflects his commitment to a holistic understanding of mission.[60] In part he sees a function of missional hermeneutics as asking difficult questions of the contemporary church that try to articulate how that group of believers works out its participation in the *missio Dei* in their particular community.

57. Bauckham, *Bible and Mission*, 53–54.

58. So, for example, Peskett and Ramachandra, *Message of Mission*, chapter 9; Burnett, *Healing of the Nations*, chapters 6–7; Bosch, "Hermeneutical Principles," 442–43, 447–48.

59. See Wright, *Mission of God*, chapter 8–9. See also Michael Gorman's work on justice and righteousness in Gorman, *Becoming the Gospel*.

60. See Barram, "Located"; *Missional Economics*.

He lists a number of examples of the kind of questions he means, some of which are related specifically to issues of poverty and justice, as he would conceive them for his own context:

> In what ways does this text proclaim good news to the poor and release to the captives, and how might our own social locations make it difficult to hear that news as good?
>
> Does our reading of the text reflect a tendency to bifurcate evangelism and justice?
>
> Does our reading of this text acknowledge and confess our complicity and culpability in personal as well as structural sin?
>
> In what ways does the text challenge us to rethink our often-cozy relationships with power and privilege?
>
> How does this text expose and challenge our societal and economic tendencies to assign human beings and the rest of creation merely functional, as opposed to inherent, value?
>
> Does the text help clarify the call of gospel discipleship in a world of conspicuous consumption, devastating famine, rampant disease, incessant war, and vast economic inequities?[61]

In chapter 1 I noted the importance of the themes of poverty and social justice for a holistic understanding of mission. My framing of a missional hermeneutic in terms of mission, therefore, builds on these assumptions and relates closely with elements of scholars such as Bauckham, Wright and Barram. Despite different nuances, each sees important connections between the missional nature of the Bible and issues of poverty, power and justice. They therefore give precedent for poverty to be a topic of interest in a missional reading of biblical texts.

As a way into the question of social justice in the book of Job I have chosen the motif of the treatment of the poor, which I address in considerable depth in chapter 6. Clearly this particular angle does not cover all aspects of social justice or broader issues important to holistic mission such as care for creation. Nevertheless, I will show that the treatment of the poor is worthy of specific attention, and functions in important ways not only in missional discussions, but also in the book of Job itself. Not least, in the book of Job we observe an individual making the downward

---

61. Barram, "Located."

descent to marginalization, which intensifies his association and commitment to the poor.

Having outlined certain characteristics of the biblical story that will impact a missional reading, I now need to return to more particular questions concerning how the rendering of reality articulated by the biblical writings encounters alternative renderings. The overarching, missional narrative of the Bible presents a metanarrative, a biblical "worldview" that is set in contrast with alternative renderings of reality. Within the biblical story there are many examples of direct and indirect "encounters" between these renderings. This idea now needs to be teased out in more detail.

The "Missionary Encounter" of Biblical Texts: The Biblical Story as an Alternative Rendering of Reality

Either implicitly or explicitly, in the texts of the OT Israel's worldview, or its "rendering of reality" is assumed, described and promoted.[62] The task of articulating the biblical rendering of reality was not simply an intellectual exercise. Its purpose was to reinforce and pass on faith in Yahweh. It was there to persuade. As I have already established, the writing and collating of these texts were not conducted in a cultural, political, historical or social vacuum. More often than not it seems that the authors and editors of the biblical material set about their tasks in the midst of, and in response to challenges to their rendering of reality and threats within and to their community. In this sense the rendering of reality put across by the biblical writers was both rhetorical and polemical. It both countered threatening alternative worldviews, but also assumed that it was (to borrow the language of Newbigin) to be "public truth" that described reality

---

62. By "worldview," I mean a culture's body of beliefs it shares concerning how they understand reality and their place within it. It will have elements that are consciously articulated, but often it is simply assumed. Indeed, a worldview is not just a set of suppositions readily acknowledged by a culture (though it will involve these); at its basic level, a worldview is the means through which a society perceives reality. Wright describes worldviews as embracing "all deep-level human perceptions of reality" in that they relate to "the presuppositional, pre-cognitive stage of a culture or society" (Wright, *New Testament*, 123, 122). A worldview not only articulates belief but also directs behavior in that they set a context—and, often, a faith commitment—in which individuals and communities live out their lives. See Goheen and Bartholomew, *Crossroads*, 23.

not just for Israel but for the whole of creation.[63] It was therefore common for the Yahweh-rendering to encounter other renderings of reality assumed, described and promoted by other cultures.

In chapter 1 I identified this tendency when discussing the missional dimensions of the biblical writings; specifically when noting the Bible as a "product" of mission. Though not employing the language of "mission," this struggle to articulate a Yahweh-shaped rendering of reality has been usefully framed by Sanders, who describes Israel and the early church as producing and shaping writings using a process of "monotheizing over against . . . polytheism."[64] Sanders characterizes the Bible as "a monotheizing literature" and it is this monotheizing characteristic that gives the Bible "its principal and hermeneutic shape" and, I would add, its missional edge.[65]

Sanders's canonical approach aims to detect two categories of "precursor" material in particular texts: the home-grown "community traditions" and the borrowed "international wisdom traditions."[66] The interpreter then tries to understand "the hermeneutics by which those identified traditions function in the passage, how they were adapted, represented, and resignified."[67] Sanders considers it as a positive thing that the Bible appropriates idioms and wisdom from other cultures, and suggests that this leads to a "newly perceived underlying hermeneutic" that understands "God as Creator of all peoples, as well as Redeemer in Israel and in Christ. Those are the two basic hermeneutic axioms operating in the Bible."[68] These points relate closely to the discussion on the particular-universal theme in the Bible, noted above. Indeed, considering the more affirmative, "open" meeting points of such encounters, this may also contribute to a defence of the notion of a biblical metanarrative, and may prove to be especially important if such texts are drawn on to reflect upon contemporary missional praxis. Sanders also helpfully observes that the biblical writers tended to be operating in the context of weakness and threat, under the shadow of more dominant powers.[69] Like

---

63. Newbigin, *Truth to Tell*.
64. Sanders, *Canon and Community*, 36.
65. Sanders, *Canon and Community*, 43.
66. Sanders, *Canon and Community*, 47.
67. Sanders, *Canon and Community*, 47.
68. Sanders, *Canon and Community*, 48.
69. Sanders, *Canon and Community*, 54–55. He notes how this was often the experience of individuals as well as the nation as a whole. Interestingly, for my purposes, he

Bauckham, Sanders speaks of God's consistent use of the marginalized throughout the Bible, which, as I have shown, may also commend the notion of a biblical metanarrative.[70]

By "wisdom" Sanders means "that which passes over national borders and reaches deep into the common human experience."[71] Although it "pervades the Bible," wisdom is "parallel" to the particular stories of Israel and Christ (the Gospel).[72] So wisdom in this sense is not restricted to the Wisdom Literature, but may be found in laws, narratives, and other types of literature in the Bible.[73] The key point of interest for Sanders, however, lies not in the existence of this cross-border usage, but in how the biblical writers adapted the material and what this would have signified to their readers.[74]

Although Sanders does not use "mission" language, this meeting of cultures he describes as evident throughout the Bible is, it seems to me, profoundly missional since intercultural engagement is such a core characteristic of mission.[75] A missional reading of a biblical text will, I would suggest, seek to draw out the nature and significance of such encounters, examining issues including the degree of encounter, the ways in which it functions, and even ways in which such an encounter may inform contemporary encounters in mission. Sanders's suggestion of a process of adaption may be useful here.[76] Although they would not necessarily have articulated such a process and would not even have gone through each step each time, the biblical writers tended to adapt non-Israelite material by removing references to other deities, asserting the presence and action

---

notes the character of Job in this connection: "Themes such as the Suffering Servant in Isaiah or a man called Job, clobbered four times over, fit well into the story of Israel's struggle to monotheize in the middle of deprivation and suffering" (Sanders, *Canon and Community*, 55).

70. Sanders, *Canon and Community*, 54. See also Bauckham, *Bible and Mission*, 49–54.

71. Sanders, *Canon and Community*, 48.

72. Sanders, *Canon and Community*, 48. Although parallel, he notes that they often "mingle."

73. Sanders, *Canon and Community*, 48.

74. Sanders, *Canon and Community*, 48–49.

75. Although he takes it in a different direction, this close relationship between missional encounters and cross-cultural encounters is noted by Brownson, "Response."

76. Sanders, *Canon and Community*, 56.

of one God, naming that God, "Yahweh," and setting it within an Israelite context.[77]

As I have established there was clearly a process occurring in the Bible which sought to articulate a rendering of reality based around the identity and character of Yahweh. But what is the essence of this articulation? If the Bible is indeed a monotheizing literature, what is the substance of its monotheism and, more particularly, what does it mean in the context of Job?

It has been well-established that the Enlightenment word "monotheism" as a term describing a belief in only one God, is problematic and anachronistic when applied to the ANE.[78] A more appropriate definition of OT monotheism is to understand it as being closely associated with Yahweh's uniqueness in himself rather as an assertion of the existence, or otherwise, of other gods: "an understanding of the uniqueness of YHWH that puts him in a class of his own, a wholly different class from any other heavenly or supernatural beings, even if these are called 'gods.' I call this YHWH's transcendent uniqueness."[79]

When Deuteronomy, for example, talks about Yahweh's uniqueness, it is understood as emerging from his incomparable power and authority (see, for example, 4:35, 39; 7:9; 10:14, 17; 32:39), which should be understood in relation to Israel and to other gods.[80] To this I would add that Israel's conception of Yahweh's one-ness was not merely a contest of "whose God is best?" but a form of cultural and political critique against the deities and derived exercising of power by other, more dominant peoples.[81]

The notion of "transcendent uniqueness" is exemplified in the ideas that Yahweh alone created all things (so everything else is created by him) and that Yahweh alone is sovereign over all things (and so everything

---

77. Sanders, *Canon and Community*, 56–57. He describes this process as "depolytheizing, monotheizing, Yahwizing, and Israelitising" (57). See also Glaser, *Bible and Other Faiths*, 121.

78. McConville, *God and Earthly Power*, 19; Bauckham, "Monotheism," 189; Wright, *Mission of God*, 72.

79. Bauckham, "Monotheism," 210.

80. Bauckham, "Monotheism," 192–95.

81. McConville, *God and Earthly Power*, 20–29.

else is subservient to him).[82] To monotheize is, then, to assert Yahweh's unique nature and status in contrast with any other beings.[83]

By conceptualizing OT monotheism in this way, Bauckham is able to read biblical texts that use non-Israelite religious imagery as still working within the monotheizing paradigm. It seems to me that he opens up the discussion in profoundly missional ways, in that his approach reflects the constant task of "asserting and characterizing the transcendent uniqueness of Yhwh."[84]

Building on this notion of monotheism as Yahweh's transcendent uniqueness, Wright then applies it to biblical concepts of mission.[85] Citing texts such as Deut 10:14; 2 Kgs 19:15; Jer 32:27; Isa 54:5; Gen 18:25; Ps 47:7, Wright suggests that in the OT we see a picture of Yahweh who, "made all, owns all, rules all. . . . The uniqueness and universality of yhwh are foundational axioms of Old Testament faith, worship, and mission, which in turn are foundational to New Testament Christian faith, worship, and mission."[86]

This is a helpful way of connecting the monotheism of the OT with the mission of God, because it associates the uniqueness of Yahweh with his universality. Wright highlights the exodus and the return from exile as two key events that enabled Israel to "know" Yahweh. Exodus 6:6–8 functions, for Wright, as "God's mission statement" concerning the exodus narrative, in that it outlines his desire to liberate them from Egyptian bondage; to enter into a relationship with them; and to bring them to the promised land.[87] These events, according to Exodus 6:7, will cause Israel to know Yahweh as God, a sentiment expressed in retrospect in Deuteronomy 4:32–35.[88] Through the exodus, Israel came to know certain key characteristics of Yahweh (drawn mainly from Exod 15; Deut 4): that he is incomparable in his power (Exod 12:12; 15:11); that his rule counters claims to kingship by other beings and is one of benevolence (Exod 15:18; Deut 10:14–19; Ps 72); and that his uniqueness is true, not

---

82. Bauckham, "Monotheism," 211.

83. Bauckham, "Monotheism," 211. Bauckham is consciously using Sanders's term at this point.

84. Bauckham, "Monotheism," 215. In Beeby's language this is an example of his third category of "missionary friction." See below.

85. In particular, see chapters 3–5.

86. Wright, *Mission of God*, 71.

87. Wright, *Mission of God*, 76.

88. Wright, *Mission of God*, 76.

just in Israel but also in the whole world (2 Sam 7:22; Ps 86:8, 10; Isa 46:9; 1 Kgs 8:23, 60).[89]

Concerning the return from exile, Yahweh's universality and uniqueness are confirmed in that he is shown to be sovereign over history by directing both the fortunes of Israel and, significantly, of other nations as well (for example, Isa 41:2–4, 25; 44:28—45:6).[90] Secondly, Yahweh's word is authoritative, as had been seen at creation (Gen 1; Ps 33:6, 9), but was now seen in the exilic language of, for example, Isa 40–55 with its declarations of salvation from Babylonian captivity.[91] Thirdly, through the return from exile Yahweh protects his name from being profaned among the nations (Ezek 36:22–23; Isa 43:25), and ensures that his name is universally known (Isa 45:5–6).[92] Fourthly, it is affirmed that Yahweh is sovereign over all of creation (Jer 10:10–12; see also Ps 33; Isa 40:21–26; 45:11–13).[93] Finally, the return from exile confirms that Yahweh entrusts to Israel the task of witnessing to his uniqueness and universality in the presence of the nations (Isa 43:9–12).[94]

The notion of Yahweh's uniqueness and universality is a helpful contribution to framing the substance of Israel's witness to God (that is, its rendering of reality), which it sought to articulate in response to alternative renderings. However, such a process, as we have seen, was not one characterized exclusively by negative comparison. In Sanders's model we detect both positivity and negativity towards other cultures, which is indicative of the dynamic of the meeting points between the biblical rendering of reality and those of other cultures. While the overall effect of these encounters was to assert the Yahweh-shaped rendering of reality over and against alternative renderings, within that broad opposition there could be included elements of both affirmation and critique. This is an important element to recognize in missional readings: to what extent and in what ways does the text engage with alternative renderings of reality, both in affirmation and critique?

How are we to talk about such encounters? My preference is to use more neutral (if a little bland) terms such as "encounter" or "meeting."

---

89. Wright, *Mission of God*, 76–83.
90. Wright, *Mission of God*, 84–85.
91. Wright, *Mission of God*, 85–87.
92. Wright, *Mission of God*, 88–89.
93. Wright, *Mission of God*, 89–90.
94. Wright, *Mission of God*, 90–91.

The language with which these issues are discussed is instructive and brings out something of the nuanced nature of the issue and the degree of openness that is perceived. Scholars discuss the nature of intercultural encounter in the Bible or in contemporary contexts using a range of vocabulary reflecting themes such as competition, resistance, subversion, clash, polemic, missionary friction, embrace and opposition, borrowing, and missionary encounter.

All of these terms seem appropriate at least some of the time. Beeby, for example, sets out three types of "missionary friction" in the Bible, which he thinks plays an important part in "missionary interpretation": first, Scripture can be seen as emerging from cross-cultural encounters; for example, the polemical nature of the creation accounts or the use of the term, *logos* in John's Gospel.[95] Beeby understood such "transformed borrowing" as "a form of cultural encounter which was a form of mission."[96] Secondly, having influenced the formation of the Bible, these cross-cultural encounters resulted in friction within the biblical community that were sometimes addressed using the language of the other cultures (see, for example, Hos 2:21–23).[97] Finally, there is a friction, "wherever the words, images and presuppositions of scripture meet the words, images and presuppositions of the world's cultures," although we should perhaps be cautious about assuming an agenda every time these coincidences occur.[98]

For Goheen, grasping the biblical story as a coherent, overarching narrative "will enable us to resist our idolatrous cultural story."[99] Elsewhere, drawing on the work of missiologist Lesslie Newbigin, Goheen speaks in more explicitly missional terms, which is particularly striking in the context of my study: "The mission of God's people involves a missional encounter with culture which both embraces the treasures and

---

95. Beeby, "Missional Approach," 280.

96. Beeby, "Missional Approach," 280. Wright also writes about a critical "borrowing" which adapts ANE texts and ideas but does so through a filter of Israel's distinctive beliefs. See Wright, *Mission of God*, 443–47.

97. Beeby, "Missional Approach," 281.

98. Beeby, "Missional Approach," 281. For further examples of such transformed borrowing, see also Beeby, *Canon and Mission*, 87–88.

99. Goheen, "Urgency," 478. Drawing on the work of N. T. Wright and Bauckham, he also uses the ideas of "subversion" and "resistance" to opposing metanarratives. See Wright, *New Testament*, 132; Bauckham, *Bible and Mission*, 97.

opposes the idolatry of all cultures."[100] Such an encounter represents "a clash of stories" and the offering of "an alternative and an invitation" into the story defined by Yahweh faith.[101] It involves a process of "affirmation and critique of other cultural stories," the former of which being exemplified by "embrace of the cultural insights of the nations . . . in the wisdom literature."[102]

A missional reading of the book of Job will explore the extent, variety and function of intercultural encounter in the text. It will seek to establish the ways in which the biblical book encounters the beliefs and even specific texts of other cultures, and will ask what Job does with those. What does the writer of Job affirm? What is distinctive about the biblical book and the Yahweh-shaped rendering of reality it promotes? How does it assert the uniqueness and universality of Yahweh? To use the phrasing of Newbigin and Goheen, to what extent and in what ways does the book of Job exhibit a "missional encounter" with ideas of other cultures, and indeed, within Israel as well. As an additional question in this regard we may also ask, how does the book of Job model missional encounter for the contemporary church?

In order to draw out this missional encounter, in chapter 5 I address the question of the relationship between the book of Job, and the literature and ideas of other cultures in the ANE. I show that the book operated with a stance that was both open and critical in relation to other renderings of reality.

In a positive sense the author of Job could be said to be using certain literary conventions and motifs that would have been familiar to others, building on and, by implication, affirming certain aspects of ideas or approaches already circulating in the ANE. This process, however, would have been discriminative:

> This common oriental heritage was subjected to a far-reaching process of "creative assimilation." The Hebrew genius adopted those elements in the surrounding culture which it found valuable, modified what was potentially useful, and rejected what it recognized as fundamentally alien. Hence, the similarities are often illuminating with regard the details, but it is the differences that go deeper and are more significant.[103]

---

100. Goheen, "Notes."
101. Goheen, "Notes."
102. Goheen, "Notes." See also Goheen, "Urgency," 478.
103. Gordis, *God and Man*, 55. A very similar point is made by Wright when

More negatively, this process also suggests an element of polemic on the part of the author of Job when engaging with ideas in the ANE, which may be discerned by looking at the distinctives of his work.[104] Focusing particularly on the portrayal of Yahweh, although Job complains of a certain degree of divine inscrutability, he is still aware of what is required of him to live an ethical life, upon which his righteousness is based (for example, Job 29; 31).[105] In contrast sufferers in the ANE texts are never fully aware of what is required of them, and they tend to conclude that the will of the gods is ultimately unknowable.[106]

Yahweh is portrayed in fundamentally different terms than the gods of the ANE. Of great importance in the biblical work is the justice of God and this is thoroughly probed by Job; indeed his commitment to God being just fuels his vexation and argument (24:1).[107] However, in the ANE texts the issue of the justice or ethics of the gods is not a significant theme, which would seem to be because there never seems to be a point at which the human cannot be assumed to be at fault. Human beings are sinful by design and cannot know all that is required of them.[108]

It seems, therefore, that Job is asking fundamentally different questions about the nature of suffering and what it questions about the moral governance of God.[109] And his quest for answers is fuelled by his understanding of who God is, particularly in relation to God's commitment to justice and righteousness.

Israel's monotheistic worldview is clearly an important factor in its distinctive portrayal of these issues. Yahweh is not just one personal god to whom Job turns as his representative who might intercede on his behalf amongst the pantheon of other deities.[110] Neither is Job's situation

---

considering the missional nature of the Wisdom Literature, although he does not deal with the book of Job in a sustained way in this regard. See Wright, *Mission of God*, 50, 442–48.

104. The question of intentionality is important here. Do the distinctives of Job signify a deliberate attempt at polemic against ANE texts?

105. Hoffman, *Blemished Perfection*, 259.

106. Hoffman, *Blemished Perfection*, 259. See also Walton, *Job*, 35; Bricker, "Mesopotamia," 202.

107. Walton, *Job*, 36.

108. Bricker, "Mesopotamia," 214. See also Gordis, *God and Man*, 61–62; Newsom, *Job*, 77.

109. See Hoffman, 260–61. See also Gordis, *God and Man*, 62; Bricker, "Mesopotamia," 214; Bricker, "Egypt," 100.

110. Hoffman, *Blemished Perfection*, 261; Hartley, "Job 2," 360. See also Walton,

purely personal to him and his relationship with his particular personal God.[111] Although the circumstances of his suffering are specific to him, Job's commitment to God's uniqueness in the world necessarily moves his questions from the particular to the universal.[112]

As I will demonstrate in greater depth in chapter 5, one particularly stark element of Job in relation to other treatments of unattributed suffering is the encounter with Yahweh experienced by Job, the sufferer.[113] In this encounter Yahweh comes to Job and asserts his freedom to govern the world in a way that he sees fit. Perhaps in this regard the inclusion of a sustained speech direct from God in the book of Job (in contrast to ANE texts) is also significant.[114]

The portrayal of Yahweh in the book, though ambiguous, depicts him as standing alone as the God who creates, who is the source of true wisdom, and who is the arbiter and director of earthly matters. While the ways in which he governs the world are not within humanity's grasp to fully understand, Yahweh's authority and control cannot be missed.

Through the book of Job we see the articulation of Israel's monotheized and monotheizing worldview, that sought to preserve the faith and identity of the people of God in contrast to idolatrous and false ideas. For the writer of Job, it was not enough to join the conversation; he had to present the truest word. What seems particularly striking here is that the book of Job contains a strong polemic for Yahweh at the very moment when Israel is asking the most difficult questions of their God. Perhaps questions of the dissonance between the Wisdom Literature and other parts of the OT are not quite so stark when set against this ANE context.

It is part of the missional mandate of the Church to articulate the true rendering of reality in the midst of alternative renderings. One aspect of this task can be evidenced in how the people of God encounter alternative views on suffering. In this sense perhaps the book of Job could also be seen as a model for cultural engagement, which could be applied (along with others) in the sphere of missional activities.

Job, 36; Wright, *Mission of God*, chapters 3–5.

111. Hoffman, *Blemished Perfection*, 261–62.

112. Hoffman, *Blemished Perfection*, 262.

113. See Newsom, *Contest*, 238; "Job," 334.

114. Segal, *Life After Death*, 153. See also Perlstein, *God's Others*, location 6041–44.

By way of conclusion to this section on the missional direction of the biblical story, Wright offers a helpful summary of the implications of this line of inquiry for a missional reading, which also highlights what I consider to be a specific problem with the approach in relation to a text like Job:

> This is the great overarching framework of the biblical narrative, which renders to us the mission of God.... A missional hermeneutic will work hard to read any text in the Old Testament canon within this overarching narrative framework, discerning its place within that framework, assessing how the shape of the grand narrative is reflected in the text in question, and conversely, how the particular text contributes to and moves forward the grand narrative itself.[115]

This, it seems to me, is a very useful way of understanding the implications of "the missional direction of the story," especially in drawing out the two ways of seeing the relationship between a text and the grand narrative of the Bible. However, it also illustrates a difficulty with this line of inquiry. Wright's choice of words—"a missional hermeneutic will work hard"—is illuminating. Some texts will require harder work than others in order to fit them into the narrative framework of the Bible.

Clearly this line of inquiry is immensely important in the developing conversation of missional hermeneutics. But how can Job be placed meaningfully within the narrative rendering of God's mission? How can we assess "how the shape of the grand narrative is reflected in [Job], and conversely, how [Job] contributes to and moves forward the grand narrative itself"?

Job does not progress the chronological storyline of the *missio Dei*, but there are other ways to relate to it. Is it, for example, a narrative "pause"?[116] Even if, as has been noted, we could associate the book with a particular point in the chronological story, what would this tell us?

Of particular significance is the idea that a text must fit *within* the narrative. I would understand Job as relating importantly with the grand narrative but in a way that stands apart from, and speaks into that narrative. A crucial function of Job is embodied in the Prologue in which the question is asked, "Is it for nothing חִנָּם that Job fears God?" (Job

---

115. Wright, "Mission and OT Interpretation," 184.

116. Loughlin, *Telling God's Story*, 62. See also Bartholomew and Goheen, "Story and Biblical Theology," 160.

1:9b). It seems to me that the accuser's question about the possibility of genuine piety is a question about the possibility of a genuine relationship between God and humanity. This is of critical importance to the *missio Dei*. Is it a sham? Is the whole project of the mission of God flawed from the start? Is the reconciliation that God is working towards in the *missio Dei* an illusion? This is a question that, at some point in the *missio Dei*, has to be asked. And it falls to the book of Job to ask it. In the book of Job, therefore, *the very mission of God is at stake*.

My critique of this line of inquiry is based on how it has been explored thus far. Far from negating it, my discussion seeks to bring out further ways in which it can be explored in relation to texts that do not simply fit into the biblical storyline. As this chapter has demonstrated, I also consider this line of inquiry to be too broad to be taken on its own. Because of the number and type of issues that it covers it seems unhelpful to package them together under one heading, especially in comparison with some of the other lines of inquiry articulated by the forum. In particular I would want to see as a separate line of inquiry the question of how biblical texts encounter the belief systems, grand narratives or worldviews of other cultures. This is a theme that occurs across the discussion on missional hermeneutics, but I believe it should have a more privileged place in the conversation, perhaps as a separately articulated line of inquiry.

The issue of intercultural encounter is particularly acute when considering the book of Job and affords some very important and promising questions. The Wisdom Literature as a whole opens up the question of international engagement helpfully.[117]

Of particular note is the non-Israelite motif in the book of Job. In addition to the non-Israelite location of Uz, Job and his comforters all appear to be non-Israelites. In chapter 4 I discuss the missional significance of this phenomenon.

It is also a common task in Job scholarship to examine the relationship between the biblical book and similar works from the ANE. While, as I will argue, there does not seem to be evidence of a direct literary relationship between Job and these texts, there does seem to be an engagement with the ideas and questions considered in other belief systems. In Job we see evidence of affirmation and critique and the "transformed

---

117. See the discussion in relation to this in chapter 2.

borrowing" of ideas, if not of specific texts. This will be addressed in chapter 5.

The Missional Purpose of the Writings

> The *aim* of biblical interpretation is to fulfill the equipping purpose of the biblical writings.[118]

> The ways in which the biblical text is shaped for the purpose of forming a people of God who are called to participate in God's mission to the creation.[119]

This line of inquiry is most closely associated with missiologist Darrell Guder, whose writing on missional hermeneutics emphasizes the formative function of the Bible as it seeks to shape the church, which, from its inception has always been missional by nature. As such it ties closely with the concept of the Bible as a means by which mission is carried out, as well as the missional contexts of the biblical writings.

Guder has an emphasis on the NT and defines missional hermeneutics as "a way of interpreting Scripture that starts from the assumption that the NT communities were all founded in order to continue the apostolic witness that brought them into being."[120]

For Guder, there is great heuristic value in reading the Bible in this way, recognizing that, "The New Testament writings were addressed to communities already in mission; the purpose of the canonical Scriptures was (and is) to enable them to continue that mission. The Scriptures are thus the warrant for the church's mission by engaging their situations, their challenges, and their struggles."[121]

The evangelization of the early church, therefore, "inexorably moved into catechesis."[122] New communities of believers were taught how to be faithful witnesses in their context, meaning that each one understood itself to be, "at its core and in a comprehensive sense missional."[123]

118. Hunsberger, "Proposals," 313.
119. GOCN, "Forum on Missional Hermeneutics."
120. Guder, "Missional Pastors."
121. Guder, *Missional Church*, 223.
122. Guder, "Missional Authority," 107. See also Guder, "Biblical Formation," 61–62.
123. Guder, "Missional Authority," 107. See also Guder, "Biblical Formation," 61–62.

For Guder, this is a foundational assumption in the discussion of missional hermeneutics, as it applies to the material of the NT, whose task "was to deal with the problems and the conflicts, the challenges and the doubts as they emerged in particular contexts, so that these communities could be faithful to their calling."[124]

The key hermeneutical question when a reader approaches the Bible with this perspective is therefore, "How did this particular text continue the formation of witnessing communities then, and how does it do that today?"[125] Guder sees this hermeneutical task as combining, "interpretative translation with missional connectedness"[126] in that, "the Gospel is constantly being interpreted into and for a particular context . . . [yet] it is the same Gospel, the continuation of the same story, the same good news that connects every community to each other."[127]

In sum, the biblical writings have "a continuing, converting, formative role in the church's life."[128]

Guder contributes to what is in my view a convincing case for the shaping and equipping function of the NT writings. However a significant weakness in his approach (especially for my purposes) is that it pays little attention to the OT.[129] In what sense could OT texts be understood to be shaping and equipping God's people for their participation in God's mission?

Clearly, in order to relate this line of inquiry to OT contexts, we must move away from the language of discipleship or apostolic witness and strategies. However, it does not seem out of place to appropriate Guder's approach in order to speak of the OT writings, which, as I have shown, certainly sought to engage "their situations, their challenges, and their struggles."[130] Thus, Israel's writings had a formative and equipping function, illustrated, for example, by the encounters with alternative renderings of reality noted above or by more internal concerns, articulated helpfully by Goheen:

---

124. Guder, "Missional Authority," 108. He also sees this as the function of the Gospels, which were written to shape the discipleship of believers.
125. Guder, "Missional Authority," 108.
126. Guder, "Missional Authority," 108.
127. Guder, "Missional Authority," 108–9.
128. Guder, "Biblical Formation," 59.
129. As noted, for example, by Schertz, "Response," 122; Hunsberger, "Proposals," 313; Wright, "Mission and OT Interpretation," 185.
130. Guder, *Missional Church*, 223.

It is precisely in order that Israel might fulfill her missional calling and be a light to the nations, that the law ordered its national, liturgical, and moral life; that wisdom helped to shape daily conduct in conformity to God's creational order; that the prophets threatened and warned Israel in their disobedience and promised blessing in obedience; that the psalms brought all of Israel's life into God's presence in worship and prayer; that the historical books continued to tell the story of Israel at different points reminding Israel of and calling them to their missional place in the story.[131]

Of particular importance in this formative conception of the biblical writings is the relationship between ethics and mission. The people of God were to exhibit and thereby witness to the character and values of Yahweh in the midst of the nations.[132]

This conception of the missional relevance of Israel's ethical conduct opens up important avenues for missional readings. In the case of the book of Job, it will be important to understand in what ways the book may be attempting to shape the thought and conduct of its readers. Clearly this is a sizeable area of study and so, as I have already indicated, I will investigate the ethical relevance of Job by examining two particular areas of conduct. The first is what the book teaches about how the people of God, as individuals and communities, can process the vexing issue of unattributed suffering in their own experience or the experience of others. The second theme is an examination of how the motif of the treatment of the poor functions in Job. As I will argue, both themes enable the people of God, in their relationship with God, to speak to God in all honesty, for themselves and on behalf of the world.

To borrow Guder's language and applying it to my study, the line of inquiry promoted in this section asks the question, "How did [the book of Job] continue the formation of witnessing communities then, and how does it do that today?"[133] That is, how did (and how does) the book of Job intend to shape and equip its audience for their participation as the people of God in the mission of God? I would understand this to involve an examination of the ways in which the book sought to articulate, as

---

131. Goheen, "Continuing," 92; Wright, "Mission and OT Interpretation," 185–86. See also Hunsberger, "Proposals," 313–14.

132. For example, Gen 18:16–19; Deut 4:5–8; 10:12–22; Wright, *Mission of God*, esp. chapter 11; "Mission and OT Interpretation," 185–86. For a recent, book-length treatment of this topic, see Salter, *Mission in Action*.

133. Guder, "Missional Authority," 108.

discussed above, a correct, Yahweh-shaped rendering of reality in relation to its particular themes, and in contrast to alternative renderings. I would also understand it to involve an examination of the ways in which the book sought to shape the ethical behavior of the people of God. Although my focus will be on the original audiences, some space should be allowed for how the text may shape and equip the contemporary church as it engages in God's mission today. As part of the latter question, we may also probe the extent to which and the ways in which the book of Job may provide models for mission practice.

How much do we need to know about the original audience of the book in order to understand its teaching? Discerning the original audience of Job is a complex task. Dating the book is notoriously difficult and it is beyond my scope to go into the debate in any great depth. Ezek 14:14, 20 contain the only OT references to Job outside of the book itself. In those sixth-century texts Job appears alongside the non- or pre-Israelite Noah and Dan'el, an Ugaritic hero of antiquity, which seems to show that Job was a known, ancient exemplar of righteousness, and was not a reference to the book of Job itself.[134]

It is generally agreed that the book of Job has a patriarchal setting, which is suggested by a number of details in the story, such as the way Job's wealth is quantified in animals and servants[135] or his longevity (42:17).[136] It seems reasonable to suggest, then, that Job was a known figure in the ancient world, presumably as some kind of righteous sufferer, and that the biblical book's archaised setting evokes the prior traditions associated with him. However, this does not address the composition of the biblical book.

Views regarding the dating of the book itself vary considerably, although most modern scholars would place it somewhere between the tenth and second centuries.[137] A particularly important marker is whether the book can be seen as a response to the Babylonian exile, so that Job symbolizes, in some way, the misfortunes of Israel as a whole.[138] However, the book need not be understood in this way; indeed this understanding

---

134. See Driver and Gray, *Job*, xxix. On the question of the three figures in Ezekiel 14, see Pope, *Job*, 6; Block, *Ezekiel 1-20*, 446-59. See also Greenberg, *Ezekiel 1-20*, 257-58; Duguid, *Ezekiel*, 193-94; Rowe, "Scribes, Sages," 97-98; Lo, *Job 28*, 59.

135. Longman, *Job*, location 1592; Hartley, *Job*, 21.

136. Pope, *Job*, xxxi.

137. See Clines, *Job 1-20*, lvii; Habel, *Job*, 40; Eaton, *Job*, 65; Newsom, "Job," 325.

138. Janzen, *Job*, 5.

is rather problematic given the insistence on Job's innocence (contra the people of Israel) and the lack of explicit connections made to the nation of Israel in the book.[139] As I will demonstrate in chapter 5, Job is part of a long-established tradition in the ANE of wrestling with the question of suffering. Such arguments mean that an exilic or post-exilic dating is not necessary, but neither do they entirely negate the possibility.

Even the apparent links between Job and books such as Isaiah and Jeremiah do not point conclusively to an exilic dating, as the nature and priority of the relationship between these texts is disagreed over.[140] However, even if Job were (post-)exilic, the book is composed in such a way as to offer few clues concerning its author's era or circumstances.[141]

Nevertheless, despite the ambiguity surrounding its composition, it is still possible to infer some useful points about the circumstances which prompted the emergence of the book of Job, and those whom the book was seeking to shape. To this extent, I would argue that this potential missional dimension, as it relates to Job at least, is not a dead end.

First, as I will demonstrate more fully in chapter 4, I would understand the stripping of certain elements of specificity to be functioning in a positive way as it serves in Job to universalize the book.[142] And this universalizing impulse is, I will argue, part of the book's missional function. Ordinarily, as discussed above, a book's historical context is an important aid to understanding how the text is a product of God's mission. However, in the case of Job, it is in the very concealment of certain details that its missional potential is most fully realized. Rather than diminishing the potential for missional reflection, the ambiguities take us in a new and more profound direction.

Secondly, we do not necessarily need to know the book's precise historical details in order to have a reasonable appreciation of what it is trying to teach and, therefore, some of the issues to which the author sought to respond. Lo, for example, sets her discussion of the audience of the book of Job by appealing to the notion of the "implied reader"; that is, "the one who responds to the expectations of its implied author."[143] The

139. Walton, "Job 1," 343–44.

140. Lo, *Job 28*, 60. See also, for example, Hartley, *Job*, 15, 19, who thinks Job was written first. See also Gordis, *Book of Man*, 216; Kynes, "Job and Isaiah 40–55," 94–105, who consider Isaiah to have priority.

141. Clines, *Job 1–20*, lvii; Lo, *Job 28*, 61.

142. See also Habel, *Job*, 42; Lo, *Job 28*, 61.

143. Lo, *Job 28*, 62. Lo builds on the notion of the implied author as conceived in

book's rhetorical audience, for Lo, are those readers who will respond to and manifest the change envisaged by the author.[144] This has relevance for discerning the missional purpose of Job because, by isolating the main issues being addressed in the book, we are able to portray, albeit tentatively, the circumstances to which the book was responding. I do not mean by this that I will try to build up a picture of a particular socio-historical situation. Rather, we may be able to infer certain false beliefs the author of Job was attempting to correct, and therefore something of the circumstances to which the book was reacting. While we may not be able to be as specific about the compositional context of Job as we can be for some other texts, this does not mean *a priori* that there is nothing to be said.

Given the concentration of the book on different, often inadequate views on the relationship between suffering and God's governance in the world, this would seem to indicate that the author's intended audience either held or encountered some or all of these perspectives, which he was attempting to correct.[145] Such a corrective confronted the audience with an alternative articulation of truth about God in a world marked by suffering. It sought to bring a change in its audience concerning what they believed about suffering and God's governance, and to equip them to confront it in other alternative renderings.

The book's equipping purpose is also seen in that it is not simply about how the people of God might understand suffering and God's governance, but how they may seek to live in the light of their own suffering.[146] It is, after all, a book of wisdom. Waters's work on the missional potential of a faithful, suffering believer is instructive here.[147] However, his concentration on Job's submissiveness in the Prologue as, "the proper response to suffering" is problematic in that it does not sufficiently account for Job's engagement with the issues in the rest of the book.[148]

Also concerning the shaping purposes of the book, in chapter 6 I examine in depth the theme of the treatment of the poor in Job. As I will argue, implicit in this theme is an attempt to shape its audience's

---

Booth, *Rhetoric of Fiction*, 138.

144. Lo, *Job 28*, 82.
145. Lo, *Job 28*, 69.
146. See also Clines, *Job 1–20*, lxii.
147. Waters, "Missio Dei."
148. Waters, "Missio Dei," 25.

relationship with the plight of the poor in the light of God's governance of the world.

This chapter has demonstrated that the emerging method of missional hermeneutics offers a number of potentially fruitful ways of addressing the relative neglect of Job in BMS. The survey of the two most relevant lines of inquiry pursued by advocates of missional hermeneutics was framed using the taxonomy suggested by Hunsberger and adopted by the GOCN forum. While this categorisation of approaches has some limitations, it does provide a useful way of framing the discussion.

In this concluding section I give a brief outline of the way forward for my own missional reading of Job, integrating aspects of the lines of inquiry that focus on the missional nature of the biblical story and the missional purposes of the text.

Despite the complications of considering the book of Job as part of the unfolding narrative of the Bible I still consider this approach to be extremely important. However, I see in Job a challenge to how this has often been applied in missional readings, and will look to provide a more nuanced understanding of the relationship between the book and the biblical story and, therefore, the *missio Dei*. Our interest in Job should not simply be to ask how the book fits into and progresses the biblical story. Rather I will demonstrate in chapter 4 how Job stands apart from, and speaks into that grand narrative. As part of this discussion I have articulated the importance of understanding the function of the particular and the universal in the biblical text, as well as the way a holistic understanding of mission sensitizes the reader to issues of poverty and justice.

The question of how Job contributes to an articulation of a Yahweh-shaped rendering of reality will also be examined. This will be carried out in chapter 5 by looking at the book's missional encounter with alternative renderings evident in the ANE, meeting them in both affirmation and critique.

The discussion of the missional purpose of the book of Job will be highlighted in several discussions. As indicated, I have isolated the treatment of the poor in Job as an appropriate theme of examination because of its importance in a holistic understanding of mission, but also its significance within Job itself. This coincidence of interests provides fertile ground for the discussion in chapter 6.

4

The Universalizing Impulse in the Book of Job

I HAVE PREVIOUSLY ESTABLISHED that the biblical story of God's mission encompassed universal concerns and purposes. It is fitting, then, that a missional reading will seek to discern how a biblical text will reflect, exhibit and even achieve these universal concerns, or embody this particular-universal movement, albeit within the context of the election of Israel. The book of Job is of special note in this regard because it is not immediately obvious how it fits into the narrative of the biblical story and, perhaps most intriguingly, it appears to be set outside of Israel. Connected to the universal scope of the mission of God, in this chapter I examine the extent and significance of the non-Israelite theme in Job. I address this particularly in a treatment of the book's Prologue, and conclude that the theme has the effect of universalizing the characters, setting, and aims of the book. Supporting this, I look at what I consider to be further universalizing features of the Prologue, including its archaic setting and literary artistry. Crucially, the question posed by the accuser in 1:9b is also considered, and connects to a reflection on the relationship between the book of Job and the *missio Dei*. As I read it, the question, "is it for nothing that Job fears God?" is not only vital to the whole book, it is also an important way of understanding how the book of Job relates to the biblical story of God's mission. Of particular note is the way in which the author of Job employs the particularities of the book's setting to universalize themes, thereby allowing the book of Job to speak "to and for all humanity," which I would argue is an essential element of our participation in the mission of God.[1]

By employing the term, "universalizing impulse" I mean, therefore, that within Job there is a dynamic at play that suggests the book presents itself as addressing universally relevant questions in a peculiarly universalized way, while also maintaining a distinctively Israelite approach. Indeed, it is ultimately this distinctive perspective that means that Job has something universally significant to say.

Having established that Job sets itself up in universally significant terms, I then examine the distinctive message of the book in chapter 5. In order to keep this focused, I concentrate on the ways in which the book could be considered to be having a "missional encounter" with surrounding cultures. As I have demonstrated in previous chapters, this line of inquiry seeks to discern how a biblical text may contribute to an articulation of Yahweh faith over and against alternative belief systems. While this will involve a process of both affirmation and critique, the end result is a contrasting of Yahweh faith with what is ultimately understood as the false religion of Israel's neighboring cultures. In chapter 5, then, I will look at the relationship between Job and the ideas of the ANE as represented by certain texts that are considered to have resonances with the biblical book. Although no direct literary relationship can be established it is possible, nevertheless, to understand Job as encountering alternative beliefs, particularly of Babylonian religion, and doing so in both affirmation and critique. I conclude that, while Job drew upon and joined the long-established "international" conversation wrestling with the theme of unattributed "innocent" suffering, it does so with a particularly Israelite understanding and exploration of the issues. Ultimately I understand the biblical book to be offering a polemic, at least implicitly, on behalf of faith in Yahweh. Of particular importance, in my view, is the function of the Yahweh speeches in Job 38–41, which are a prominent distinctive of the biblical work. Not only are they crucial to an understanding of Job, they also demonstrate the contrastive nature of the work in relation to alternative attempts in the ANE. The speeches also return the chapter to the universalizing theme with which it began, demonstrating the universally significant nature of the book.

To conclude that chapter I outline a series of missional implications which arise out of the findings from chapters 4 and 5. In particular I

---

1. Pope, *Job*, xxxviii.

highlight: Job as a universalized figure struggling with a universal problem; Job in relation to the missional narrative of the biblical story; Job as missional encounter; the missional potential and missional cost of character formation; and Job as exhibiting a missional responsibility to articulate the pain of the world.

The Extent and Significance of the Non-Israelite Theme in the Book of Job

אִישׁ הָיָה בְאֶרֶץ־עוּץ אִיּוֹב שְׁמוֹ . . . וַיְהִי הָאִישׁ הַהוּא גָּדוֹל מִכָּל־בְּנֵי־קֶדֶם:
There was a man from the land of Uz, Job was his name . . . and he was the greatest man of all the sons of the East. (Job 1:1a, 3c)

Who was this man, whose story the book of Job tells? In the opening words of the Prologue the reader is told several things. First, we are given a place and a name. Later on, amidst the glowing portrait of his piety and wealth we find that he was a man (indeed, *the* man) of the East. In these few words the reader is given a glimpse of the broad horizons of the book, and it is my contention that these horizons are missionally significant.

A study of the non-Israelite motif allows for a closer examination of certain particularities of the biblical text while also drawing this into the broader context whereby the author seeks to use the specifics of Job's situation to present a universalizing context for his work. Initially I focus on Job 1–2, which contains the majority of relevant information concerning the non-Israelite theme. The Prologue also sets a trajectory for the entire book and contains within it vital orienting information for the characters, plot and themes of the book as a whole.

I begin by establishing, as far as can be achieved, some of the cultural particularities of the book's setting and characters. The discussion is then developed considerably when I address the significance of this non-Israelite setting. Here I tease out the nuances and ambiguities of the motif and review different explanations put forward for the existence of the theme. I conclude that it has a vital universalizing function within the book, which serves the author's literary and theological purposes and, I argue, has important missional implications. To further support this understanding of the non-Israelite motif I then point to further examples of the universalizing impulse within the Prologue, including its temporal (that is, archaic) setting and certain literary features. I then attend to the crucial question of the accuser in 1:9b, "Is it for nothing that Job fears God?" which is of particular importance within the book and in relation to the biblical story of God's mission.

Establishing the Non-Israelite Motif

In this section I determine the location of Uz and, closely related to this, identify the provenance of each of Job's comforters (including Elihu), all of which leads me to conclude that the story has a strong Edomite connection. I then examine the provenance of Job himself and conclude that he is also presented as a non-Israelite, and quite possibly an Edomite.

Where Was Uz?

In the OT the term עוּץ Uz refers both to people and a place. Three people are named עוּץ, all of whom are found in Genesis: the firstborn of Aram, Shem's son (Gen 10:23; cf. 1 Chr 1:17); the firstborn of Milcah and Nahor, Abraham's brother (Gen 22:21); and a son of Dishon and grandson of Seir the Horite, who were inhabitants of the land of Edom (Gen 36:28; cf. 1 Chr 1:42).[2]

Although the location of Uz is ambiguous enough to preclude certainty, the majority view among scholars is that the land of Uz has associations with Edom. The only references to "the land of Uz" outside of Job are both in poetic texts.[3] Lamentations 4:21 שִׂישִׂי וְשִׂמְחִי בַּת־אֱדוֹם יוֹשַׁבְתִּי בְּאֶרֶץ עוּץ (Rejoice and be glad, O daughter of Edom, you who live in the land of Uz) associates Uz with Edom, although the precise connotations of the parallelism are contested.[4] Jeremiah 25:20 mentions כָּל־מַלְכֵי אֶרֶץ הָעוּץ (all the kings of the land of Uz) as recipients of Yahweh's wrath, which will also be experienced by leaders of Judah, the kings of Egypt, the Philistines, and a number of others, notably including Edom (vv. 15–26). It should be noted, however, that the authenticity of inclusion of Uz is contested.[5]

---

2. See Opperwall-Galluch and LaSor, "Uz," 959.

3. Weiss, *Job's Beginning*, 21.

4. LaSor, "Uz," 959; Alden, *Job*, 46–47; Balentine, *Job*, 44. Driver and Gray, *Job*, xxviii, go as far as to say that, if genuine, Lamentations 4:31 "decisively connects [Uz] with Edom."

5. For example, it is not included in the LXX and seems inappropriate placed

The Sabeans (שְׁבָא) of Job 1:15 are possibly of North Arabian provenance, located next to the land of Edom.[6] The term also occurs in Job 6:19, in parallel with תֵּמָא, which was also located adjacent to Edom.[7] Pope notes close association between Tema, Sheba, and Dedan, which suggests a geographical proximity (cf. Isa 21:13; Gen 10:7; 25:3).[8]

A further set of evidence for an Edomite association is provided by the provenance of Job's comforters. In each case the individual is given a name and a place of origin. Although not part of the Prologue it seems logical to include a brief treatment of Elihu's provenance here as well.

The provenance of Job's comforters

וַיִּשְׁמְעוּ שְׁלֹשֶׁת רֵעֵי אִיּוֹב אֵת כָּל־הָרָעָה הַזֹּאת הַבָּאָה עָלָיו וַיָּבֹאוּ אִישׁ מִמְּקֹמוֹ
אֱלִיפַז הַתֵּימָנִי וּבִלְדַּד הַשּׁוּחִי וְצוֹפַר הַנַּעֲמָתִי

When Job's three friends heard about all the troubles that had come upon him, each one came from his place: Eliphaz the Temanite, Bildad the Shuhite, and Zophar the Naamathite. (Job 2:11)

Eliphaz the Temanite אֱלִיפַז הַתֵּימָנִי

The first and apparently most senior of the friends is Eliphaz the Temanite.[9] The name Eliphaz is not unique to Job. In Genesis 36:1–15 Esau, the ancestor of the Edomites (vv. 1, 8–9), is said to have fathered an Eliphaz (vv. 4, 10), who in turn fathered Teman (vv. 11, 15).

Teman is a well-attested and significant Edomite place name and is even used in a representative way for the whole of that territory.[10] A further connection between the book of Job and the Edom theme of Genesis

---

where it is, so could well be a later gloss. See Day, "Edomite," 392; Knauf, "Uz," 770; Weiss, *Job's Beginning*, 22–23; McKane, *Jeremiah*, 637–38, 641.

6. Pope, *Job*, 13; Day, "Edomite," 393.

7. Day, "Edomite," 393.

8. Pope, *Job*, 13.

9. Eliphaz is the first of the friends to speak (4:1) and is singled out by Yahweh (42:7) as representative of the three comforters. See Longman, *Job*, location 12385–86.

10. See Ezek 25:13; Amos 1:12; Clines, *Job 1–20*, 57; Day, "Edomite," 393; Pope, *Job*, 24.

36 is the reference to Uz in Genesis 36:28, suggesting perhaps that the chapter was a source used by the author of Job.[11]

Bildad the Shuhite בִּלְדַּד הַשּׁוּחִי

The name Bildad is unique to the book of Job. Although it is difficult to establish any etymological connections between Bildad and other names in the OT, there are partial similarities to other non-Israelite names, which may give it the capacity to trigger the audience's imagination in a certain direction. Of particular note is the suggestion by Clines that the sound associations of Bildad may have reminded Job's audience of characters like Moabite king Balak and his hired prophet Balaam,[12] בִּלְעָם (Num 22–24); Bela, בֶּלַע, king of Edom (Gen 36:32; 1 Chr 1:43); Bilhan, בִּלְהָן, a descendant of Esau (Gen 36:27; 1 Chr 1:42); Bilhah, בִּלְהָה, a non-Israelite concubine of Jacob (Gen 29:29); and Bedad, בְּדַד, the father of Edom's king Hadad (Gen 36:35; 1 Chr 1:46).[13]

Although the significance of sound association is difficult to establish, it should be noted that this idea is returned to below in connection with other terms, notably Job's name and the significance of the use of the name "Uz."

Bildad's supposed home territory, Shuah, is also unique to Job as a place name, although there may be an intended connection with Shuah, שׁוּחַ, a son of Abraham and Keturah, and uncle of Sheba and Dedan, who were noted above in relation to Teman.[14] An Edomite association is, therefore, a possibility although it is perhaps not a strong one.

Zophar the Naamathite צוֹפַר הַנַּעֲמָתִי

Like Bildad, the name Zophar is unique to Job. Sharing the same consonants as Zophar, Zippor, צִפּוֹר, was the father of Balak, King of Moab

---

11. Day, "Edomite," 393.

12. Rather than as a matter of course for all names in this discussion, I provide Hebrew spelling where it helps to demonstrate similarity.

13. Clines, *Job 1–20*, 58–59. See also Gordis, *God and Man*, 66, 324n14; Driver and Gray, *Job*, xxxix.

14. Gen 25:1–6; 1 Chr 1:32; Isa 21:13; Gen 10:7; Clines, *Job 1–20*, 57; Pope, *Job*, 24; Day, "Edomite," 393.

(Num 22:2).¹⁵ A similarly named person is found in Esau's genealogy in Gen 36:11 (Zepho, צְפוֹ) and 1 Chr 1:36 (Zepiy, צְפִי). He was a son of Eliphaz and brother of Teman and one of the rulers of Edom. In both verses the Septuagint alters his name to Sophar, σωφαρ, the same name as the Joban Zophar, although the significance of this is difficult to establish.¹⁶

The place name Naamah is of uncertain origin. As a personal name it is used of a female descendant of Cain (Gen 4:22) and an Ammonite wife of Solomon, who was also the mother of Reheboam (1 Kgs 14:21).¹⁷ In 1 Chr 4:15 mention is made of a Naam who is said to be a descendant of Judah. This Naam was the uncle of a Kenaz, which may suggest an Edomite connection, although this may be a leap too far in the imagination of Job's audience.¹⁸

Elihu the son of Barachel the Buzite, of the family of Ram

אֱלִיהוּא בֶן־בַּרַכְאֵל הַבּוּזִי מִמִּשְׁפַּחַת רָם

Unlike Job and his three friends, Elihu receives an extended introduction focussing on his familial pedigree. The name is shared by several biblical characters including an ancestor of Samuel (1 Sam 1:1); one of the chiefs of Manasseh who deserted David on his way to Ziklag (1 Chr 12:21 [ET 20]); a Korahite temple gatekeeper (1 Chr 26:7); and one of David's brothers (1 Chr 27:18).¹⁹

---

15. Pope, *Job*, 24, suggests (albeit tentatively) that, following a *qawtal* pattern, Zophar is a diminutive form of Zippor. See also Gordis, *God and Man*, 66; Clines, *Job 1–20*, 59.

16. Gordis, *God and Man*, 66; Pope, *Job*, 24; Driver and Gray, *Job*, xxxix; Clines, *Job 1–20*, 59. Day considers the possible significance of the LXX rendering of Genesis 36:11 but rightly cannot draw firm conclusions: "Did the author of Job, like the LXX read *ṣpr* (Zophar) instead of *ṣpw* (Zepho) here? If so, the case for seeing Zophar as an Edomite would be a good one, but we cannot be sure of this" (Day, "Edomite," 394n10).

17. Gordis, *Job*, 23.

18. Clines, *Job 1–20*, 58.

19. Hartley, *Job*, 482.

Although the personal name Barachel is not found anywhere else in the OT several other names come from the same verb root, ברך, "bless" including Berechiah, Barchi, Beracah, Baruch and Jeberechiah.[20]

Buz is attested several times in the OT, both as the name of a person and a place. In Genesis 22:21 Buz is named as a brother of Uz and nephew of Abraham. As a location Buz is found in Jeremiah 25:23 in connection with Dedan and Tema. Although they seem distinct from Edom in this passage, later on in Jeremiah 49:7–8 Dedan and Tema are found within an oracle concerning Edom. It would seem, therefore, that Buz was associated with Edom.[21]

Ram was the name of an ancestor of David (Ruth 4:19; 1 Chr 2:9–10), although there may not be a direct connection here with Elihu's ancestry.[22] This Ram also had a nephew of the same name (1 Chr 2:25, 27).

It seems that in the light of connections noted above, and especially those with the name Buz, Elihu may be conceived as having Edomite associations. As such it may be feasible to consider him as a non-Israelite like Job's other comforters.[23]

Job's Provenance

While acknowledging an element of caution, there does seem to be sufficient evidence to make a strong connection between the land of Uz and Edom, based particularly on the names and provenance of Job's comforters and how they relate to genealogies in the book of Genesis.[24]

I will now examine whether Job himself was a non-Israelite and, more specifically, whether he was an Edomite. Part of this treatment will discuss a further, potentially complicating issue: given the historically troubled relationship between Israel and Edom, particularly in light of the exile, is it reasonable to suppose that the author of Job would want to link his story and characters with Edom?

I then address the question towards which the whole discussion has been moving inexorably: Why has the author of Job sought to employ a non-Israelite, even Edomite setting for his work? It is in answering this

---

20. Clines, *Job 21–37*, 713.
21. Clines, *Job 21–37*, 713; Hartley, *Job*, 482; Day, "Edomite," 394.
22. A helpful caveat made by Habel, *Job*, 448.
23. Wilson, *Job*, 361; Clines, *Job 21–37*, 713.
24. See below for a related discussion on the archaic setting of the book.

question that I demonstrate the presence of a universalizing impulse within Job, which I understand to be a crucial element in a missional reading of the book.

Given that the land of Uz has close associations with Edom, does this imply that Job himself was Edomite? As with the comforters, Job's provenance will be probed by looking at his name, but I will also consider the phrase, בְּנֵי־קֶדֶם (the sons of the East) in 1:3c.

אִיּוֹב (along with its older forms) appears to have been well-known in the ANE as a Semitic name.[25] Indeed, for the readers it may "have had a foreign and archaic ring to it."[26] Unlike Eliphaz, for example, whose name had clear associations with Edom, no certain connections can be made with אִיּוֹב.[27]

Apart from the book of Job itself, the name Job appears only in Ezekiel 14:14, 20, alongside the non- or pre-Israelite Noah and Dan'el, an Ugaritic hero of antiquity.[28] In this prophetic oracle, the three well-known figures are evoked as supreme models of righteousness; not even their presence in Jerusalem would save the city from God's coming judgment. Job, it seems, was a familiar character in the broader milieu of the ANE to whom such archetypal appeals could be made.[29]

The meaning of Job's name does not provide much in the way of evidence concerning his geographical and, therefore, cultural provenance. אִיּוֹב has been variously thought to mean, "enemy,"[30] "hated/persecuted one,"[31] "penitent one,"[32] or even, "where is my/the father?"[33]

---

25. Pope, *Job*, 6; Albright, "Northwest-Semitic Names," 226; Gordis, *Job*, 10. Clines cites a range of examples of close variants of *Ayab*. "The name Job is not attested elsewhere in Hebrew. But it is known from several extrabiblical sources as a Semitic name" (Clines, *Job 1–20*, 10).

26. Newsom, "Job," 344.

27. Although note, for example, Longman, who assumes, because of the Edomite setting of the book, that Job's name is likely to have been Edomite originally, though now rendered in Hebrew for the audience's sense of familiarity. See Longman, "Job 4," 372.

28. There are not thought to be any connections between Job and Jobab, יוֹבָב, in Genesis 10:29 or Yob, יוֹב, in Genesis 46:13. See Driver and Gray, *Job*, xxix. On the question of the three figures in Ezekiel 14, see Pope, *Job*, 6.

29. Pope, *Job*, 6; Habel, *Job*, 85. See also Joyce, "Noah, Daniel, and Job," 118–28.

30. Tur-Sinai, *Job*, xvii.

31. Gordis, *Job*, 10.

32. Hartley, *Job*, 66; Pope, *Job*, 5.

33. A number of scholars note the work of Albright, who, in a 1954 article, claimed

The degree to which significance can be assigned to Job's name is difficult to establish. Weiss, for example, considers the true import of the phrase אִיּוֹב שְׁמוֹ to be not etymological but in the unusual order of the words (that is, the act of his naming) indicating that the Job of the story is a particular, known Job.[34] Weiss seems overly dismissive of the idea of literary exploitation of the name. Similarly, other scholars consider it an unnecessary or unwise line of inquiry because the author of the biblical book would have inherited the name Job for his character because of the prior tale of Job.[35]

When dealing with the significance of the name, Uz (see below), Weiss helpfully points to the term's "associative capacity," drawing together its "aural effect, and the etymology based on it."[36] It seems reasonable that the same could be said of Job's name, even if it was inherited by the author of Job, with the biblical author exploiting the rich potentiality of Job's name for his literary and theological purposes. The idea, in my view, cannot be dismissed as readily as some suppose. Indeed, it may be in the various options that a note of artistry can be detected. In this regard, Balentine's conclusions seem appropriate and also anticipate my view of the function of the universalizing theme, which I shall develop below:

> One might reasonably conjecture, however, that ancient readers would have readily discerned multiple connections, both literal and symbolic, between this archaic name and this story. Job is the legendary paragon of righteousness whose life is marked by both invocation ("Where is God?") and accusation ("You treat me like an enemy"). His stance before God is that of the innocent sufferer whose petition for help is representative of the unjustly persecuted across the ages.[37]

One final point relating to Job's name is the absence of any genealogical background, in contrast to the general custom of patriarchal times.[38] The wording of Job's introduction is more ambiguous that that

---

that Job's name in its original form, 'Ayya-'abu(m) (meaning "Where is (my) father?"), can be found in an Egyptian record of Palestinian chiefs. See Albright, "Northwest-Semitic Names," 226.

34. That is, "this specific, famous, righteous Job" of the prior stories (Weiss, *Job's Beginning*, 20–21). See also Habel, *Job*, 85–86; Wilson, *Job*, 16.

35. Hartley, *Job*, 66; Habel, *Job*, 86. See also Pope, *Job*, 5–6.

36. Weiss, *Job's Beginning*, 23.

37. Balentine, *Job*, 46. See also Janzen, *Job*, 34.

38. For example, Abraham in Genesis 11:26–28; Hartley, *Job*, 66.

of his comforters, and Elihu especially (2:11; 32:2). This rather unusual phenomenon may contribute towards the author's intention to present Job as a representative figure of humanity, an issue that will be dealt with more fully below.[39]

In the above discussion on the location of Uz I referred briefly to Job 1:3c in which Job is said to be "the greatest of all the sons of the East." The phrase בְּנֵי־קֶדֶם is ambiguous enough that any specific referents cannot be identified without a clear sense of context. For example, it can refer to Mesopotamian people as a whole (1 Kgs 5:10 [ET 4:30]), but also nomadic desert tribes east of the Jordan river.[40] Similarly, it could be applied to Arameans (Gen 29:1), southerly areas (including Edom, Isa 11:14), and even Midian (Judg 6:3).[41] Thus, "No more specific location than east of Israel can be established from the term."[42] Despite the flexibility of the term, therefore, it is reasonable to conclude that the phrase relates to non-Israelites.

Does the phrase וַיְהִי הָאִישׁ הַהוּא גָּדוֹל מִכָּל־בְּנֵי־קֶדֶם necessarily imply that Job was one of the sons of the East, or are the sons of the East distinct from Job, functioning rather as a point of comparison and not identity? In 1 Kings 5:10 [ET 4:30] Solomon's wisdom is described as greater than the wisdom of the sons of the East and all the wisdom of Egypt and this is used by Clines as a note of caution that the verse in Job "does not necessarily imply" that Job is one of the sons of the East.[43] However, the points of comparison are different in Job. Strictly, it is Solomon's wisdom that is compared with the wisdom of Easterners and Egyptians, whereas in Job it is the man himself that is being compared with the sons of the East.[44] More importantly, however, the context of Job's non-Israelite setting in Uz contrasts vividly with that of Solomon. It therefore seems evident that,

---

39. See also, for example, Hartley, *Job*, 66; Estes, *Handbook*, 28; Reitman, *Unlocking Wisdom*, location 1000–1003. See also Dhorme, *Job*, xv, who thinks the author did not feel a genealogy was necessary because Job was a non-Israelite.

40. Rogers, "קָדִים," 873.

41. Clines, *Job 1–20*, 14–15. See also Day, "Edomite," 392; Wilson, *Job*, 21; Driver and Gray, *Job*, xxvii; Mitchell, *Job*, xxxi.

42. Clines, *Job 1–20*, 15.

43. Clines, *Job 1–20*, 15. Though he still maintains that assuming Job to be one of them "is a natural interpretation."

44. Though, of course, these are closely related; it is Job's wealth and implied wisdom that make him great. See Clines, *Job 1–20*, 14. Longman, *Job*, location 1597–98, sees the verse focusing on Job's wealth; cf. Weiss, *Job's Beginning*, 267, who prefers a focus on Job's wisdom.

although Clines's caution may be valid on linguistic grounds, the context strongly suggests that interpreting Job as belonging to the sons of the East is by far the most natural reading of the verse.[45]

While it is true that the book of Job does not say explicitly that Job either was or was not an Israelite, the most natural reading of the weight of evidence would suggest that he is portrayed as a non-Israelite.[46] Though perhaps one could argue that Job is an Israelite who happens to live outside of the borders of Israel this seems to me to be unnecessarily strained.[47]

Furthermore, given the probable Edomite context of the setting of the book it would therefore seem reasonable to suppose that Job was himself an Edomite. However, is it similarly reasonable to suppose, in the light of historical tensions between Israel and Edom, that this Israelite writer made his hero an Edomite? In an article-length treatment of this question, Day defends an Edomite Job against objections that, assuming a later dating for the book, Hebrew authors would not have countenanced an Edomite Job, given the traditionally negative view of Edom, especially following the exile (e.g., Ps 137:7; Lam 4:21–22; Obad; Jer 49:7–22; Isa 34:5–17).[48] In my view he makes a good case, offering four main arguments that an Edomite association is feasible. First, the more "internationally minded" wisdom writers responsible for Job, "may not have had 'hang ups' about Edomites.... Job was a foreigner, for Wisdom was characteristically universalistic."[49]

Edom was known for its wisdom (Obad 8; Jer 49:7) and "Israel's wise men were doubtless partly indebted to Edomite Wisdom (cf. the Wisdom of nearby Massa, taken up in Proverbs 30 and 31), so it should not be surprising that the Israelite wise men were tolerant towards the Edomites."[50]

Secondly, because the root narrative of the book was a previously-known story, it may be that Job's Edomite identity was already fixed and

---

45. Mitchell, *Job*, xxxi, for example, sees this as a certainty. See also Wilson, *Job*, 21; Driver and Gray, *Job*, xxvii.

46. See Clines, *Job 1–20*, 10, 15.

47. Clines, *Job 1–20*, 10.

48. Day, "Edomite," 396. In particular, he highlights Lamentations 4:21, which references Uz when chastising Edom for its role in the destruction of Jerusalem. See also Pope, *Job*, xxxiv.

49. Day, "Edomite," 397.

50. Day, "Edomite," 397–98.

was "part and parcel of this tradition."[51] Thirdly, Job is depicted as worshipping Yahweh, which may have been more acceptable. Indeed, this may even be seen as "yet another instance of Israel's Yahwization of an originally non-Yahwistic figure."[52] Finally, Day suggests that the ancient setting of the book in the "more amicable" distant past may have been acceptable, even if the book was shaped in a context more generally hostile to Edom.[53]

Though not without a degree of speculation, on the whole Day's points seem plausible and confirm that an Edomite setting, and even an Edomite provenance for Job himself, is reasonable. However, there remains an element of ambiguity in the discussion. We simply do not know conclusively where Job is from. Presumably the author could have been more explicit but he was not. Although I will expand on the Edom theme a little more below, I will also move the discussion further by addressing this element of ambiguity in Job's provenance, concluding that this is an important function of the book.

The Significance of the Non-Israelite Motif in the Book of Job

Having established the existence of a non-Israelite theme in relation to the setting and characters in Job, it is now important to understand its significance. To address this I begin with a brief survey of explanations given by scholars, including: the non-Israelite setting was inherited from the "original" story; it allows the author to explore difficult themes more easily; it promotes the theme of wisdom; it promotes an openness to God working in and through non-Israelites; and it universalizes the book. It is the last view that I consider to be the most compelling in that it demonstrates how the non-Israelite theme and, more specifically, Job's non-Israelite provenance plays a crucial role in universalizing Job into an "everyman" figure. That is, although he suffers in a unique and specific manner, he is portrayed as doing so in a way that represents humanity and the vexing and universal problem of unattributed suffering.

---

51. Day, "Edomite," 398.

52. Day, "Edomite," 398. This point is particularly notable given themes present in this volume, such as the monotheizing or Yahwizing process of certain biblical writers and also the theme (discussed below) of Job as a non-Israelite who has aligned himself with the worship of Yahweh.

53. Day, "Edomite," 398–99.

To give further support to this interpretation, I also examine a selection of other elements of the Prologue that appear to promote this universalizing theme, including the archaic setting, certain literary features of the narrative, and the crucial question asked by the accuser in 1:9b: "Is it for nothing that Job fears God?"

A Review of Scholarly Opinion on the Non-Israelite Motif in Job

When discussing the non-Israelite setting of Job scholars assign varying degrees of significance to the theme and give a range of possible reasons why the author of Job may have employed it. In this brief survey of the literature I isolate the main reasons given and conclude with a view I consider to be the most persuasive. Although I have separated them for clarity, no explanation should be understood as entirely independent of others. While I will demonstrate that the universalizing theme is the principal reason for the non-Israelite setting, a work of the sophistication of Job would certainly allow for other, overlapping purposes. It is also worth noting that there may be a distinction between what the author intended and the effect his choices have had on his audiences.[54] This does not, however, undermine my conclusions.

THE "ORIGINAL" STORY THE AUTHOR INHERITED/INCORPORATED HAD A NON-ISRAELITE SETTING THAT HE RETAINED

Although there are variations on this line of thought it could be that the author incorporated, utilized and developed a previously known folk tale about a righteous sufferer named Job. The assumption is that this story he chose to employ would already have had a non-Israelite setting, which he did not change.

Assuming this to be the case, the crucial question would be, given his predominantly Hebrew audience, why did the author decide to retain the non-Israelite setting? It seems to me there are two main possible explanations: either he wanted to change the setting but did not feel he could, or he could have changed it but preferred not to.

It is generally accepted that, prior to the writing of the book of Job, there existed a traditional folk tale of a righteous sufferer named Job, which would have been a precursor to what is now the frame narrative of

54. Clines, *Job 1–20*, 10.

the biblical book.[55] It would seem reasonable to suppose that this original story was set outside of Israel and, given the associations with Edom evident in Job, perhaps an Edomite setting is the most likely candidate.[56]

One possibility is, therefore, that the setting of the original story (whether Edom or elsewhere) was so well-known that the author of the biblical book did not feel able to change it, for fear of distracting or jarring his audience to such a degree as to undermine the impact of his work.[57]

While there may be some validity in this argument it is, of course, impossible to know the extent to which it accurately reflects the situation facing the biblical author. It also seems problematic to assume that if the author could have changed the setting he would inevitably have chosen to do so. In my view, a more appropriate assumption would be that, although the author may have felt some degree of constraint, he had more positive and strategic reasons for retaining the non-Israelite setting. To this end, whether he could have changed the setting or not becomes a moot point. Possible, more constructive reasons will now be explored.

The Non-Israelite Setting More Easily Facilitates an Exploration of the Book's Difficult Themes

It could be that casting Job as a non-Israelite was a literary device used to ease the tension readers may presumably have experienced when encountering the extremities of his words later in the book. In doing so the author may have afforded himself the freedom of having his main character say whatever needed to be said and, thereby, making his harsh words and extreme positions more palatable because they were on the lips of a Gentile.[58]

However, this would seem to undermine a crucial tenet of the book of Job which is that, whatever his provenance, Job is declared righteous from the outset and that his protests need to be understood in this

---

55. Day, "Edomite," 398. See also Pinker, "Core Story," 1; Newsom, "Job," 321–22; Pope, *Job*, xxi–xxviii.

56. Day, "Edomite," 398. See also Good, *Tempest*, 3–4.

57. See Day, "Edomite," 398.

58. Hoffman, for example, sees this as the context for the frequent use of foreign and unusual details in the book which create "a feeling of distance and strangeness which accompanies the reader throughout the length of the book" (Hoffman, *Blemished Perfection*, 203). See also Pinker, "Core Story," 5.

context.⁵⁹ Although his words may have caused a degree of discomfort, is this not the point? The book of Job shocks the reader because it articulates loudly and without compromise what its readers only tend to whisper.⁶⁰ Nevertheless, perhaps the author found the non-Israelite setting useful as a starting point for his readers. As I say below, the non-Israelite theme (especially in relation to the provenance of Job himself) is at points a type of mask or disguise that allows the author to think daringly and creatively in Israelite ways, and in some way to universalize the characters of his work.⁶¹

If casting Job as a Gentile was, in part at least, to accommodate the audience's sense of what was acceptable for an Israelite, it should be noted that the book is able to achieve what it does *precisely because of* the non-Israelite setting. Job needed to go to such extremes to have an effect. As Habel so strikingly puts it, "the author introduces us to a monumental figure who has the capacity and courage that provoke God to emerge from his hidden transcendence and to confront a mortal personally in a whirlwind."⁶²

The Non-Israelite Setting Promotes the Wisdom Motif

Why did the author use the term Uz, rather than the location's 'official' name, Edom? Why did he place the events in a 'land' rather than narrow it down to a particular city or rural setting? Weiss detects in these choices a deliberate strategy to serve the author's purposes.⁶³ His starting point for understanding the author's intentions is to examine "the associative capacity of the name Uz," discerned particularly in the "aural effect, and the etymology based on it."⁶⁴

Weiss suggests that the main sound association of עוּץ is with עֵצָה "council" or "wisdom," which is highly suggestive given the connections between Edom, Teman and wisdom (Jer 49:7; Obad 8), the link between

---

59. See Weiss, *Job's Beginning*, 22n5; Brenner, "Job the Pious," 40.

60. I am developing here a phrase by Duquoc: "The author of the Book of Job knows what people think, what people say in whispers—and not just in Israel" (Duquoc, "Demonism and the Unexpectedness of God," 83).

61. Perlstein, *God's Others*, location 5062–69.

62. Habel, *Job*, 42.

63. Weiss, *Job's Beginning*, 23.

64. Weiss, *Job's Beginning*, 23.

"the East" (Job 1:3) and wisdom (1 Kgs 5:10 [ET 4:30]), and that "the conceptual starting point of the story (and of the entire book) is the world of Wisdom literature."[65] All these associations help to fulfil the author's aim, which is to show that Job "lived in the world of Wisdom."[66] If this were the case it is notable that this would seem to represent a degree of affirmation regarding non-Israelite wisdom as well.[67]

Weiss's points fit well within the wisdom context of Job and I see no reason why the author may not have been artistic in this way by exploiting the "associated capacity" of the term, עוץ. However, I would see Weiss's theory as complementing the reasons why the author chose this particular location rather than being the driving force behind it. In this sense, Weiss does his views a disservice by stopping where he does.

The Non-Israelite Setting Promotes an Openness to God Working In and Through Non-Israelites

Could it be that the author of Job opted for a non-Israelite setting in order to challenge his audience about the possibility of God working in and through people beyond the borders of Israel? Is the author of Job trying "to teach that perfect fear of heaven is not solely the possession of the Jews"?[68]

That Job was a non-Israelite who nevertheless had a belief in and relationship with God is a common observation in BMS, as demonstrated in chapter 2 of this volume. Job is described as "a saintly pagan,"[69] "a true servant of Jehovah,"[70] and an example of a godly non-Israelite who worships and pleases God without explaining how he knows God.[71] Rétif and Lamarche's reflection on universalism and Job seems apposite here:

---

65. Weiss, *Job's Beginning*, 23, 24; Crenshaw, *OT Wisdom*, 100. See also Clines, *Job 1–20*, 59.

66. Weiss, *Job's Beginning*, 24. See also Alter, *Wisdom Books*, 11.

67. Wilson, *Job*, 17. See also Wright, *Mission of God*, 442–43.

68. Weiss, *Job's Beginning*, 22n5. See also Rétif and Lamarche, *Salvation of the Gentiles*, 64, 96; Horton, *Bible*, 159; Montgomery, *Bible and Missions*, 27.

69. Legrand, *Unity and Plurality*, 25.

70. Montgomery, *Bible and Missions*, 27.

71. Schultz, "Mission im AT," 41. See also Schnabel, *Jesus and the Twelve*, 58 (citing Job 1:8); Wright, *Salvation*, 173; Glaser, *Bible and Other Faiths*, 39; Wright, *Thinking Clearly*, 45; Widbin, "Salvation for People," 80–83.

> A man who lives on the borders of Arabia and Edom, who does not belong to the race of Israel, is nevertheless engaged in a dramatic argument with God. It is such a gentile whom God puts to the test and who bows down in worship of him without wanting to find a human explanation of the problem of suffering.[72]

Furthermore, concerning the relationship between the non-Israelite setting, the Yahweh speeches and the "missionary potential" of Job, Beeby states, for example:

> The writer seems to be grappling with the missionary problem of how a non-Israelite is to stand before Israel's God. His conclusion is that it must be in conjunction with what is common to all men, namely nature, rather than in conjunction with Israel's history which the outsider might wrongly see as only of interest to Israel.[73]

Beeby's point relates to a particular discussion concerning Job's provenance; namely, whether Job can be considered to be a "righteous pagan" and what this might be teaching the people of God, or more particularly for some, what this might imply about the salvation of "outsiders" or the "unevangelized." Elsewhere Beeby cites Job as an example of OT "missionary literature" stating that "in it a theophany produces repentance and restoration to a non-Israelite."[74] Unfortunately he does not develop this line of argument in a sufficient manner.

As I demonstrated in chapter 2, this discussion is one issue that emerges out of the relatively limited engagement with Job in BMS. Verkuyl, for example, includes Job alongside Melchizedek, Ruth, and the Ninevites in the book of Jonah as examples in the OT of non-Israelites who

> by a word-and-deed witness were won over to trust and serve the living God who had shown them mercy . . . [and whose stories] are windows, as it were, through which we may look out on the vast expanse of people outside the nation of Israel and hear the faint strains of the missionary call to all people already sounding forth.[75]

---

72. Rétif and Lamarche, *Salvation of the Gentiles*, 96. See also Horton, *Bible*, 159; Montgomery, *Bible and Missions*, 27.

73. Beeby, *Mission and Missions*, 32–33. This is the basis for Beeby's claim that "the missionary motive is explicitly seen" in the book of Job.

74. Beeby, *Canon and Mission*, 89.

75. Verkuyl, *Missiology*, 95.

Elsewhere he describes the faith of Melchizedek, Job, Balaam and others as examples of the work of the Holy Spirit and the light of Christ "far beyond the borders of Israel."[76]

For Widbin such figures could be described as "God-fearers" (Job, Melchizedek, Jethro, and Abimelech in Gen 20) or "venerable, righteous Gentiles" (Noah, Dan'el, and Job in Ezek 14:14).[77] Furthermore, Hedlund understands Job to be "a representative of the nations . . . [who] has the knowledge of the true God" which is evidenced in his awareness of God as "Creator and Sustainer and as the source of wisdom."[78] Hedlund sees Job as offering a confession of faith in God as "the Almighty, the Redeemer" (Job 14:14, 16–17; 19:25–26) and becoming personally aware

> of God's grace and mercy in the forgiveness of sins and catch a glimpse of belief in the resurrection that is rare in the Old Testament. The missionary significance of Job is that he, a representative of the Gentile world, was a recipient not only of God's general revelation but also of redemption. Job was a representative of those who seek and find for he had come to hope in the living God.[79]

Understandably in this light, Job is sometimes included in broader studies on the possibility of the salvation of those outside the people of God. Writing on this theme, Pinnock refers to Job as a "pagan believer" and includes Job in lists of "godly pagans," "pagan saints" that feature in the Bible.[80] For Pinnock, the existence of such believers outside of Israel demonstrates that salvation is not the preserve of the "formal covenant communities" and contributes to his inclusivist stance on the question of salvation.[81] Tiessen also asserts that figures such as Job, Abel, Melchizedek, Naaman, Rahab, and Ruth were "saved" although he prefers not to use the term, "holy pagans" as most had some kind of special revelation from God.[82] For him the cases of Job and Melchizedek are particularly

---

76. Verkuyl, "Kingdom," 76.
77. Widbin, "Salvation for People," 80–83.
78. Hedlund, *Mission of the Church*, 134–35.
79. Hedlund, *Mission of the Church*, 135.
80. Pinnock, *Wideness in God's Mercy*, 60, 40, 94, respectively.
81. Pinnock, *Wideness in God's Mercy*, 162; cf. Hedlund, *Mission of the Church*, 81. For a critique of Pinnock's views, see Strange, *Possibility of Salvation*.
82. Tiessen, *Who Can Be Saved?*, 170.

intriguing as there is no indication of such a revelation and, more generally, there is no indication of how their relationships with God arose.[83]

Although (among others) O'Collins considers figures such as Melchizedek, the widow of Zarephath, the Ninevites, Naaman and Ruth, he reserves a special designation for Job, naming him "the holy 'outsider' par excellence."[84] Such a superlative is based on his observation that

> the OT contains no other story like this: the long story of a blameless non-Israelite ... [which] drives home two lessons: the just person is not necessarily an Israelite nor even visibly related to Israel; the revelation of God can be mediated through creation and is not limited to particular historical events.[85]

Similarly, Perlstein reserves a special status for Job in comparison with Melchizedek, Jethro and Ruth, whom he selects as other examples of "righteous" non-Israelites.[86] Whereas "Melchizedek ... and Jethro play only brief, supporting roles in the Bible," Job "is a star!" who even "far outdistances Ruth," whose book has only four chapters compared with Job's 42.[87] Moreover, Job's book has the "very unusual distinction" of making "no mention of Israel, Israelites or Jews."[88]

There is a certain degree of logic in pointing to Job as an example of someone from outside of the covenant community who has aligned themselves with the living God. His story does provide a fascinating case study in this regard, especially in light of the exemplary description of his piety in 1:1–5 which, presumably, would put many within the covenant community to shame. However, so much is left unsaid about the background to Job's faith that it is difficult to draw conclusions concerning its significance without a considerable degree of speculation. There is, therefore, an inherent danger in the use of Job as a support to differing arguments in the debate. Would it be significant for the purposes of the discussion if, for example, the Job of the biblical book were understood not as a historical figure but as a literary creation? While I would not

---

83. Tiessen, *Who Can Be Saved?*, 149.

84. O'Collins, *Salvation for All*, 54, 66–67.

85. O'Collins, *Salvation for All*, 55, 66.

86. Perlstein, *God's Others*, location 5044–57. See also Hedlund, *Mission of the Church*, 37.

87. Perlstein, *God's Others*, location 5048–50. See also Hedlund, *Mission of the Church*, 66.

88. Perlstein, *God's Others*, location 5055–57.

want to dismiss entirely the attempts made to draw Job into these discussions I would also not want to reduce him to this. In my view simply placing Job in the category of a "righteous Gentile" fails to recognize the complexity with which he is portrayed and considerably underplays the missional significance of both him as a character but also the book as a whole. As such, this particular line of thought seems to reflect the effects of the author's use of the non-Israelite theme rather than his reasons for employing it.

Although calling Job a "saintly pagan," Legrand takes this idea in a more fruitful direction. Reviewing the function of the wisdom literature in the context of universalism Legrand exploits Job's non-Israelite provenance to make him into a universalizing figure: "Job's problem is a universal problem, and the divine response, as well, has universal validity. Here indeed is a decentralized universalism, in the sapiential tradition."[89]

Job, then, is more than just a righteous Gentile. He is more, even, than the best of righteous Gentiles. In my view, Job should be considered in an altogether different category because his particularity as a non-Israelite exhibiting faith in Yahweh serves a universalizing purpose that makes him representative of humanity.[90] The same idea cannot be applied to any of the other figures mentioned, and it is to this universalizing theme that I now turn.

The Non-Israelite Setting Universalizes the Book

The most commonly held and, in my view, persuasive reason given for Job's non-Israelite setting is that it functions as a device to universalize the book. The point has already been made that the Wisdom Literature has a more "international" tone than other parts of the OT.[91] Setting the book of Job outside of Israel is in keeping with this tendency and associating it with Uz, as was shown above, includes at least some associations with international wisdom.[92]

Setting the story outside of Israel's borders removed the necessity of dealing, explicitly at least, with such matters as covenant, election, and

---

89. Legrand, *Unity and Plurality*, 25.

90. See, for example, Hedlund, *Mission of the Church*, who understands Job to be "a representative of the nations."

91. Wright, *Mission of God*, 443; Hartley, "Job 2," 346.

92. Wilson, *Job*, 17; Weiss, *Job's Beginning*, 23–24.

Israel's history.[93] The author of Job was thus able to transcend certain peculiarly Israelite concerns that may have distracted the audience from the core human dilemma at play in the book.[94] Additionally, perhaps, as Beeby has noted above, if the book had exhibited more overtly Israelite trappings it may not have appealed to a wider, international audience. While it is difficult to assess this as a principal aim of the author, it does not seem unreasonable that this would have been an effect of the setting. The setting of the book, therefore, enabled the author to probe the divine-human relationship aside from, or at a level deeper even than covenant.[95]

As is demonstrated by the survey of ANE material in the following chapter, neither suffering nor reflecting on suffering was unique to Israel. In writing the book of Job the author was, in his own Israelite way, making a contribution to humanity's wrestling with this most universal of experiences. Setting the action outside of Israel would therefore seem to be an entirely appropriate way of internationalizing his work as it took its place among other attempts to probe the universal and vexing questions it addressed.[96]

The literature discussing Job 1:1 often contains lengthy treatments of the precise location of Uz, but this question seems much less important than what Uz represents. Granted, the choice of Uz (and, by extension, Edom) may have afforded the author of Job some helpful associations. There is the known association between Edom and wisdom, and the sound capacity of Uz (noted by Weiss, above) is suggestive of wisdom as well. Edom also seems an appropriate choice because it retains the "not Israel" status while also still being somewhere an Israelite could relate to as it was "just next-door."[97] Therefore the proximity of Edom enabled the author to highlight certain connections with Israel which made it familiar enough to "draw in" its audience.[98]

However to focus on the specific location of Uz is, ultimately, a distraction from the main significance of the author's choice of a

---

93. Gordis, *God and Man*, 213; Janzen, *Job*, 5; Moberly, "Solomon and Job," 10.

94. Clines, *Job 1–20*, 10, 59. Ticciati, for example, builds on the work of Barth and speaks of Uz "as a sort of contextless context, being taken as a license to extract Job from his historical context and consider him solely in relation to God" (Ticciati, *Job*, 19).

95. Janzen, *Job*, 11–12, 21.

96. See Hoffman, *Blemished Perfection*, 203; Wilson, *Job*, 17–18.

97. Clines, *Job 1–20*, 59.

98. Perlstein, *God's Others*, location 5165–66.

non-Israelite context. The primary importance in this setting is not tied to its specificity, Edomite or otherwise. In essence, the significance of this choice is literary and theological rather than geographical.[99] The crucial factor in choosing Uz is that it is not Israel, which signals to the audience that the book has a horizon beyond their own borders.[100]

The effect of the non-Israelite setting is to create "a sense of narrative distance" which is emphasized by the ambiguities of the text.[101] This theme of ambiguity has been interpreted in a variety of ways by scholars. Brenner, for example, sees the non-Israelite motif as offering a signal that the piety of Job in the Prologue should be treated with suspicion, whereas the lack of historical detail points Penchansky to the author's desire to undermine more mainstream voices at the time of composition.[102] Such is the nature of ambiguity that the gaps can be filled in a variety of ways.

This "not Israel" motif functions as part of a broader strategy of the author, who exploits both what is known (that it is not Israel) and what is left unknown or ambiguous. Contra Brenner and Penchansky I would understand this as a means of universalizing his book in order to create in Job a representative or paradigmatic figure.[103] Job embodies in himself and his circumstances the "movement from the particular to the universal."[104] Despite the very particularities of his situation, Job becomes a personification of the human dilemma when faced with suffering: "Job is no longer man; he is humanity!"[105]

Job's representative function is made all the more evident because his identity and provenance cannot be tied down definitively. As Long puts it so poignantly:

> In his story of anguished suffering and troubled faith, symbolically Job is neither Jew nor Greek, male nor female, ancient nor

---

99. Balentine, *Job*, 40.

100. Moberly, "Solomon and Job," 10; Clines, *Job 1–20*, 10.

101. Newsom, "Job," 345. See also Janzen, *Job*, 5; Brenner, "Job the Pious," 40.

102. Brenner, "Job the Pious," 40; Penchansky, *Betrayal of God*, 32–33.

103. "His life circumstances are left deliberately vague so that they can represent any person at any point in time; people of any era in any location can identify with Job and learn the lessons that wisdom has for them" (Konkel, "Job," 30–31).

104. Borrowing the phrase from Bauckham, *Bible and Mission*, 13.

105. de Lamartine, cited in Balentine, *Job*, 5. See also Hartley, *Job*, 67; Estes, *Handbook*, 28; Balentine, *Job*, 46; Moberly, "Solomon and Job," 10. Indeed, resonances between Job's location "in the East" and Genesis 2:8 may further suggest themes of representation, creation, and divine design; a connection noted by Balentine, *Job*, 44.

modern. Job is from the land of Uz, a place where no one can find on a map but a place where nearly everyone has spent some time. Job is every person, transcending particularity of time and place.[106]

The present language of "representative" and "paradigm" requires clarification. It is my view that the author presents Job in a universalized and universalizing manner in order to create in him a representative of suffering humanity, but also a paradigm for how a person of faith could engage with the vexing and universal experiences of suffering. Although the two ideas are closely linked, they seem to me to evoke certain passive and active nuances respectively. Addressing the question of Job's provenance, Pope states:

> The author of the Book of Job cannot be precisely placed temporally or geographically, but this is of no great consequence for he speaks to and for all humanity about a problem that has perplexed thinking and feeling men in all times and places.[107]

However, I would want to tweak the wording to say that the ambiguity is of *great* consequence *precisely because* it enables Job to speak "to and for all humanity" in a clearer and more compelling way.

Yet at the same time I would want to argue that as well as his everyman status, Job does represent something particularly Israelite. Despite his provenance, Job is depicted as a worshiper of Yahweh and the book, we may assume, had Israelites as its primary audience. As I will demonstrate later in the following chapter the Israelite nature of the book of Job can be seen especially in the light of other ANE texts on innocent suffering. There is an assumption of Israelite monotheism that drives the book of Job, and its turning point occurs in an encounter with Yahweh himself.

The relationship between particularity and universality in Job is, therefore, a subtle one that works in both directions. The particularity of Job's provenance and circumstances function to universalize the book. Yet at the same time the book deals with its universal theme in a particularized way, thereby driving the reader struggling with universally relevant questions and concerns to the very particular God of Israel.[108]

---

106. Long, *What Shall We Say?*, 94. See also Clines, *Job 1–20*, 10; Reitman, *Unlocking Wisdom*, location 1000–1003.

107. Pope, *Job*, xxxviii.

108. See Glaser, *Bible and Other Faiths*, 122.

Other Universalizing Elements of the Prologue

To demonstrate further the presence of a universalizing impulse in the book of Job it would be helpful to show how the author achieves this in ways other than the use of the non-Israelite motif. This could be done in a number of different ways but I have chosen to focus on certain features of the Prologue that give the book of Job a more universalized trajectory. In particular I will address the archaic setting of the book, the Prologue's literary artistry, and the crucial question voiced by the accuser in 1:9b.

The Archaic Setting

Although they differ over the extent to which and ways in which the author has developed it for his purposes, scholars generally agree that the Prologue-Epilogue of Job is based on an earlier, traditional story.[109] While the application of precise terminology such as "folk tale" or "legend" receives a degree of attention, many point to the sophisticated and didactic nature of the narrative.[110] My own view is that the prose frame functions as a didactic story that features archaising elements that may well have been, in part at least, inherited from a known, traditional story or stories about a righteous sufferer named Job. Where I talk about genre, my focus will be on the ways in which this promotes the universalizing theme that I am addressing.

It is widely held that the book of Job has a patriarchal setting, which is suggested by a number of details in the story. Job's wealth, for example, is quantified in animals and servants.[111] Presumably in the absence of priest or sanctuary Job, as the head of his household, is responsible for the religious activities of his family, including sacrifices.[112] The Prologue uses the terms, שְׁבָא (Sabeans, 1:15) and כַּשְׂדִּים (Chaldeans, 1:17), depicting them as nomadic, as yet unsettled peoples.[113] Looking ahead to the Epilogue, the term, קְשִׂיטָה in 42:11 is considered to be an archaic term for

---

109. See Gordis, *God and Man*, 65–75.

110. Newsom, "Job," 343; Newsom, *Contest*, 38–41; Clines, "False Naivety," 735–44; Habel, *Job*, 39–40.

111. Longman, *Job*, location 1592; Hartley, *Job*, 21.

112. Longman, *Job*, location 1616–17; Walton, *Job*, 23; Hartley, *Job*, 21.

113. Clines, *Job 1–20*, 32; Walton, *Job*, 32; Hartley, *Job*, 21;

currency that is only found in early texts.[114] Additionally, Job's longevity (42:17) may point to an ancient time.[115]

Overall the prose story appears to have an "ancient epic" feel to it, exhibiting poetic details even though it is broadly prose.[116] Examples of this include assonance and alliteration (for instance, בְּאֶרֶץ־עוּץ in 1:1; הַשָּׂטָן הֲשַׂמְתָּ in 1:8; 2:3; and וַיָּקָם ... וַיִּקְרַע in 1:20); parallelism (1:10; 1:22); poetic phrasing (1:21; the use of תִּפְלָה in 1:22 and לְבַלְעוֹ in 2:3); symmetrical structuring (1:6–12 and 2:1–7; 1:1, 8, and 2:3; 1:14–19); symbolic numbers (sevens, threes, and, by combination, tens in 1:2–3; 2:11, 13); mention of the divine council; and the theme of the daughters in the Epilogue.[117]

We see, therefore, that Job's character and story are placed in the context of an ancient, "heroic" setting. Functioning very closely with the non-Israelite theme, this archaic motif creates a temporal distance that contributes to the narrative distancing noted above. In so doing it removes the requirement to deal with issues specific to Israel's covenant history, which enables the author to "pose the problems raised in the book in general human terms," and to allow his audience, "to experience vicariously the primal nature of God," which in turn will inform them about how they perceive their covenant relationship with God.[118] This setting may also function to facilitate a theme of ignorance or limited knowledge on the part of Job, as if the narrative were transporting the audience to a time (and place) "when mortals were first struggling to know God."[119]

While the book appears to place itself within a particular era, that of the patriarchs, this still allows for a certain degree of ambiguity. Just as it is unnecessary to place Uz on a map, it is also unnecessary to date the setting of the story any more specifically than to say that it occurred before the time of the covenant. Given that the action of the book is already taking place outside of Israel, it could be argued that this archaised

---

114. See Gen 33:19; Josh 24:32; Walton, *Job*, 32; Clines, *Job 38–42*, 1236; Hartley, *Job*, 21; Dhorme, *Job*, xxi.

115. Pope, *Job*, xxxi; Hartley, *Job*, 22.

116. Sarna, "Epic Substratum," 15.

117. Sarna, "Epic Substratum," 14–24; Hartley, *Job*, 22; Hoffman, *Blemished Perfection*, 47–48. See also Newsom, *Contest*, 53.

118. Janzen, *Job*, 5; Habel, *Job*, 40. See also Janzen, *Job*, 21; Ticciati, "Does Job Fear God for Naught?," 355.

119. Habel, *Job*, 30. See also Allen, "Missionary Message," 18–31.

setting is unnecessary. In my view, however, the overall impression of the archaic setting adds a further (albeit minor) layer of distance to the story, deepening the impression that the book of Job is not "here and now" but "there and then" or, more precisely, "anywhere and anytime," with Job being "anyone"; that is, "representative of all who suffer."[120]

Literary Artistry

While certain details of the text noted above may be seen simply as archaic (or archaising) features of the Prologue, these phenomena may also be placed within a broader discussion of the way in which the author of Job has constructed his work.[121]

In recent years much work has been done to draw out the sophisticated literary features and theological significance of the Prologue.[122] Hoffman, for example, focuses his attention on the tension in the frame narrative between "mimetic" and "anti-mimetic" elements within the story; that is, elements that represent or cohere with reality and those that undermine a sense of recognition.[123] Concentrating particularly on 1:1–2:7; 42:12–17 he understands the author to be creating an "anti-mimetic mood" using "numerous schematic and symmetrical elements," many of which I have noted in the above section, such as symbolic numbers, repetition and chiasm.[124] He also sees an anti-mimetic tendency evidenced by the hyperbolic description of Job's righteousness and the inclusion of the satan (who "seduces" God) and the "tableau of the sons of God."[125]

Notably he understands the Uz setting as combining elements of mimesis and anti-mimesis, which reflects the complex nature of the Prologue.[126] Given the deep mimesis displayed in the Dialogues it was crucial to give the book some degree of historical rootedness; hence the (albeit loosely) known place of Uz.[127] Yet, building on Weiss's argument

---

120. Hartley, *Job*, 67.
121. See, for example, Habel, *Job*, 81.
122. See Newsom, "Re-considering Job," 159.
123. Hoffman, *Blemished Perfection*, 267–76.
124. Hoffman, *Blemished Perfection*, 271.
125. Hoffman, *Blemished Perfection*, 272, 273.
126. Hoffman, *Blemished Perfection*, 271–72.
127. Hoffman, *Blemished Perfection*, 272.

on the wisdom motif, Uz can also be understood symbolically to portray Job as an archetype of wise piety.[128]

Hoffman sees these elements functioning as a device by which "the author deliberately wrote a story that seemingly declares of itself 'I am not true,' 'I am not an imitation of any reality,'" the purpose of which is to afford himself "maximum freedom" to pursue the themes of his book: "When the righteous man, his happiness and his suffering are 'absolute,' one may examine the subject in a 'purer' way."[129]

It could be argued that even the phrasing of 1:1a contributes towards this "unreal" tone of the book. The narrative opens with the unusual phrase אִישׁ הָיָה which has parallels only in Nathan's parable (2 Sam 12:1) and Joash's tale (2 Kgs 14:9).[130] On this (admittedly slight) evidence it could be that the phrasing indicates that the audience should expect some kind of fictional story rather than a historical account.[131] Another explanation is that the use of אִישׁ here emphasizes the humanity and vulnerability of Job, although this is perhaps overly speculative.[132] However it may be meant more as an indication that the story is not part of the continuing narrative of the history of Israel.[133] In this case the opening may not prove historicity one way or the other but still contributes to the narrative distancing of the Prologue.

In an influential essay entitled, "False Naivety in the Prologue to Job," Clines demonstrates, correctly in my view, that certain seemingly simplistic features in the Prologue actually evidence a sophisticated literary hand.[134] The author, he suggests, gives the text "the appearance of artlessness to convey a subtle message."[135] The language is naive (especially in comparison with the Dialogue), containing very few colloquialisms or metaphors (with 1:10; 2:4 as exceptions).[136] The style is naive, using very few adjectives (for example, תָּם and יָשָׁר in 1:1, 8; 2:3; גְּדוֹלָה in 1:19; and רָע in 2:7) and employing repetition as its most prominent device

---

128. Hoffman, *Blemished Perfection*, 271–72.
129. Hoffman, *Blemished Perfection*, 271, 273. See also Newsom, *Contest*, 53.
130. See Clines, *Job 1–20*, 9.
131. So, Gordis, *Job*, 10; Rowley, *Job*, 28; Newsom, *Contest*, 41.
132. An explanation offered by Alden, *Job*, 46.
133. Clines, *Job 1–20*, 9–10. See also Pope, *Job*, 3.
134. Clines, "False Naivety."
135. Clines, "False Naivety," 735.
136. Clines, "False Naivety," 735.

(as noted above).¹³⁷ Further, Clines points to certain simplistic details to demonstrate the supposed naivety of the plot:

> Job must be the *greatest* of the sons of the East, *none like him* on earth, *blameless* and upright; he must lose *all* his possessions in *one* day, he must be afflicted *from the sole of his foot to the crown of his head*. His downfall must result from a *divine* conspiracy against him, of which he must have not the slightest suspicion. And to his fate he must respond with inscrutable oriental submissiveness.¹³⁸

Finally, the structure seems particularly naive, being divided into five scenes which alternate between earth and heaven, including a "four-fold messenger scene" plus several two-member dialogues, all of which point to "the utmost simplicity of construction."¹³⁹

However, for Clines, the naivety of the narrative is "false" because the Prologue is actually, "a well wrought narrative that plunges directly into issues of substance that reach as deep as the fraught dialogues themselves."¹⁴⁰

It is not my intention here to work through the details of Clines's treatment of the elements of the Prologue noted above. Instead, because of the way it demonstrates the movement from Job's particularity to universal concerns, I will focus on his concluding comments about the implications of the Prologue's sophisticated handling of the question of Job's suffering.

While Job may wrestle with the reasons behind his suffering throughout the book, the reader is in no doubt whatsoever. In one sense there is no mystery at all in Job's experiences. In Job's particular case he is suffering because, as is explicitly stated in the Prologue, it has been decreed in heaven:

> Read naively, the prologue must mean that no question about the meaning of Job's suffering remains . . . [and therefore] Job's suffering is irrelevant to human suffering in general, for there is a distinct and known reason for it. . . . What then does the prologue offer for the problem of human suffering? Naively read, what it is doing is to proffer the reason for Job's suffering: more

---

137. Clines, "False Naivety," 735.
138. Clines, "False Naivety," 735.
139. Clines, "False Naivety," 735.
140. Clines, "False Naivety," 735.

subtly read, what it is doing is to offer no reason for any suffering at all—except Job's.[141]

Thus, read in a simplistic fashion, the Prologue can only tell us why *Job* suffered. Yet this cannot be what the author intends. However, if the Prologue, and indeed the whole of the book, are "read with an ounce of subtlety," it become clear that the book probes the broader question of human suffering and not just the specific question of Job's.[142]

At points in the rest of the book Job himself made this move from his own particularities to universal questions (3:20; 7:1; 14:1; 24:1–17) and the reader is invited to do the same.[143] In Clines's view, the Prologue appears to teach, in light of the Dialogue, that there is a divine reason behind human suffering, even if it is not the same as the particular divine reason in Job's case, which is merely an exemplar.[144] Moreover, although Job's suffering is gratuitous (חִנָּם) in one sense (2:3), from the divine perspective it is necessary, meaning that Job's response in suffering could actually be said to be benefiting God.[145] Perhaps, suggests Clines, Job is paradigmatic in this sense as well:

> Why else should God authorize the persecution of Job if not because it is only Job who can solve the question that has been raised in heaven? In a word, Job suffers for God's sake. May not the prologue, read as the framework for the dialogue, be saying the same thing about innocent suffering in general? If innocent suffering is for God's sake, to grant him some undivulged benefit, to win him some unguessed at boon, then does not undeserved suffering acquire a fresh and startlingly positive valuation—for the sufferer in his particularity and for humankind at large?[146]

Both Hoffman and Clines note the motif of hyperbole in the Prologue in relation to Job's characterisation and circumstances. It seems to me this is also an important contribution to the universalizing of Job's

---

141. Clines, "False Naivety," 743.
142. Clines, "False Naivety," 743.
143. Clines, "False Naivety," 743.
144. Clines, "False Naivety," 743–44.
145. Clines, "False Naivety," 744.
146. Clines, "False Naivety," 744. Thus, the book of Job "lays undeserved suffering on God's majestic shoulders. No attempt to explain either enigma is made; the story seems content to affirm disinterested righteousness and to acknowledge vexing instances that lack a positive correlation between sin and punishment" (Crenshaw, *OT Wisdom*, 103). See also Yancey, *Bible Jesus Read*, 62, 65–68.

character and book. In 1:1 the narrator describes Job as תָּם (blameless) and יָשָׁר (upright), וִירֵא אֱלֹהִים (fearing God) and וְסָר מֵרָע (turning from evil). This loading of commendable attributes, which are repeated by Yahweh in 1:8 and 2:3, makes Job into "a paragon of devotion and integrity" or an idealized wisdom figure.[147] Indeed, no other figure in the OT (Israelite or otherwise) receives such accolades of integrity, illustrating Yahweh's view that there really is no-one on earth like Job (1:8; 2:3).[148]

To this idealized figure is added an idealized life-circumstance of wealth and familial harmony, illustrated by symbolic amounts of possessions and offspring, and an example of Job's scrupulous attention to religious practice.[149] Job's initial character and circumstances are expressed most of all by hyperbole, which is then matched by descriptions of the breadth and depth of losses and grief he endures. Job is a man of extremes, and so, functions as a paradigm for everyone in between, providing the most effective "control" experiment for probing the nature of true piety.[150] Furthermore, it is not just the existence and origins of his suffering that make him representative. It could also be argued that the depth and breadth of his pain is so all-encompassing that, to some degree, he embodies a totality of human suffering and, so, makes him a paradigm in this way as well.[151]

Reviewing certain aspects of the literary artistry of the Prologue appears to demonstrate further evidence of a universalizing impulse within the book of Job. Using different motifs and techniques, the author clearly seems to be setting up Job as a representative or paradigmatic figure. One further example of this impulse will be addressed; namely, the way in

---

147. Walton, *Job*, 58; Weiss, *Job's Beginning*, 25; Habel, *Job*, 86.

148. Balentine, *Job*, 46–47. See also Moberly, *Bible*, 84; Hoffman, *Blemished Perfection*, 272.

149. Attempts to show that 1:5 evidences a suspiciously "over-pious" tendency in Job are, in my view, over-reading the idealized nature of the descriptions. For examples of these readings, see Wolde, *Mr and Mrs Job*, 13–14; Brenner, "Job the Pious," 44.

150. Moberly, *Bible*, 87.

151. This helpful insight is suggested by Hartley: "Beyond the sheer severity of his physical suffering, two factors explain why Job's suffering could be representative of all human suffering. First, there is the principle that the severity of his suffering increases inversely in relationship to one's success. Since Job was the most exalted person of ancient times by reason of his standing in the community (29:7–10, 21–25) and his wealth (1:2–3), his downfall was the most dramatic possible in the human sphere. Second, Job endured terrible suffering on all levels of human experiences: the physical, the spiritual, the social, and the emotional" (Hartley, "Job: Theology of," 782).

which the initial question of the accuser in 1:9b functions to universalize the significance of both Job the individual and the book as a whole. As I will show, understanding this crucial text becomes a significant way of discerning the missional function of the book of Job.

The Crucial Question: Is It for Nothing חִנָּם that Job Fears God? (1:9b)

I have chosen to highlight this particular text due to its prominence in scholarly discussions on Job, but also because it is, in my view, a significant example of the universalizing impulse within the book of Job. As I argue throughout this volume, I view the question as a key to understanding the complex relationship between Job and the *missio Dei*. By illustrating the role of Job within this broader question of the *missio Dei* this also enables me to consider the book in relation to the theme of what I have termed "the missional potential and cost of character formation," which I highlight in the concluding section of the following chapter.

Following the introductory scene on earth, which orients the reader to the character and original circumstances of Job, the narrative of the Prologue shifts to heaven in a supposed meeting of the divine council in 1:6–12. Among the sons of God, בְּנֵי הָאֱלֹהִים, is a figure called the accuser, הַשָּׂטָן, whose role it seems is to scour the earth, checking on the integrity of human beings.[152]

In a manner which seems to invite a counter claim, Yahweh asks the accuser if he has considered his servant Job, whom he assesses to be unique on the earth, confirming the combination of righteous traits the narrator has already highlighted (vv. 1, 8). Thus Job is set up as the greatest of the sons of the East by the narrator, and someone beyond compare in all the world, according to God himself. Here is an archetypal, pious human being.

The accuser does not doubt that Job appears to be pious.[153] Rather, he casts doubt on the genuineness of his piety and, so, on the nature of piety itself:

---

152. It is not my intention here to detail the lengthy discussion on the precise identity of this figure or the assembly more broadly. My view is that הַשָּׂטָן is an ambiguous figure who has the particular responsibility among the angelic beings of bringing to light human failings. See Clines, *Job 1–20*, 19–23; Weiss, *Job's Beginning*, 31–46; Balentine, *Job*, 48–53; Walton, *Job*, 63–67.

153. Gutiérrez, *On Job*, 4; Jones, *Job*, 53.

הַחִנָּם יָרֵא אִיּוֹב אֱלֹהִים "Is it for nothing that Job fears God?"

This question has, rightly in my view, been recognized by many as the critical point in the book of Job. Ticciati, for example, sees it as "pivotal" not only for the opening narrative but also as a means of setting the agenda for the entire book.[154] Similarly, others have described it as "the critical issue around which the whole story revolves,"[155] and as propelling[156] or functioning as a "key" to the whole work.[157] As such the accuser's question acts as a necessary catalyst and context for the unfolding events and speeches in the book. Once uttered it cannot be taken back and must be seen through to resolution: "there is no turning back either for God or for Job."[158]

חִנָּם is a nuanced term that can mean doing something for no payment or price (Gen 29:15; Exod 21:2; Isa 52:3); purposelessness or vanity (Prov 1:17; Mal 1:10); or doing something *gratuitously, without cause, undeservedly,* esp. of groundless hostility or attack" (1 Sam 19:5; 2 Kgs 2:31; Ps 35:7; Prov 1:11; Lam 3:52).[159] In addition to its use in 1:9, חִנָּם occurs three other times in the book of Job. In 2:3 Yahweh accuses the accuser of inciting him to destroy Job for no reason; in 9:17 Job complains that God multiplies his wounds for no reason; and in 22:6 Eliphaz accuses Job of exacting pledges from his brothers for nothing. In 1:9 it seems to be both the first and third nuances that are at play in the accuser's question. Does Job fear God for no reward? Surely, considers the accuser, Job has every reason to serve God.

The significance of the question, particularly in relation to its universalizing or paradigmatic impulse, can be examined by highlighting two key aspects. First, it is clear that while it is casting doubt on the nature of Job's piety, the question is really probing the nature of all human piety. If Job is Yahweh's exemplar of integrity then he is also the accuser's potential exemplar of doubt. The basis of the accuser's suspicion concerning Job's piety is his doubt about piety full stop.[160] Is Job's character and

---

154. Ticciati, "Does Job Fear God for Naught?," 353.

155. Moberly, *Bible*, 85.

156. Brueggemann, *Theology of the OT*, 387.

157. Gutiérrez, *On Job*, 4.

158. Ticciati, *Job*, 50.

159. BDB 336. See also Dhorme, *Job*, 7; Wilson, *Job*, 23; Rowley, *Job*, 32; Fretheim, "חנן," 203–4).

160. Selms, for example, makes this point in the reverse: "In the opinion of the

piety, indeed any human character or expression of piety, "nothing more than a sham?"[161]

Secondly, the question casts doubt on the integrity of God as well as that of Job and, by extension, humanity because "Job's character is necessarily intertwined with Yahweh's character."[162] It looks to the accuser as if God is, in effect, buying Job's loyalty in exchange for protection and prosperity.[163] Is the very relationship between God and humanity a sham too? Obedience, it seems, is not enough on its own; what is required is genuine relationship.[164]

It may be argued that the real target of the accuser's question is God himself. If human beings can only be bribed into line, does this imply that God is not "intrinsically worshipful"?[165] Perhaps God is not in himself enough to elicit "the free adoration and love of humankind,"[166] or is not capable of creating a being that would recognize his qualities sufficiently to choose worship.[167]

Clearly, then, much is at stake. The very integrity of God himself is under question, as is the integrity of the way God relates to humanity. Therefore, it is precisely because these are such fundamental questions that they needed to be asked and answered.[168]

For whose benefit is the question being asked? I do not think satisfying the accuser is, in itself, sufficient reason to pursue the question, given his subordinate status and his disappearance from view after the Prologue. Could it be, as some suppose, that it is Yahweh who "needs" to know the answer, as if to address some kind of divine doubt?[169] While it may be the case that Yahweh as a literary character within the book "needs" proof, something else seems to be at play. Perhaps because the

---

Adversary, Job's piety, *and therefore all human piety*, is a refined form of egoism" (Selms, *Job*, 24, my italics). That the accuser has all humanity or general human nature in view is evident also in his declaration in 2:4.

161. Brown, *Character*, 52.
162. Brown, *Character*, 52; Lo, *Job* 28, 40; Ticciati, *Job*, 74.
163. Jones, *Job*, 53.
164. Brueggemann, *Theology of the OT*, 387.
165. A phrase used by both Balentine, *Job*, 74; Janzen, *Job*, 38.
166. Balentine, *Job*, 74
167. Janzen, *Job*, 38.
168. Weiss, *Job's Beginning*, 37; Clines, *Job 1–20*, 25.
169. Weiss, *Job's Beginning*, 42. See also Mitchell, *Job*, xi; Clines, *Job 1–20*, 26; Perlstein, *God's Others*, location 6056–58.

issue is one of integrity, this issue cannot just be discussed. In order to deal with the accuser's suspicion, Job's integrity must be demonstrated, "out there in public view."[170]

Ultimately, it is the audience of the book of Job that needs to consider the question and be formed both by its asking and by its answer. It is therefore part of the formative purpose of the book of Job, in which "God lets us be real and show ourselves, show the world, and show God."[171]

What we have seen is that the question posed by the accuser is a further instrument of universality, employed by the author to transform Job's particularity into a representative or paradigmatic figure. Job becomes the test case in an examination of an absolutely fundamental issue, as developed in several aspects. If God's confidence in Job is vindicated, this allows for the possibility that other human beings may also be obedient and fear God for no reason other than for who God is.[172]

The accuser's question is, therefore, an essential one to be asked in relation to the mission of God. If there is no such thing as the possibility of genuine piety, this throws into question the integrity of the relationship between God and humanity. Would such a sham relationship amount to nothing more than idolatry?[173] In the *misso Dei* God's purpose is to restore the broken relationship between humanity and himself. However, if this relationship turns out to be a sham, then the project of the *missio Dei* is likewise a sham, rendered meaningless by an unattainable goal. It is at this pivotal moment in the mission of God that Job plays his part. His is a role of great cost, yet has a value that is "fresh and startlingly positive."[174]

This, I believe, is an essential and particularly Joban contribution to biblical reflection on mission. It also makes a more satisfying connection between Job and the biblical story of God's mission. Rather than trying to find how the book fits into and progresses the story of God's mission in a temporal sense, and by way of awkward historical associations, the book of Job can be understood as standing apart from it and speaking into it. As a way of relating Job to the *missio Dei* this seems to account more appropriately and fully for the book on its own terms. As such Job tackles head on a question that threatens the validity of the entire project

---

170. Goldingay, *Job*, 20. See also Moberly, *Bible*, 87–88.

171. Goldingay, *Job*, 20. See also Brown, *Character*, 51.

172. Gutiérrez, *On Job*, 4. He also notes that, similarly, Job's underserved suffering opens up the possibility of the unjust suffering of others.

173. Gutiérrez, *On Job*, 5. See also Janzen, *Job*, 41.

174. Clines, "False Naivety," 744.

of the mission of God. Read in this way it becomes clear that, in the book of Job, nothing less than the mission of God is at stake.[175]

I have so far demonstrated that the book of Job presents itself as addressing universally significant (and therefore missionally relevant) concerns, seen especially through the paradigmatic function of the non-Israelite theme. I have also highlighted the missional importance of the crucial question in 1:9b. However, I have yet to explain what the book actually says about these. Do we find, for example, that the piety of Job and, therefore, the integrity of God's mission, is vindicated? How does the book address the question of unattributed or innocent suffering in a way that makes a significant contribution to the international conversation?

In the next chapter I turn to matters of content, focusing especially on the extent to which the book of Job exhibits a missional encounter with ANE beliefs. I will show how Job meets them in affirmation and challenge, ultimately contending for a distinctive, Israelite view on the issue in contrast to alternatives. This is seen especially through the speeches of Yahweh and Job's responses (38:1–42:6), which also provide a way of answering the questions posed in the early stages of the book.

---

175. See also Jones: "Indeed the honor and glory of his entire redemptive programme are at stake" (Jones, *Job*, 54). Similarly, Yancey suggests: "A piece of the history of the universe was at stake in Job and is still at stake in our own responses. . . . How we respond *matters*. By hanging onto the thinnest thread of faith, Job won a crucial victory in God's grand plan to redeem the earth" (Yancey, *Bible*, 66).

5

A Missional Encounter with Cultures in Job

> The Joban drama is perhaps the longest-running story in the history of human experience. The biblical Job is but one, even if one of the best, of a cast of characters who has played this role. ... This wider context for encountering the Bible's version of the story keeps us mindful that the Joban problem is no aberration; instead, it stands at the center of what it means to be human. For as long as men and women have walked this earth, they have shared the journey with someone, somewhere, named Job.[1]

> Living as a contrast community will mean a missionary encounter with our culture. In a missionary encounter, the gospel challenges the cultural story instead of allowing the cultural story to absorb it. Thus to be faithful we will need to understand our particular cultural context well.[2]

As I demonstrated in the first part of this volume, one question that can be probed as part of a missional reading is the extent to which a biblical text engaged with and critiqued the worldviews and ideas of Israel's neighbors. When the biblical writers articulated a rendering of reality that reflected their monotheistic or Yahwistic beliefs they were, implicitly or explicitly, telling an alternative story that encountered and competed with alternative renderings.

1. Balentine, *Job*, 4–5.
2. Goheen, *Light to the Nations*, 211.

It follows, therefore, that the relationship between Job and similar ANE texts would be an appropriate topic of study. Furthermore, this seems to be a natural direction in which to take the prior discussion on the universalizing impulse of the book. Having established that Job presents itself in universally significant ways it follows that an examination of the distinctive contribution of this Israelite work would be appropriate.

A Survey of Selected ANE Texts

In this section I outline a number of ANE texts that are considered to be similar enough to Job to be worth comparing and contrasting with the biblical book. The survey shows that, although there does not seem to be conclusive evidence of a direct relationship between Job and these works, there are nevertheless some instructive points of similarity and contrast that can be observed. I will demonstrate that, while Job stands in continuity with a tradition of ANE wisdom by dealing with the universal phenomenon of human suffering, it also has a unique, Israelite contribution to the issue. This distinctive element evidences a critique or "missionary encounter" with certain ideas and worldviews exhibited in the ANE texts and, in evidencing themes of affirmation and critique, provides some insights for missional reflection with which the paper concludes.[3]

My purpose is not to be exhaustive in my coverage; rather, I have sought to be selective in my choice of texts, highlighting six that feature consistently across the literature.[4] In particular I have focused most attention on two Babylonian works that seem to relate most closely to the book of Job: *I Will Praise the Lord of Wisdom* (*Ludlul bēl nēmiqi*) and *The Babylonian Theodicy*.

A note of caution should be sounded at this point concerning the extrapolation from a particular text of a culture's religious beliefs.[5] Beliefs

---

3. While the note of polemic, implicit or otherwise, is highly significant, it should be noted that elements of affirmation and acceptance should be shown as well. This is an important part of Wright's understanding of critique, and leads to a more nuanced and missiologically fruitful encounter with other cultures. See Wright, *Mission of God*, 442–46. See also Glaser, *Bible and Other Faiths*, 59–66, which considers some of the positive elements of intercultural engagement in Genesis 1–11, including some notes on how they may provide some wise examples of how Christians may engage with people of other faiths.

4. For examples of other texts, see Hartley, "Job 2"; Clines, *Job 1–20*, lix–lx; Vicchio, *Job*, chapter 1; Crenshaw, "Job, Book of," 864–65.

5. A caution noted helpfully by Clarke, "Misery Loves Company," 91.

in any culture may change over time, there may have been texts with contrasting views that that have not survived, and the ideas expressed in any text may in fact be attempting to subvert rather than exhibit or support a culture's religious norms.[6] However, qualified with suitable care it is still appropriate and useful to compare and contrast these works, which exhibit something of the wrestling of ancient sages with the universal and vexing experience of suffering. What will become evident is that Job does indeed "meet" the literature and ideas of neighboring cultures in both affirmation and critique. As such, in the terms that I have framed in my study, we may discern a missional encounter between the biblical work that is borne out of Yahweh faith, and alternative explorations of the suffering theme in the ANE. It is to these alternative explorations that I now turn.

A Dispute over Suicide/The Dispute of a Man with His *Ba*[7]

This Egyptian text recounts an argument between a man and what may loosely be described as his "soul."[8] The text presents the "deep self-reflection" of the suffering character, who has become overwhelmed by the suffering and injustice he sees and experiences in the world, leading him to contemplate suicide.[9] Although the initial section is missing, the poem builds a conversation with the man yearning for death, and his

---

6. See Lambert, *Babylonian*, 1–20; Clarke, "Misery Loves Company," 85, 91, 92. See also Seow, *Job*, 56; Newsom, "Job," 333.

7. *COS* 3:321–25; *ANET* 405–7. This Egyptian text dates from either the end of the third millennium or the beginning of the second and is evidenced by one papyrus in particular. See *ANET* 405; Longman, *Job*, location 899–900; Vicchio, *Job*, 15. Its text is partial and, at times, obscure, which has led to a range of translations and interpretations. See *COS* 3:321; Longman, *Job*, location 902–3; Hartley, "Job 2," 354; Bricker, "Egypt," 91.

8. However, note Shupak, who suggests that it may be better to think of the text as "a monologue reflecting the internal struggle of a despairing man. The man, weary of life as a result of private misfortune, wrestles with two opposing perspectives of life versus death. This being the inner psychological situation of the man, one should not look for systematic thought or a rational plot in the composition" (*COS* 3:321). Even if a distinction were to be maintained, the concept of *ba* is still not quite analogous to the idea of a "soul." Though overlapping, the Egyptian concept of the *ba* is rather more complex. See Hartley, "Job 2," 354; Longman, *Job*, location 903–7. The text involves a combination of three principal genres: "Prose, symmetrically structured speech, and lyric poetry" (Shupak in *COS* 3:321).

9. Hartley, "Job 2," 354. See also Vicchio, *Job*, 15.

ba trying to persuade him otherwise. Both the *Dispute* and Job could be said to have the form of "a prose prologue and epilogue punctuated by a poetic soliloquy of the unknown sufferer," yet these function differently in each case, for example in the addressees of each speech.[10]

Following four poems that detail the man's suffering and despair, and celebrate the preference for death over life, the *ba* seems to relent and agree to remain with him in this life and the next.[11] In general terms, this desire for death is also seen in the biblical work. In chapter 3, for example, Job longs for the release from his torment that death would provide, although Job's understanding of the afterlife is not as developed as the protagonist's in the *Dispute,* and he certainly never frames this in terms of suicide.[12] Crucially, Job moves away from his initial death wish in chapter 3, to the extent that, by the end of the dialogue, his energy and focus is towards vindication, and hence life.[13] Such a distinction seems much more stark than any similar features or themes.

The Protests of the Eloquent Peasant[14]

Like Job, the Egyptian *Protests of the Eloquent Peasant* has a narrative frame surrounding a series of poetic speeches. The victim of an exploitative confrontation with Nemty-nakht, a greedy and opportunistic landowner, the titular peasant, Khu-u-Anup, appeals for vindication to

---

10. Vicchio, *Job*, 16. See also Hartley, "Job 2," 355. Shupak suggests that "the juxtaposition of the sufferings of our hero and the replies of his *ba* call to mind the figure of the tortured righteous man and the dispute between him and his friends in the book of Job" (*COS* 3:321). While this may be true in a general sense, the details of these resonances (seen, for example, in Shupak's cross-references in the *COS* text) suggest similarity rather than dependence.

11. The theme of the first poem (lines 86–103) is the awful state of the man's reputation; the second (lines 103–30) laments his loneliness due to the lack of true, virtuous friends; and the third poem (lines 130–42) describes death using attractive and various metaphors. In the final poem (lines 142–247) he focuses on the privileged status of the one who lives in the next world. See *COS* 3:323n38; Hartley, "Job 2," 354–55.

12. Hartley, "Job 2," 355; Viccio, *Job*, 16.

13. For example, Job 27:2–4. "In contrast to the Egyptian who yielded to despair at life, Job came to prize a full life, which he believed would return upon his vindication" (Hartley, "Job 2," 355).

14. *COS* 1:98–104; *ANET* 407–10. An Egyptian text dating from the Middle Kingdom, around the twenty-second to eighteenth centuries. See Viccio, *Job*, 16; Longman, *Job*, location 879–80; Hartley, "Job 2," 358; Bricker, "Egypt," 93.

Rensi, a high official and dispenser of justice in that region.[15] Following an account of the initial situation, the central part of the text is made up of a series of nine speeches by Khu-u-Anup that aim to convince Rensi to give him justice.[16] The story concludes with Khu-u-Anup receiving vindication and recompense, albeit following some confusion.

As well as a very broad similarity in its overall structure, *Protests* resonates with several themes that also occur in Job, although these do not seem to indicate anything more significant than shared interests. That the character Khu-u-Anup is not Egyptian seems reminiscent of Job being a non-Israelite.[17] However, the action is still set in Egypt which differs, by parallel, with Job.

Justice is seen as a virtue in both books; for example, in his first speech to Remsi, Khu-u-Anup says of his hearer, "If thou embarkest on the lake of justice, mayest thou sail on it with a fair breeze! . . . Because thou art the father of the orphan, the husband of the widow, the brother of the divorcee, and the apron of him that is motherless," which has some resonances with biblical texts such as Job 29:11–17 or 31:13–23.[18]

In a similar vein to *Dispute*, above, it is worth noting the movement from despair to a certain type of hope or confidence in Job, in contrast with the protagonist of the Egyptian text, whose speeches seem to be

---

15. Nemty-nakht had forced him to go a certain precarious way through his property, which resulted in Khu-u-Anup's donkey eating a small amount of grain, for which Nemty-nakht demands disproportionate compensation. Khu-u-Anup was travelling to Egypt because of famine in his own land.

16. Unbeknownst to him, Rensi keeps Khu-u-Anup longer than necessary so that his eloquent speeches can be recorded for the entertainment of the Pharaoh, who agrees to provide for Khu-u-Anup and his family (albeit anonymously) while this is going on. That this has some resonance with God's limiting the extent of the accuser's testing of Job seems a little slight. See Hartley, "Job 2," 359.

17. As observed in Hartley, "Job 2," 358.

18. See Hartley, "Job 2," 358; Vicchio, *Job*, 16–17. Although note that in Job these passages are a defense of the speaker's integrity rather than attributes applied to the hearer. Balentine, *Job*, 11, draws this into a helpful, broader context by saying that a number of social justice issues are raised by both texts. Other potential resonances include Khu-u-Anup's appeal to the highest level of justice through eloquent speech; that he is met with persistent and confusing silence; that his tone becomes less polite, and that he ultimately receives intervention from a high official are all suggestive but do not lead to anything like evidence that the texts are themselves related. See Hartley, "Job 2," 358–59, for these ideas. Because of the different dynamics at play in both texts, making comparisons seems to me to be deeply problematic. The quote is from the *ANET* translation.

marked by a continuing despair.[19] It may also be noted that it is, finally, an earthly king who restores the peasant, in contrast to Job's divinely initiated restoration.[20]

Man and His God[21]

This Sumerian poem begins with a general exhortation that one should revere one's god ("Let a man utter constantly the exaltedness of his god . . . (For) a man without a god would not obtain food").[22] It then illustrates this with a story of a righteous young man that suffers bitterly, experiencing sickness, hostile enemies, and abandonment by his friends. He wants to stand before his god and complain about his suffering, yet "My god, to you, who are my father that begot me, let me [lift] my eyes. . . . How long will you not care for me, will you not look at me?"[23]

Yet the sufferer recalls the words of the wise that, "Never has a sinless child been born to its mother"[24] and realizes that, ultimately, he must have sinned in some way and that the way out of his suffering is confession (line 115). Having done so, the narrator informs the reader that the man's prayer of confession was acceptable to his god, who withdrew his hand of punishment and placed his protection on him instead (lines 120–32).

While there are obvious parallels between this suffering, vexed and righteous individual and the biblical Job, ultimately the focus of *Man and His God* on the connection between sin and suffering sets them apart. The man accepts this contention of the wise, acts on it in confession, and is restored. It was the task of the sufferer, therefore, to plead with their god to show them their sin and confess all. This seems, then, to negate

---

19. Hartley, "Job 2," 359.
20. Viccio, *Job*, 17.
21. See *COS* 1:573–75; *ANET* 589–91. It is generally understood as an early second millennium copy of an older composition. See Balentine, *Job*, 6; Longman, *Job*, location 921–22. Kramer calls it a "Sumerian Variation of the 'Job' motif" (*ANET* 589). It is occasionally referred to with an indefinite article in the title, *A Man and His God*. See Walton, *Job*, 32.
22. Lines 1, 9 *ANET*.
23. Lines 98, 100 *COS*.
24. Line 104 *COS*.

the concept of divine injustice, since suffering can always be attributable to human sin.[25]

Dialogue Between a Man and His God[26]

This early, incomplete text tells the story of a man who cries out to his god for relief from his suffering, and sets the story broadly in the form of a dialogue between the man and his personal god. Following a description of his misery and pleading, the man claims, "My Lord, I have debated with myself, and in my feelings . . . of heart: the wrong I did I do not know! Have I . . . a vile forbidden act?"[27]

Unfortunately there is a large gap in the text soon after this. However, the man seems to assume that even though he is unaware of any specific sin in his life, his illness must be the result of such sin and so sees his calamity as bringing his shortcomings to his attention, "How much you have been kind to me, how much I have blasphemed you, I have not forgotten."[28]

After another gap in the text the man's restoration is recounted, followed by a declaration of divine confirmation of this, and a reminder of his dependence on the god:

> The path is straight for you, mercy is granted you.
> You must never, till the end of time, forget [your] god
> Your creator, now that you are favored.[29]

The god then instructs the man to provide for those in need out of the prosperity he will gain in the future, which may be a form of penance.[30]

---

25. "Since there is none without guilt there is no innocent sufferer, only an ignorant one" (Bricker, "Mesopotamia," 199). See also Hartley, "Job 2," 347; *ANET* 589. Klein suggests that the lack of dialogue is the main difference between Job and *Man and His God* (*COS* 1:573). Perhaps this should be qualified as the main difference in form. Ultimately the theological idea seems to be the most significant point of comparison.

26. See *COS* 1:485. Also known as "The Pious Sufferer," this text is dated to around the seventeenth century and is the earliest known Akkadian text to look at the issue of suffering. See Bricker, "Mesopotamia," 201; *COS* 1:485; Hartley, "Job 2," 351.

27. Lines 12–14 *COS*.

28. *COS* translation. See Hartley, "Job 2," 351.

29. *COS* translation.

30. Bricker, "Mesopotamia," 202.

It is striking that, as in Job, the god himself speaks to the sufferer in this text.³¹ However, there are distinctive elements to both stories. In Job the story is resolved without specific instructions to the sufferer like this (apart from praying for the friends) or the assurance (at that stage) from God that Job's future will be any better.³² Crucially, the *Dialogue Between a Man and His God* retains a clear sense of retribution, even if it might mean retribution for unknown sin, with piety being a best defence against calamity.³³

The Poem of the Righteous Suffer/The Babylonian Job/I Will Praise the Lord of Wisdom (Ludlul bēl nēmiqi)³⁴

In this lengthy poem, the speaker, Subshi-meshre-Shakkan, recounts how he had suffered greatly but had been restored by Marduk. The poem is framed with praise for Marduk and has the intention of encouraging the hearer to grasp both the deity's anger and kindness: "I, who touched bottom like a fish, will proclaim his anger. . . . I will teach people that his kindness is nigh, May his favorable thought take away their [guilt?]."³⁵ Subshi-meshre-Shakkan goes on to recall how he was afflicted with terrible suffering, ranging from social, familial and divine abandonment and hostility, and distressing illness (tablets 1 and 2). But just as he was about to slip into death, Marduk sent three messengers to assure him, which preceded his restoration (tablets 3 and 4).

Ludlul exhibits several features in form and content that resonate with Job. Both texts, for example, contain vivid descriptions of the physical suffering experienced by the main character.³⁶ In *Ludlul*,

---

31. Indeed, Hartley, "Job 2," 35, notes this is the only instance of this happening in the Akkadian literature of this type. See also Newsom, *Contest*, 238.

32. "These contrasts underscore the central concern of the book of Job, which is Job's ongoing relationship with God regardless of whether he was prospering or suffering" (Hartley, "Job 2," 351).

33. Bricker, "Mesopotamia," 203.

34. See *COS* 1:486–92; *ANET* 596–600. The poem is thought to have originated in the second millennium, although it is known from texts dating around the seventh or eighth century and seems to have been a popular work during the period in which the book of Job could have been written. See Balentine, *Job*, 6; Lambert, *Babylonian*, 26; Hoffman, *Blemished Perfection*, 66.

35. 1.39, 41–42; *COS* 487; Hartley, "Job 2," 348. Translations are from *COS* unless stated otherwise.

36. The length of Job's suffering is unclear, whereas in *Ludlul* it lasted for over a

Subshi-meshre-Shakkan recalls in some detail a variety of ailments such as disease (2.50), headache (2.52), coughing (2.53), muscular problems (2.61), convulsions (2.63), digestive and breathing problems (2.65–66) a lack of mobility (2.75–79) and appetite (2.87–89). He declared, pitifully, "My afflictions were grievous, the blow was severe! . . . From writhing my joints were separated, My limbs were played and thrust apart. I spent the night in my dung like an ox, I wallowed in my excrement like a sheep" (2.99, 104–7). In relative terms Job focuses much less on describing his physical suffering, which was exhibited in sores and skin disease (1:7–8; 7:4–5; 30:28, 30), a wasting away (19:20), lack of sleep due to pain (30:17); and inner turmoil (30:27).[37] More common in Job are poignant descriptions of social ostracism and hostility at the hands of various parties, including family, which is also a significant theme in *Ludlul* (Job 12:4; 16:7, 10, 20; 17:2, 6; 19:13–22; 30:1–15; *Ludlul* 1.55–104).[38]

Both Job and *Ludlul* deal with the unexpected, intense suffering of an individual who considers themselves to be pious and, therefore, undeserving of such treatment. The process by which each sufferer defends their integrity is instructive. Subshi-meshre-Shakkan speaks of the care he took over cultic matters such as prayers, sacrifices and other rites, as well as reverence for the king and deities (2.23–32). Neither he nor diviners, interpreters of dreams or exorcists could discover the causes of, or help reverse the divine displeasure under which he lived (2.4–9). Later on, however, Subshi-meshre-Shakkan seems to imply or assume that he must have committed certain infractions in 3.60: "He made the wind bear away my offenses."[39] It is as if the central character's confidence in his own integrity finally gives way to the force of the retribution principle.

In contrast to Subshi-meshre-Shakkan, Job rarely makes recourse to his cultic credentials in order to defend his integrity, although 1:5

---

year (*Ludlul* 2.1); Hartley, "Job 2," 349.

37. Commenting on Job 20:19a, Seow observes that Job's physical torment is closely tied to his more general "shattered state" (Seow, *Job*, 801).

38. Hartley, "Job 2," 348; Sedlmeier, "Ijob," 111.

39. *COS* 1:490. See Bricker, "Mesopotamia," 205. Longman also detects a possible allusion to some form of cultic sin, as suggested by a fragment inserted by Foster (in *COS* 1:491) in tablet 4: "I proceeded along Kunush-kadru Street in a state of redemption. He who has done wrong by Esagil, let him learn from me. It was Marduk who put a muzzle on the mouth of the lion that was devouring me. Marduk took away the sling of my pursuer and deflected his slingstone" (Longman, *Job*, location 954–57). However, Longman notes the sense earlier that Subshi-meshre-Shakkan did consider himself to have honored the gods in the cultic setting.

suggests this could have been an option.[40] Instead Job focuses on the way his life was characterized by the attitudes and actions of righteousness and justice, articulated particularly in his final defence of chapters 29 to 31.[41] Furthermore, when Yahweh chastises Job (38:2) it is for being presumptuous rather than committing wrong.[42] Job withdraws his complaint (42:6) but this does not equate to the confession of a particular sin and neither is Yahweh said to have forgiven Job for any wrongdoing.[43]

A further point of comparison between the two texts is the supposed involvement of the gods in relation to the suffering and recovery of the protagonists. In *Ludlul* Marduk became angry with Subshi-meshre-Shakkan, which caused his protective deities or spirits to abandon him (1.4–46; 2.4–5, 112–13), leaving him vulnerable to human and demonic hostility (1.51–112; 2.49–72).[44] Recovery occurred through the intervention of three intermediaries sent from Marduk (3.9–60), although no direct word from the god is spoken.

Although the accuser is said to be the instigator of Job's suffering it is nevertheless Yahweh who has the final authority (1:11–12; 2:3–6). Job understands Yahweh to be directly involved in his misfortunes (6:4; 16:7–14) and the dynamic of greater or lesser gods or the notion of demonic activity are absent in the biblical book.[45] Just as the cause of Job's suffering is not seen in cultic terms, neither does Job seek the solution to his situation through religious ritual. Instead he yearns for vindication through an encounter with God, even though at points such a prospect seems to overwhelm Job (9; 16:18–22; 19:25–29; 23:1–7). A clear distinctive between the texts is the sustained and unmediated encounter with God experienced by Job in the biblical book (chapters 38–41), to which I will return below. This relates to a further point of comparison, which is the nature of restoration seen in each work. In contrast with *Ludlul* the biblical text does not dwell in great detail on Job's social and physical restoration; indeed it does not mention it, although it may be inferred.[46]

---

40. Hartley, "Job 2," 349; Clarke, "Misery Loves Company," 87; Weinfeld, "Job," 224.

41. See especially 29:11–17; 31:1–40. Hartley, "Job 2," 349; Weinfeld, "Job," 224.

42. Hartley, "Job 2," 350.

43. Hartley, "Job 2," 350. Indeed, in contrast to his comforters, Job receives divine vindication (40:7).

44. This is also closely tied to the loss of favor of the king (1.55–58). See Toorn, "Theodicy," 78; Sedlmeier, "Ijob," 111.

45. Hartley, "Job 2," 350.

46. Thus in *Ludlul*, tablets 3 and 4: "My windpipe, which was tight and choking

Rather Job appears to concentrate on the reconciliation between different parties, seen especially between Job and his friends and family (42:10–11), although it could be argued that this also takes place between Job and God (42:1–6), Job and his comforters, and the comforters and God (42:7–9).[47] While the language of "reconciliation" is rather broad, it does seem evident that communion between parties, whether human or divine, is an important theme at the end of Job.[48]

A key dilemma for Subshi-meshre-Shakkan in relation to the gods and their involvement in the world is expressed in tablet 2:

> I wish I knew that these things were pleasing to a god!
> What seems good to one's self could be an offense to a god,
> What in one's own heart seems abominable could be good to one's god!
> Who could learn the reasoning of the gods in heaven?
> Who could grasp the intentions of the gods of the depths?
> Where might human beings have learned the way of a god?
> (2.33–38 COS)

Although the ultimate tone of *Ludlul* is one of praise for Marduk this passage illustrates *Ludlul*'s view of the human predicament that, despite our best efforts, the ways of the gods are inscrutable and so life seems arbitrary.[49] The human dilemma, then, is not just that we may sin without realizing it, but that the gods who set the criteria for what is right and wrong are not, from a human perspective, consistent.[50] The logic of Subshi-meshre-Shakkan's statement suggests that the notion of

---

... He made well and lit it si[ng] ... My intestine, which was ever empty for want ... accepts nourishment, holds drink ... he made my body like a perfect athlete ... I proceeded along Kunush-karu Street in a state of redemption ... The Babylonians saw how [Marduk] can restore to life" (*COS* 1:490–92). The exact placement of these texts is ambiguous. See Hartley, "Job 2," 350–51.

47. So suggested in Hartley, "Job 2," 351. My hesitation to apply the theme to all parties is due to it being less explicit in the latter cases.

48. See Hartley, "Job 2," 350.

49. Lambert, *Babylonian*," 22; Longman, *Job*, location 961–62. See also Crenshaw, "Job, Book of," 864; Balentine, *Job*, 7; Hartley, "Job 2," 349; Toorn, "Theodicy," 80.

50. For Moran, this was a "radically new twist" on Mesopotamian belief: "Not only are the gods inscrutable, but they hold man to norms of behavior that they would not reveal and he could not discover. Indeed, it even appeared that good was evil and evil good. Here is an *Umwertung aller Werte* if there ever was one, but it is the logical conclusion of two convictions: one, the possibility of innocence according to known norms; two, suffering is a consequence of personal sin" (Moran, "Babylonian Job," 190).

retribution is consistent from the divine perspective, but because humans are not privy to this we cannot be sure we are always on safe ground.[51]

It should also be noted that the two texts have different aims. *Ludlul* functions as a hymn of praise to Marduk, beginning and ending with exaltation for the "lord of wisdom" who exhibits anger, mercy, and a powerful knowledge of and influence over lesser gods, who restores life and is worthy of praise (1.1–36; 4.33–48).[52] In its description of praise for the deity and the testimony of the depths of suffering and the joy of restoration, *Ludlul* seems more akin to biblical psalms of thanksgiving than Job, which is a much more sustained and probing examination of the nature of God's governance in the world in the light of the existence of unattributed suffering.[53] While *Ludlul* includes a question concerning the principle of retribution, Job finds in this theme its *raison d'être*.

The Babylonian Theodicy[54]

The Babylonian Theodicy contains certain resonances with the book of Job in both form and content. In the Babylonian text a sufferer engages in a dialogue with a learned friend to complain about personal misfortunes as well as the apparent inconsistencies between the principle of retribution and what actually happens in the world. Orphaned as a child, he was left without protection and has suffered greatly (stanza 1), even though he has sought to act piously (stanzas 5, 7). Despite this he observes the fortune of those unconcerned about the gods (stanza 7). Often the world

---

51. Seow, *Job*, 52–53, contra Toorn, "Theodicy," 80, 81, who takes *Ludlul* as being much more undermining of the retribution principle, although in my view he overstates the case.

52. See the argument of Moran, "Babylonian Job," 186–87, who understands the text as exhibiting a struggle with the sufferer's personal gods, indicating a move away from traditional personal religion to a proclamation and adherence to Marduk himself. The hymn of praise to Marduk in tablet 1 declares his great wisdom, implying that although it may seem mysterious and unattainable, there is a purpose or plan in the mind of Marduk, even if human beings or even other gods cannot know it. See Moran, "Babylonian Job," 192, 197; Sedlmeier, "Ijob," 117–18. Marduk has total sovereignty whereby he can, as declared in 1.23–24, cause a person to sin but also absolve them. See Moran, "Babylonian Job," 196.

53. Weinfeld, "Job," 217–22; Newsom, "Job," 329; Sparks, *Ancient Texts*, 62.

54. See *COS* 1:492–95; *ANET* 601–4. It is probably from around the year 1000 and comprised 27 stanzas in the form of an acrostic. See Lambert, "Theodicy," 63. It seems to have been well-known, as evidenced, for example, by a later commentary on the work. See Newsom, "Job," 330.

order seems upside-down (stanza 12) with the wicked prospering (stanza 25). Although appreciative of his friend's attempts, the sufferer's situation seems unresolved by the end and he invites his friend once again to consider his suffering, and pleads for the gods to take pity on him (stanza 27).

The friend meanwhile seeks to encourage the sufferer by offering wise words. Ultimately, we will all die yet the one without a protector can look to his god (stanza 2). The sufferer is like a child and cannot hope to discern the ways of the gods (stanzas 6, 8, 24), yet there is still a mechanism of retribution in the world so he should humble himself, seek after his god and, so, look forward to good fortune which can be delivered in an instant (stanzas 6, 8, 20, 22). Towards the end, however, the friend does admit that the falsehood and lies that mark humankind are there by the design of the gods, and that the gods made humans to suffer (stanza 26). Ultimately, however, no resolution is found.

At first glance the *Theodicy* does seem to parallel certain aspects of Job. The dialogue form, between a suffering individual and a friend who seeks to comfort and teach him, is the most immediately evident similarity. Such a form lends itself well to exploring different, even contradictory, views on the nature and significance of suffering.[55] Unlike Job's several participants, the *Theodicy*'s dialogue is only shared by two characters. This is indicative of the greater complexity evident in Job, not least when the book is viewed in its entirety.[56] With a few exceptions, the dialogue in *Theodicy* is cordial, sympathetic and respectful, unlike the cantankerous exchanges observed in Job, especially as the book progresses.[57] This can also be related to the sense of solidarity shared by the interlocutors. By the end of the *Theodicy* the sufferer and the friend's relationship is maintained, with the friend even becoming persuaded to some extent by the plight and points of the sufferer (stanza 26).[58] Such agreement is absent in Job, which exhibits a breakdown in both the debate and the relationships.[59]

---

55. Seow, *Job*, 55.

56. On the greater complexity of the Joban dialogue alone, see Seow, *Job*, 56; Newsom, "Job," 333. See also Newsom, *Contest*, chapter 3.

57. *Theodicy* 1.4–6; 2.12; 3.23–24; 5.45; 7.67–68; cf. Job 8:2; 15:2–3; 16:3; 22:5. See Hartley, "Job 2," 352; Balentine, *Job*, 10; Newsom, *Contest*, 81.

58. Clifford, *Wisdom Literature*, 71; Gray, "Job," 258; Newsom, "Job," 332.

59. See the third cycle of speeches (chapters 22–27) in particular. Balentine, *Job*, 10; Seow, *Job*, 56.

The sufferer cannot understand why the gods do not seem to uphold the principle of retribution in the world. He has been faithful to the gods[60] yet has suffered physical, societal and financial misfortune (3.27–33; 7.76–77), and while he feels abandoned by the gods he observes the thriving of the disobedient and unjust:

> The parvenu who multiplies his wealth, Did he weigh out precious gold to the mother goddess for a family? [Have I] withheld my offerings? I prayed to my god, [I said the blessing over my goddess]. (5.52–55)

> Those who seek not after a god can go the road of favor, Those who pray to a goddess have grown poor and destitute. Indeed, in my youth I tried to find out the will of (my) god, With prayer and supplication I besought my goddess. I bore a yoke of profitless servitude: (My) god decreed (for me) poverty instead of wealth. (7.70–75)

> God does not block the progress of a demon. . . . What has it profited me that I knelt before my god? It is I who must (now) bow before my inferior! (23.244, 251–52)

> They extol the words of an important man who is accomplished in murder, They denigrate the powerless who has committed no crime. They esteem the wicked to whom tr[uth] is abhorrent, They reject the truthful man who he[eds] the will of god. They fill the oppressor's [st]rongroom with refined gold, They empty the beggar's larder of [his] provisions. They shore up the tyrant whose all is crime, They ruin the weak, they oppress the powerless. And as for me, without means, a parvenu harasses me. (25.267–75)

> Though I am humble, learned, suppliant, I have not seen help or succor for an instant. I would pass unobtrusively through the streets of my city, My voice was not raised, I kept my speaking low. I did not hold my head high, I would look to the ground. I was not given to servile praise among my associates. (27.289–94)

Job, too, expresses his vexation at what he sees as the reversal of how God should be ordering the world. The wicked do enjoy full and prosperous lives (21:7–34), often at the expense of the poor (24:1–25), whereas

---

60. The grounds for his integrity seem more general and less explicitly cultic than, for example, *Ludlul*. See Weinfeld, "Job," 224; Clarke, "Misery Loves Company," 86–87.

Job's life has moved from bliss to wretchedness despite his consistent faithfulness and integrity (chapters 29–31).

In the *Theodicy* the friend responds to the sufferer's complaints in a variety of ways that attempt to defend the orthodox principle of retribution and encourage him to persevere. He accuses the sufferer of perverse and even blasphemous thinking, disregarding the divine design and ordinances (8.78–81; 20.212–14; 24.254–55; cf. Job 8:2; 11:2–6; 15:2–4). He assures the sufferer that, by committing his way to the gods, he will experience a reversal in his fortunes and that the wicked will also receive their just punishment in the end (20.219–20; 22.235–42; cf. Job 5:19–26; 8:5–7, 11–22; 11:13–20; 15:20–35; 18:5–21; 20:4–29; 22:21–30). While these attempts resonate with those of the friends in the Job, the biblical work contains a greater variety of approaches, including the notion that the sufferer's experiences are educational (5:17–18; 33:29–30) and, related to the combative tone of the book, a more direct accusation of the sufferer's supposed wrongdoing (22:5–9).

Of great significance in the *Theodicy* is the friend's view that ultimately the gods and their ways are inaccessible to humanity:

> You are a mere child, the purpose of the gods is remote as the netherworld. (6.58)

> The strategy of a god is [as remote as] innermost heaven, the command of a goddess cannot be dr[awn] out. (8.82–83)

> Divine purpose is as remote as innermost heaven, It is too difficult to understand, people cannot understand it. (24.256–57)

By implication, therefore, humans can never know the precise reasons for things and so it could be that the exceptions to the rule described by the sufferer are merely part of the inaccessibility of the transcendent gods (cf. Job 11:5–9; 36:22–26).[61]

In his final speech the friend admits that the perversity evident in humanity is there by divine design: "Enlil, king of the gods, who created teeming mankind, Majestic Ea, who pinched off their clay, The queen who fashioned them, mistress Mami, Gave twisted words to the human race, They endowed them in perpetuity with lies and falsehood" (26.276–80).

This seems particularly striking as it makes the notion of divine and human responsibility for wickedness more ambiguous, especially in light of his and the sufferer's prior assumptions that the gods were responsible

---

61. Hartley, "Job 2," 353; Toorn, "Theodicy," 72–74; Newsom, "Job," 332.

for maintaining justice.⁶² Ultimately the issue is not resolved and the *Theodicy* ends with the sufferer reiterating that he has lived appropriately, and prays for help from the gods: "May the god who has cast me off grant help, May the goddess who has [forsaken me] take pity, The shepherd Shamash will past[ure] people as a god should" (27.295–97).⁶³

Although making uncomfortable observations that imply the failure of the gods to maintain a just order in the world, the sufferer tends not to state this explicitly and never directly to the gods.⁶⁴ In contrast, Job complains explicitly and vehemently both to his friends and to God directly that God has caused his suffering and does not keep up his commitment to the just maintenance of society.⁶⁵

Given that the *Theodicy* seems to be the closest to Job of the known ANE works, it is notable that the gods are only ever *discussed* in the text. Balentine highlights well this contrasting element with Job:

> The gods never speak, never intervene, never have more than a spoken-about presence in this debate about innocent suffering. By contrast, the *first* and *last* "character" to speak in the biblical Job's story is God (1:7; 42:7). Moreover, although the dialogue between Job and his friends is extensive (Job 4–27), the dialogue on which the book turns is that between God (who, speaking with hurricane force, most clearly does intervene) and Job (Job 38–42).⁶⁶

Furthermore, these instances of God's speech function climactically and transformatively in the broader context of God's "active presence" in the book in which Yahweh is portrayed as initiating and concluding the events of the drama.⁶⁷ I will say more about the function of this crucial distinctive feature of Job below.

---

62. Bricker, "Mesopotamia," 207–8; Lambert, *Babylonian*, 65; Newsom, "Job," 332. See also the similar point made above on *Ludlul* 1.2–4. Contra Job 1:1, 8, which sees the possibility at least of human beings leading lives that are blameless and upright. See Vicchio, *Job*, 21.

63. Newsom, "Job," 332. Whether he concludes the dialogue because he has now been heard (so, Newsom, "Job," 332) or because he is faced with the "theological contradiction" of the justice of the gods (so, Sparks, *Ancient Texts*, 63) is unclear, although it seems reasonable to suppose that the two are related.

64. Balentine, *Job*, 10.

65. For example, Job 10; 12:13–25; 16:6–17; 24:1–17; 30:19–23. Balentine, *Job*, 10.

66. Balentine, *Job*, 10.

67. Clifford, *Wisdom Literature*, 73; Newsom, "Job," 333–34; Gray, "Job," 268–69; Longman, *Job*, location 988–89.

Job and "Similar" ANE Texts: Themes of Continuity and Distinctiveness

Having outlined some of the ANE texts most commonly associated with Job, it is now possible to draw together some broad conclusions concerning the extent and significance of their relationship, thereby suggesting some ways in which a missional encounter may be detected between the book of Job and ANE ideas. As such I will address the issues of literary form, subject matter, and perspective.

Literary Form and Subject Matter

It seems evident that there was no single way of exploring the nature of suffering in the ANE, not least in the book of Job which combines a number of different literary forms within its complex whole.[68] From the brief survey above certain literary features do appear to be shared between Job and other works. Like the two Egyptian texts, for example, the structure of Job features a narrative frame surrounding a series of poems. The use of Dialogue is a common feature across the texts, which may not be surprising as it is a literary form that allows for different viewpoints to be expressed and interacted with.[69] Job, however, seems to employ the device in a more complex manner, given the number of participants in Job and the fractured nature of the dialogue which appears to embody the breakdown in the discussion. Parallels with smaller literary units may also be observed, such as the description of the central figure's suffering in *Ludlul*, or the prospering of the wicked in the *Theodicy*. More broadly scholars have noted similarities between, for example, Job's speech in chapter 31 and the "Declaration of Innocence" found in the Egyptian *Book of the Dead*,[70] and between texts such as the Yahweh speeches and ANE catalogue or name lists.[71]

The exact significance of such overlap is difficult to determine. While it may suggest evidence of a direct literary relationship between Job and prior ANE texts, this is by no means the only available conclusion. In my

68. See Crenshaw, *Reading Job*, 10–12.

69. See Seow, *Job*, 55.

70. See Clines, *Job 21–37*, 1013; Longman, *Job*, location 9245–53; Habel, *Job*, 428–42; Crenshaw, "Job, Book of," 865.

71. Hoffman, *Blemished Perfection*, chapter 4; Murphy, *Wisdom Literature*, 44; Clines, *Job 38–42*, 1087.

view it seems quite possible that the author of Job gathered together different genres that he had observed elsewhere without meaning to make a direct connection. He was clearly someone with a rich knowledge of literary traditions and texts, presumably including some that have not survived.[72] Certainly, Job was part of an ANE literary tradition of sorts, but Hoffman seems reasonable in supposing that the author of the biblical book may have struggled with conventional literary forms as a vehicle for his unconventional message, and so may have shaped

> a new literary model . . . from available types of materials: the hymn, the lamentation, the catalogue, the proverb literature, the speech, and the narrative. . . . As a result, the new literary framework that took shape and the problem of faith . . . with which he came to grapple were combined with one another.[73]

Related to connections of literary form, a number of common themes may be observed between the book of Job and the other texts. While not necessarily present in every text, certain motifs emerge such as a suffering individual who is vexed by their plight and tries to understand what is happening in relation to the gods, who appear to be inscrutable, by speaking to or with another party, often with some kind of resolution by the end.[74] Hoffman, for example, focuses his treatment of the similarities on *Ludlul* and the *Babylonian Theodicy* and points to a number of features shared by these two texts and Job (and, to a lesser extent, *Man and His God*): all three texts feature afflicted individuals who describe their suffering in great detail (for example, cf. *Ludlul* 2.68–77; *Theodicy* 2.27–32, 137–43; Job 29–30); all three individuals wonder why they are suffering and struggle to find an answer (*Ludlul* 2.4–10; *Theodicy* 2.108–11); in all three texts the sufferer protests his innocence (*Ludlul* 2.12–33; *Theodicy* 2.54–55, 72–74; Job 29, 31); both Job and the *Theodicy* struggle with the prosperity of the wicked (*Theodicy* 2.52–53, 70–72; Job 19, 24); all three exhibit a sense of crisis in which the principle of retribution does not seem to be working, which makes the ways of the gods difficult or impossible to discern (*Ludlul* 2.34–41; *Theodicy* 2.256–57); in the *Theodicy* and Job those coming alongside the sufferer maintain the link between sin and suffering and give advice based on this assumption (*Theodicy* 2.21–22, 2.79–80, 1.66); in *Ludlul* and Job there is an appearance either of

---

72. Hoffman, *Blemished Perfection*, 263.
73. Hoffman, *Blemished Perfection*, 114. See also Newsom, *Contest*, 78.
74. Walton, *Job*, 33. See also Gordis, *God and Man*, 59–60.

a god or of his representatives (*Ludlul* 3.40-44; Job 38-41); in *Ludlul* and Job there is a scene of restoration at the end (*Ludlul* 3.49; Job 42); *Ludlul* and Job both have "hymns" that exalt the gods through creation language (*Ludlul* 4.37-42; Job 38-41).[75]

It is also worth noting that, as with the coincidence of literary forms, the existence of certain common thematic elements does not in itself prove a direct relationship between Job and the other texts.[76] The more cautious approach is to consider the book of Job as standing in a tradition of texts attempting to probe the question of suffering, as expressed helpfully by Crenshaw:

> These explorations of the governance of the universe and unjust suffering may have provided an intellectual stimulus.... [The] structural similarities (framework enclosing poetic disputes) and common ideas place the biblical work in the wider context of intellectual and religious foment.[77]

Suffering was a universal and vexing problem in the ancient world, so it should not be a surprise to find such texts in each culture, evidencing that these concerns "agitated the sages" across the ANE, and led to texts with "similarities in outlook, mood, and form of expression."[78]

However, it seems unlikely that the author of Job would have had no knowledge at all of any of the ANE texts in one form or another, and especially the Babylonian examples.[79] It seems reasonable that he would have been aware of certain ANE texts, or certainly the ideas and worldviews behind them, and that he may have used these as stimuli for his own thinking and imagination. The key point is that it is not necessary to establish a direct link between Job and similar ANE texts in order to show that the biblical book encounters alternative beliefs, both in affirmation and critique. The lack of evidence for a direct literary relationship need not diminish the significance of the Job's missional encounter with ANE ideas.

---

75. Hoffman, *Blemished Perfection*, 253-58.

76. Balentine, *Job*, 12; Viccio, *Job*, 16; Gordis, *God and Man*, 55, 59-60; Longman, *Job*, location 983.

77. Crenshaw, "Job: Book of," 865.

78. Gordis, *God and Man*, 55. See also Balentine, *Job*, 12; Vicchio, *Job*, 24-25; Hartley, "Job 2," 360; Crenshaw, *OT Wisdom*, 271.

79. See Hoffman, *Blemished Perfection*, 263.

The complexity of this idea of stimulus is important to acknowledge as it can be understood positively and negatively, which relates to the idea of "open" critique voiced, for example, by Wright, Goheen and Glaser earlier in this volume. It is at this juncture that the monotheizing or Yahwizing process may be seen at work.

In a positive sense the author of Job could be said to be using certain literary conventions and motifs that would have been familiar to others, building on and, by implication, affirming certain aspects of ideas or approaches already circulating in the ANE. This process, however, would have been discriminative:

> This common oriental heritage was subjected to a far-reaching process of "creative assimilation." The Hebrew genius adopted those elements in the surrounding culture which it found valuable, modified what was potentially useful, and rejected what it recognized as fundamentally alien. Hence, the similarities are often illuminating with regard to details, but it is the differences that go deeper and are more significant.[80]

This phenomenon makes the question of the Joban author's familiarity with ANE texts and ideas more nuanced as it suggests that it may be the distinctive elements and not the similarities that provide a more compelling case for prior knowledge and fruitful interpretation. More negatively, this process also suggests an element of polemic on the part of the author of Job when engaging with ideas in the ANE, which may be discerned by looking at the distinctives of his work. This will become more evident as I look at the distinct perspectives of the Israelite work.

A Distinct Israelite Perspective

Upon closer inspection the approaches taken by the texts to supposed common themes do evidence different perspectives. The nature of the origins of the sufferer's problems is one such example. ANE texts tend to portray the innocence of their characters as resting on correct cultic behavior which leads to confusion because this behavior was supposed to lead to divine protection. In contrast, the theme of cultic behavior is

---

80. Gordis, *God and Man*, 55. A very similar point is made by Wright when considering the missional nature of the Wisdom Literature, although he does not deal with the book of Job in a sustained way in this regard. See Wright, *Mission of God*, 50, 442–48.

marginal at best in Job, with his innocence being based upon his moral character and his devotion to God (that is, his righteousness), and even the arguments of his friends tend not to draw on the cult.[81] Job is described by both Yahweh and the narrator as תָּם וְיָשָׁר וִירֵא אֱלֹהִים וְסָר מֵרָע, "blameless and upright, fearing God and turning from evil" (1:1, 8; 2:3), whereas in most of the above ANE texts there is a presumption of guilt concerning the individual or mankind as a whole, even if the specific wrongdoing is unknown.[82] While Job does not claim that his life has been completely free of sin (cf. 7:21; 10:6–7, 14; 13:23),[83] his vexation concerns the disproportionality of his suffering in relation to his generally upright life. With this broader view of blamelessness, Job displays an intense, defiant and sustained confidence in his innocence, unmatched in ANE texts (Job 9:20–22; 13:18; 23:2–17; 27:2–6).[84]

As noted above, the *Theodicy* seems to offer a more nuanced view on the sufferer's innocence, making it more general than cultic. However, it still seems to acknowledge an evil tendency in humanity, even if it was put there by the gods (*Theodicy* 26.276–80).

Related to assumptions about the origins of the sufferers' difficulties is how the texts understand the notion of the retribution principle. The figure in *Man and His God*, for example, accepts that he must have done something wrong to be suffering; a view which is vindicated in that his prayer of confession leads to his restoration. The sufferer in the *Dialogue Between a Man and His God* appears to operate under a similar assumption. Even though, initially at least, the particular wrongs are unknown, they are still believed to be the cause of the person's suffering. In *Ludlul* Subshi-meshre-Shakkan claims to have lived a pious life yet there is also an assumption of guilt evident later on (3.60). It seems to me that *Ludlul* still maintains a belief in some kind of retribution principle. If a person suffers it is because they have angered the gods. However, the ways of the gods are inscrutable and, strikingly in *Ludlul*, the gods may redefine what is good, thereby further compounding our inability to maintain an innocent existence. Such arbitrariness therefore throws the worshipper

---

81. Walton, *Job*, 34–35; Hoffman, *Blemished Perfection*, 258–59. See also Bricker, "Mesopotamia," 198; Gordis, *God and Man*, 64; Newsom, *Contest*, 73.

82. See *Man and His God*, line 104; *Dialogue Between a Man and His God*, lines 12–14; *Ludlul* 3.60.

83. Seow, *Job*, 649.

84. Walton, *Job*, 34.

onto the mercy of Marduk. Though he is angered, he also heals (1.1–36; 4.33–48).

As with the theme of the sufferer's innocence, the *Theodicy* appears to have a more nuanced approach to the notion of retribution than other ANE texts. From a human perspective it seems to be inconsistent and ambiguous, although its workings are ultimately inaccessible to humans because of the inscrutability of the gods.[85] This theme of inscrutability is also a crucial point of comparison. Often, the human dilemma in suffering is understood as a problem of ignorance rather than innocence.[86] In *Man and His God* and the *Dialogue Between a Man and His God* the sufferer does not know what he has done wrong and so must plead with his god to enlighten him. *Ludlul* expresses the mystery in a particularly poignant manner, while also expressing doubts concerning the arbitrary nature of the gods (2.33–38).[87] The *Theodicy*, too, expresses the notion of the inaccessibility of the ways of the gods (6.58; 8.82–83; 24.256–57).[88]

In the ANE texts, therefore, sufferers are never fully aware of what is required of them and they tend to conclude that the will of the gods is ultimately unknowable.[89] But is God understood as inscrutable in the book of Job? In one sense this is certainly the case. Although it is not because of moral or cultic wrongdoing, the reasons for Job's suffering are never disclosed to him or anyone else. Job regularly expresses a desire for a confrontation with, and explanation from God (13:3, 21–24; 23:3–17; 31:35–37), but such access to God is not up to Job.

Job's complaint is not that he must have committed an unknown sin, since he knows how he should live. Unlike the common theme in the ANE texts, Job has a confident sense of what is expected of him to live a moral life, upon which his righteousness is based (for example, Job 29; 31).[90] For Job, it is not God's standards that are inscrutable, but God's seemingly inconsistent maintenance of his commitment to justice in the world (chapter 24).

Furthermore, Job's comforters do not appear to struggle greatly with the ways of God. Through their concern to bring back their suffering

85. Walton, *Job*, 33.
86. Bricker, "Mesopotamia," 214; Walton, *Job*, 35.
87. Quoted more fully above.
88. Quoted more fully above.
89. Hoffman, *Blemished Perfection*, 259. See also Walton, *Job*, 35; Bricker, "Mesopotamia," 202.
90. Hoffman, *Blemished Perfection*, 259.

friend to orthodox views of retribution, they display a confidence in their ability to explain what God is like and how and why he acts.[91]

This leads my discussion to one of the most distinctive elements of Job in comparison with the ANE texts: the speeches of Yahweh. In Job Yahweh is not just talked about; he is involved in speech and action. This section of the book of Job (38:1–42:6) therefore requires some attention. Given its context and function within the biblical book, it also provides a helpful means of discussing the distinctive ideas of Job in more depth.

The Distinctive Contribution of the Yahweh Speeches

Although there is precedent for a god to act or speak directly in the ANE texts, none do so with such sustained, climactic presence as Yahweh in the book of Job. It would seem appropriate, therefore, to examine the function of this distinctive feature of the biblical book as a means of contributing to an articulation of Israel's faith in Yahweh. Read in the light of my missional approach to the text, we will therefore be able to detect some of the ways in which the book of Job embodies a missional encounter with alternative renderings of reality.

Throughout the book Job had been calling for a meeting with Yahweh to make his case and get answers, although he has reflected on such a prospect with a range of emotions from despair and dread to confidence and hope (9:14–20, 32–35; 13:3, 15–28; 23:2–17; 31:35–37).[92] Through two lengthy speeches (38:2–40:2; 40:7–41:34) Yahweh is said to "answer," עָנָה, Job (38:1; 40:1, 6), with Job responding briefly in each case (40:4–5; 42:2–6). As a whole the speeches conform to the disputation genre with features such as a challenge to an opponent and a series of rhetorical questions.[93] Views on the tone of the speeches are many, varied and sometimes contradictory, with Yahweh's words being labelled as brutal,[94]

---

91. So, for example, Eliphaz in 5:8–27; 15:20–35; 22:30; Bildad in 8:3–22; 18:15–21; Zophar in 11:13–20; 20:4–29. Elihu does likewise (33:19–33; 36:2–12), although he seems more ready to reflect on the majesty and inaccessibility of God in chapter 37.

92. Newsom, "Job," 595. Clines helpfully describes Job as "calling on God for a reply, wistfully, hopefully, despairingly, tauntingly, aggressively" (Clines, *Job 38–42*, 1088).

93. Job 38:2–3; 40:2; Clines, *Job 38–42*, 1087; Murphy, *Wisdom Literature*, 44; Habel, *Job*, 528–30.

94. Cornhill, *Einleitung*, 232, cited in Clines, "Job's Fifth Friend," 243.

sarcastic and impatient,⁹⁵ or even playful.⁹⁶ However, Clines rightly warns against reading into the text one's own culturally conditioned sense of etiquette, and so it seems best to be cautious in assessing this particular aspect of the text.⁹⁷

The speeches focus on two particular themes. In the first (38:2) Yahweh asks who it is that obscures his design without knowledge: מִי זֶה מַחְשִׁיךְ עֵצָה בְמִלִּין בְּלִי־דָעַת. The design, עֵצָה, refers to "Yahweh's principles for running the creation . . . implicit in the descriptions of the universe that follow in Yahweh's speech."⁹⁸ From Yahweh's perspective, Job has "darkened" or "obscured," חשׁך, the design by considering it too narrowly through the lens of the retribution principle.⁹⁹ In so doing, Job has erred because he presumes to know how the universe works, or should work, even though his knowledge is limited. It is this limited perspective that Yahweh exposes in the speech that ranges around the creation, illustrating the contrast between Job's capacity for insight and Yahweh's superlative perspective and knowledge. Yahweh's strategy, then, for answering Job's complaints about his governance of the universe is to move the debate away from the arena of "justice" and into the broader context of wisdom.¹⁰⁰ In so doing there is an implicit critique of the fundamental assumptions of Job, his friends, and those exhibited in the ANE texts. Retribution is not the defining principle of the universe and so cannot be the only way to frame how we think about our experiences in the world. Rather, the design of Yahweh is defined by the wisdom of Yahweh.

But what, then, of justice? Yahweh addresses this at the beginning of his second speech in which he asks Job, הַאַף תָּפֵר מִשְׁפָּטִי תַּרְשִׁיעֵנִי לְמַעַן תִּצְדָּק, "Do you indeed deny my justice,¹⁰¹ declare me to be wrong so that you may be in the right?" (40:8). It is close in purpose to the previous challenge in 38:2 and implies that Job has overstepped the bounds of presumption, based on an overly simplistic conception of God's role in the

---

95. Crenshaw, *Reading Job*, 149.
96. Anderson, *Job*, 271. See also Newsom, "Job," 595.
97. Clines, *Job 38–42*, 1088–89.
98. Clines, *Job 38–42*, 1096.
99. Clines, *Job 38–42*, 1096; Walton, "Job 1," 341.
100. Walton, "Job 1," 341.
101. On this rendering of מִשְׁפָּטִי, see Gordis, *Job*, 468; Hartley, *Job*, 519; Longman, *Job*, location 11900–904. Cf. Clines, *Job 38–42*, 1147, who suggests it would be "unusual" to have a personal suffix ending an abstract term.

world.¹⁰² Job had asked whether God had reneged on his commitment to justice, either for him as an individual or in the world more generally (see, for example, Job 23–24).¹⁰³ Now Yahweh challenges Job to do better by taking down the proud himself (40:9–14), which is illustrated and pressed home through meditations on those "creatures of power and pride," Behemoth and Leviathan.¹⁰⁴ These quasi-mythical¹⁰⁵ creatures are beyond human (but not divine) capacity to control (40:19).¹⁰⁶

Responding to the first speech Job declared his small status before God and recognized his inability to answer or say any more than he already has (40:4–5), although neither does he withdraw his complaint, which suggests that he is not quite ready to capitulate: Job, it would seem, is "shaken, but still steadfast."¹⁰⁷ Nevertheless, by his second response (42:2–6), Job is indeed ready to withdraw his complaint. As a consequence of the encounter with Yahweh, Job has a more profound understanding of who Yahweh is and how he works in the world: לְשֵׁמַע־אֹזֶן שְׁמַעְתִּיךָ וְעַתָּה עֵינִי רָאָתְךָ, "I had heard you with my ears, but now my eyes have seen you" (42:5).¹⁰⁸ This new perception has led Job to change his mind concerning the pursuit of his case, which he now withdraws, declaring: עַל־כֵּן אֶמְאַס וְנִחַמְתִּי עַל־עָפָר וָאֵפֶר, "Therefore I submit¹⁰⁹ and recant concerning dust and ashes"¹¹⁰ (42:6). Despite the evident difficulties in in-

---

102. Newsom, "Job," 616.

103. Clines, *Job 38–42*, 1135.

104. Newsom, "Job," 616.

105. "These are liminal creatures, betwixt and between the categories of ordinary animal and mythic being.... Even more than the wild animals of chapters 38–39, they represent the frightening and alien 'other,' bearing the terror of the chaotic in their very being" (Newsom, "Job," 615).

106. Longman, *Job*, location 11471–73.

107. Wilson, *Job*, 450. See also Hartley, *Job*, 518; Anderson, *Job*, 285; Clines, *Job 38–42*, 1139.

108. I maintain the traditional contrast between hearing and seeing as rendered, for example, by ESV; NRSV; NIV; Gordis, *Job*, 491; Pope, *Job*, 288; Longman, *Job*, location 12161–62; Hartley, *Job*, 535.

109. Following Clines, *Job 38–42*, 1207, who understands אֶמְאַס to be from the second meaning of the root מאס, "flow, melt," as opposed to the primary meaning of reject or despise.

110. Here Job "repents" of his former course of action in that he changes his mind and withdraws his case which, in the light of new information, is no longer tenable and has had its pretentions exposed. He is, after all, "dust and ashes," a reference to human mortality and vulnerability. See also Hartley, *Job*, 537; Goldingay, *Job*, 207.

terpreting this verse[111] it seems that Job is saying that he now recognizes his place before Yahweh, his limited capacity to be making judgments concerning the workings of Yahweh's governance of the world, and so withdraws his case that was premised on what he now understands to be insufficient knowledge.

Several points may be made relating to the Yahweh speeches and the themes discussed in this (and the previous) chapter. First, in Job, suffering humanity encounters its creator. In chapter 4 I established Job's "everyman" credentials, meaning that he functions as a representative of suffering humanity. As Gutiérrez puts it so poignantly, "Here is the encounter Job has so feared but also so awaited. In the person of Job, alone here before God, are all the innocent of this world who suffer unjustly and ask, 'why?' of the God in whom they believe."[112]

Job has not simply accused God of the mistreatment of Job and Job alone, but the particularities of his plight have become wrapped up in the plight of humanity. Job has questioned God's governance of the world, a charge with universal implications. Yahweh cannot, then, simply explain to Job why just he has suffered. Instead Yahweh must address the universal theme and, through this, answer not just Job but humanity.[113]

Secondly, as in the narrative frame of the book, the creator of the world and source of wisdom behind its design is named as Israel's God, יהוה, Yahweh. Although this divine name is absent from the Dialogue chapters (3–37) this is perhaps a further distancing or universalizing effect of the book's non-Israelite setting.[114] Having set up the book with reference to Yahweh in the Prologue and explored the theme using more generic divine terms on the lips of the dialogue's participants, the author now returns to an explicit assertion of Israelite monotheism, which is shaped by an understanding of the transcendent uniqueness of Yahweh.[115] In this way, the author places the universal implications of the divine

111. See, for example, reviews by Newsom, "Job," 629; Clines, *Job 38–42*, 1207–11, 1218–23; Krüger, "Did Job Repent?," 217–29.

112. Gutiérrez, *On Job*, 68.

113. It may even be that in protesting and confronting Yahweh, Job may be seen to be living up to his calling as a human being. Janzen, *Job*, 256–58; Balentine, *Job*, 695–98, for example, both note the use of the phrase, עָפָר וָאֵפֶר, dust and ashes, by Job in 42:6 (and 30:19) and Abraham in Genesis 18:27. They note that Genesis 18:27; Job 30:19; 42:6 are the only times in the MT that the phrase occurs.

114. The occurrence in 12:9 is usually taken to be a scribal error. See Hartley, *Job*, 491n5.

115. See Seow, *Job*, 105. See also Glaser, *Bible and Other Faiths*, 122.

speeches within the context of the specificity of Israel's covenant God. Through these speeches the book of Job is making claims, not only of the universal implications of what the deity says, but the universality of Yahweh himself. It is Yahweh who speaks decisively into the problem of human suffering; it is therefore in Yahweh that suffering humanity can find the ultimate answer to their vexing plight.

Thirdly, the speeches of Yahweh address the question of inscrutability. It seems to me that the author of Job is not content to conclude with resignation that the ways of Yahweh are inscrutable. The Yahweh speeches are significant in comparison with the ANE texts noted above because they allow for a degree of scrutiny of Yahweh's design. In answering Job, God takes up the challenge to defend his ways before humanity, thereby correcting ignorance. While acknowledging the limitations of human capacity to knowledge of God and his ways, the Yahweh speeches, and the book more broadly, nevertheless place this within the context of wisdom and relationship. In conjunction with chapter 28 the Yahweh speeches function in part as an invitation to Job, indeed to humanity, to recognize their limits as humans, yet to throw themselves into the arms of the wisdom of Yahweh. Yahweh is transcendent yet encountered. He has provided a way of negotiating life as he has ordered it and that way is the way of wisdom, accessed through a fear of God.[116]

It seems, then, that the book of Job offers a more profound account of the ways of God in relation to suffering. While still acknowledging the deep mystery of God's ways and the nature of unattributed suffering, humanity is offered hope in the wisdom of Yahweh. As such they are invited to Yahweh himself.

The book of Job acknowledges the mystery and transcendence of Yahweh, but this does not lead to despair. Rather it should drive us to a fear of Yahweh, which leads to hope because this fear is the beginning of wisdom. The inscrutability of the divine is, thus, reframed (even transformed) into something hopeful and relational.

Fourthly, in the speeches of Yahweh we see that encounter with Yahweh leads to vindication and transformation. Yahweh's speeches do not contain an explicit declaration of Job's guilt or innocence, or instructions about how to reverse his plight, or an assurance of divine favor or restoration. Nevertheless, implicit in Job 38–42:6 (and explicit in the Epilogue, 42:7–17) is the vindication of Job's integrity. Additionally, it becomes

---

116. See Glaser, *Bible and Other Faiths*, 122–23; Glaser, *Trauma*, 14–15.

clear that by the end of the book the crucial question posed by the accuser in 1:9b has been answered: disinterested piety is indeed possible. The speeches therefore act as an implicit vindication not just of Job, but of the divine-human relationship in general and, in a sense, of God himself. By implication the book therefore resolves the doubts over the validity of the mission of God, which has been at stake in the book: the divine-human relationship is not a sham and, therefore, neither is the mission of God to restore that relationship with humanity. The book has voiced and now answered the question that had to be asked.

As well as vindication, the speeches of Yahweh lead to transformation. In particular Yahweh's reframing of the question of his governance, from the sphere of retribution to the arena of wisdom, redefines for Job how he now perceives his place in the world. In dismantling the retribution principle as the only way of understanding how the world works Yahweh provides a corrective to Job, and to humanity, that we cannot reduce God's operation of the universe to a simplistic or mechanical application of action and consequence. As such the book of Job offers a corrective to faulty religious thinking and practice that assumes that suffering must necessarily imply sin.

The Defining Effect of Israel's Monotheism

A driving force behind the distinctiveness of the book of Job is Israel's core belief in the transcendent uniqueness of Yahweh. Whether it was meant explicitly or implicitly, we may therefore detect a monotheizing or Yahwizing process at work in Job, in continuity with the rest of the biblical canon, and in line with my understanding set out in chapter 3. To state it simply, I discern in the book of Job a distinctively Israelite contribution to the international conversation concerning unattributed suffering, which finds its discussion framed by a belief in the transcendent uniqueness of Yahweh.

In Job, Yahweh is portrayed in fundamentally different terms than the gods of the ANE. Of great importance in the biblical work is the justice of God, which is thoroughly probed by Job; indeed Job's commitment to God being just drives his vexation and argument (for example, 24:1).[117] However, in the ANE texts the issue of the justice or ethics of the gods is not a significant theme, which would seem to be because there never

117. Walton, *Job*, 36.

seems to be a point at which the human cannot be assumed to be at fault.[118] Human beings are sinful by design and cannot know all that is required of them. Given this foundational assumption, to speak of "innocent" or "righteous" suffering and, therefore, "theodicy" in relation to Babylonians texts may be seen as inappropriate.[119] The book of Job, however, exhibits an "ethical pathos" because it deals with the vexation of innocent suffering in a world governed by a supposedly just God.[120] In contrast to other works, which tend to view unattributed suffering as "a confusing and frightening state," Job takes it on as a matter of theological, ethical and philosophical importance.[121] Gordis captures the issue well stating, "The burning conviction that man's suffering in the world is an affront to the goodness of God was possible only to a Hebrew. For him alone, the essential nature of God resided in His ethical character."[122]

It seems, therefore, that Job is asking fundamentally different questions about the nature of suffering and what it implies about the moral governance of God. Hoffman may well be correct in suggesting that

> only in the book of Job is there a confrontation among central and powerful ideas presented by God and humanity, and only in it, and not in the Mesopotamian works, are the necessary conditions created for true tragedy. The rebellious nature of the book of Job, which is entirely different from the tone of elegiac submission in "I Will Praise" and "Theodicy," follows from this.[123]

The transcendent uniqueness of Yahweh, therefore, intensifies the biblical work's exploration of unattributed suffering because, "The perception of the one God as the God of justice necessarily exacerbates both

---

118. This is not to say that other ANE texts do not deal with justice themes. Rather, that justice as a characteristic of the gods is not in view in the surveyed texts. See Walton, *Job*, 35–36.

119. See Bricker, "Mesopotamia," 214; "Egypt," 100, who suggests that "innocent" suffering is virtually unheard of in Mesopotamia, and there is no such thing as "theodicy" in the Egyptian literature. See also Hoffman, *Blemished Perfection*, 260–61; Gordis, *God and Man*, 61–62. Similarly, Newsom, *Contest*, 77: "[According to Mesopotamian thought,] suffering is caused by the anger of a god provoked by a human. Though a person may be good, the nature of the human condition ensures that one will inevitably offend against deity." See Newsom, *Contest*, 73.

120. Hoffman, *Blemished Perfection*, 260.

121. Hoffman, *Blemished Perfection*, 261.

122. Gordis, *God and Man*, 62.

123. Hoffman, *Blemished Perfection*, 261.

the theological crisis and the emotional crisis."[124] Compared to other religious belief systems, Israel's monotheism made them less flexible in terms of attributing blame for misfortune; "thus, questioning the deity's justice was more unsettling and opaque in the Israelite worldview."[125]

I would add, however, that the uniqueness of Yahweh also provides the author of Job with a way out of the confusion through the definitive word of the Yahweh speeches. Yahweh is not just one personal god to whom Job turns as his representative, who might intercede on his behalf amongst the pantheon of other deities.[126] Neither is Job's situation purely personal to him and his relationship with his particular personal God.[127] Although the circumstances of his suffering are specific to him, Job's commitment to God's uniqueness in the world necessarily moves his questions from the particular to the universal.[128]

Although statements about the relative worth or profundity of one text over another should be made carefully, it does seem reasonable to suggest that, in comparison with known ANE texts, the book of Job is set apart in terms of its length, complexity and depth. Concluding his survey of ANE parallels, Anderson exemplifies some of the superlatives with which the book of Job has been described:

> Job stands far above its nearest competitors, in the coherence of its sustained treatment of the theme of human misery, in the scope of its many-sided examination of the problem, in the strength and clarity of its defiant moral monotheism, in the

---

124. Hoffman, *Blemished Perfection*, 261.

125. Clarke, "Misery Loves Company," 90. "The Bible's confession of one God, all-wise and all-powerful, makes its exploration of the problem of evil and of the righteous sufferer more pressing and more poignant than those of its neighbors. For who but the *one* God of Israel is ultimately responsible for *everything* that happens in the world?" (Clifford, *Wisdom Literature*, 73).

126. Hoffman, *Blemished Perfection*, 261, with reference to "Man and His God." Hartley, "Job 2," 360, also sees Israel's monotheism accounting for an absence of fate or demons being seen as responsible for human suffering. See also Walton, *Job*, 36; Wright, *Mission of God*, chapters 3–5.

127. "In 'I Will Praise' the understanding of god is also personal, and hence lacking in the sense of universal ethical injustice manifested in the case of the suffering righteous" (Hoffman, *Blemished Perfection*, 261–62).

128. Hoffman, *Blemished Perfection*, 262, citing Job 13:7, 16–17. Hoffman suggests that these texts "express the quintessence of the conflict involving both a theological and a personal side. These cannot be separated: in expressing the dual nature of Job's faith in God, he is both personal and universal-ethical" (Hoffman, *Blemished Perfection*, 262).

characterization of the protagonists, in the heights of its lyrical poetry, in its dramatic impact, and in the intellectual integrity with which it faces the "unintelligible burden" of human existence. In all this Job stands alone. Nothing we know before it provides a model, and nothing since, including its numerous imitations, has risen to the same heights. Comparison only serves to enhance the solitary greatness of the book of Job.[129]

Albeit with a note of caution, it may be true to say that the book of Job offers a more profound, more "true" engagement with the problem of suffering and, as such, could be seen as a gift of Israel to the world, for whose benefit they were called by God. Suffering is a universal and vexing problem and, from the perspective of Israel who had been entrusted with the true rendering of reality, the other explorations of the theme were inadequate. That is not to say that there was nothing valuable in what they said or how they said it, but until the problem was explored from the perspective of Israel's distinctive beliefs, the world did not have a wholly true way of approaching the problem of their pain.

Returning to the question of literary dependence, there is still no indication that Job borrowed from or engaged explicitly with the specific texts under discussion. However, it does seem that the ideas and worldviews expressed in these texts, and others now lost to us, would have provided the author of Job with some of the raw materials with which he wrote his work.[130] We may go as far as to say that the ANE texts and ideas functioned as a "foil" for the biblical writer as he sought to present a distinctively Israelite investigation into the question of suffering, which would act in part as a polemic against the inadequacy of alternative worldviews.[131] It is in this sense that the book of Job may be understood

---

129. Anderson, *Job*, 32; cf. Viccio, *Job*, 25; Clines, *Job 38–42*, ix–x. Although I agree in large part with Anderson's assessment, a note of caution should be given about comparing the "worth" of different works. Perhaps the relative complexity of Job can be explained in part by it being a much later work: "A masterpiece emerges not at the beginning of a movement, but at its culmination" (Gordis, *God and Man*, 59). See also Newsom, "Job," 333.

130. Addressing the theme, Newsom speaks helpfully "of a degree of cultural continuity" (Newsom, *Contest*, 72).

131. Walton, *Job*, 38. Walton sees the book of Job as exposing the "inadequacy" of ANE solutions to individual suffering and considers it "remarkable that some still speak of the book of Job as borrowing from the ancient Near Eastern exemplars. A more defensible model sees the ancient Near Eastern literature and mentality as a foil for the book of Job. Job's friends are the representatives of the ancient Near Eastern perspectives, and their views are soundly rejected" (Walton, *Job*, 32, 38).

as exhibiting a missional encounter with ANE religious beliefs. These findings can now be set within the broader context of this and the previous chapter.

Missional Reflections on the Universalizing Impulse and Cultural Encounter in the Book of Job

Chapters 4 and 5 have demonstrated some of the ways in which the book of Job can be approached using a missional hermeneutic. In so doing I have isolated several key themes important, not only to the book of Job, but relevant also to the mission of God. In this final section I draw together the insights from both chapters, and present the findings in a number of missional reflections.

The Book of Job Is Missional Because It Addresses a Universal Concern

It is evident that Israel did not have a monopoly on either the experience of suffering, or its exploration. Given the universality of such vexing human experience, it is inevitable that any culture's sages will attempt to ask questions relating to suffering in an attempt to articulate and understand it. In writing the book of Job the author joined a long-standing, "international" tradition in the ANE and showed that he "knows what people think, what people say in whispers—and not just in Israel."[132]

Such an honest engagement with the realities and complexities of the world provides a challenge for the church's contemporary engagement in the world. Through the book of Job it seems incumbent on the church to be involved in the "universal" conversations common to humanity, irrespective of cultural context. Such an honest engagement is missionally relevant because it has great potential:

> The questions that Israel's wise men and women reflected on, the answers they came up with, the dilemmas they left without final solution, the advice and guidance they offered, all of these resonate with common human experience everywhere. For that reason some missiologists and crosscultural practitioners suggest that the Wisdom literature provides one of the best bridges for biblical faith to establish meaningful contact and

132. Duquoc, "Demonism and the Unexpectedness of God," 83.

engagement with widely different human cultures around the world ... So to engage people's own answers to life's questions and then introduce them to how the Bible handles them can be a friendly, nonthreatening way of gaining people's interest in the wider truth of the biblical revelation.[133]

This is no less true for the universal experience of suffering, concerning which the people of God must provide ways of engaging and understanding.

The Book of Job Is Missional Because It Presents Itself as Universally Relevant

By setting Job within a non-Israelite context and, in particular, casting the central character as a non-Israelite, the author sets up his treatment of the universal and vexing experience of unattributed suffering in an idealized way. In addition, Job's "everyman" status is emphasized by a degree of anonymity and ambiguity surrounding his characterisation. By doing this the author is able to examine more freely the question of suffering and the justice of God without the need to refer, explicitly at least, to Israel's history or cultic traditions. Although the book is uniquely Israelite, the phenomenon of the non-Israelite motif pushes the horizon of the book beyond purely internal debates.

The missional significance of this is clear. In making Job into a representative figure, the author pours into Job the questions of humanity. Because of its covenant relationship with Yahweh, Israel was uniquely positioned before God to probe the depths of questions of suffering and justice. Setting the events of the book of Job outside of Israel allows Job to speak "to and for all humanity" more effectively.[134] In so doing, I would argue the book of Job requires and equips the church to do the same.

I have sought to distinguish between Job as representative (his suffering embodies the pain of humanity's inexplicable suffering) and Job as paradigmatic (in Job we have models of how one might suffer, process and persevere in the light of a relationship with the Yahweh). As Crenshaw so incisively puts it, one must recognize that

> the first step toward answering this question requires one's recognizing the exemplary character of Job, who must surely stand

---

133. Wright, *Mission of God*, 445.
134. Pope, *Job*, xxxviii.

for all the innocent sufferers in Israel, but his sufferings also particularize the universal situation enveloping humanity. For that reason his cries seem to arise in the depths of our being, and his longing for God who withdraws farther and farther away strikes a familiar chord in us. This means that Job's exemplary character extends to the present, transcending time and space, for his suffering resembles our own.[135]

In my view this way of understanding Job's non-Israelite provenance is a corrective to discussions that limit its significance to Job being a "righteous pagan" in a similar vein to figures such as Melchizedek, Jethro or Ruth. Certainly this perspective on Job's non-Israelite identity is important. Job is indeed an example of a commended non-Israelite engaging with Yahweh in important ways. While this phenomenon may have some contribution to make to the discussion of the Bible's dealing with "outsiders," it is my view that drawing confident conclusions for that discussion is problematic. While he could be described as a "righteous Gentile," he is so much more. As noted, my view is that reducing Job's provenance to an example of "holy outsiders" represents both an inadequate reflection of its context in Job and also a diluting of its missiological significance. As a more universalized figure than those he is usually mentioned alongside, Job is in a category of his own.

The Book of Job Is Missional Because in It the Very Mission of God Is at Stake

Particularly in the discussion on the accuser's question, "Is it for nothing that Job fears God?" I suggested that Job could be understood as of critical importance for the mission of God. As I indicated in my review of BMS earlier in chapter 2, scholars have tended to ask how texts fit into the "grand narrative" of the Bible. While this may be a fruitful line of inquiry for texts that may easily be located within the chronological storyline of the biblical narrative, it becomes difficult to know what to do with texts that do not "progress" that plot. While these kinds of texts could be connected to the narrative by association with a particular stage or person of Israel's history (such as Solomon),[136] I would understand the book of

---

135. Crenshaw, *OT Wisdom*, 112.

136. As Wright does when discussing Wisdom, although this is part of a more developed discussion on the missional significance of the Wisdom Literature, which I addressed earlier in the study. See Wright, *Mission of God*, 448.

Job to be functioning in a different, and ultimately more compelling way. Although we could attempt to place the book historically, this is no easy task for a book that has an ancient setting yet was written much later. Additionally, there is no firm conclusion about when the final form of the book was put together.

However, this does not mean that the relationship between the book of Job and the grand narrative becomes unfruitful or futile. Instead, more nuanced questions need to be asked. Rather than "where does this text fit into the grand narrative?" a more appropriate and fruitful question would be, "How does this text function in relation to the grand narrative?" or, more specifically in the case of Job, "How does this text stand apart from, and speak into the grand narrative?"

The book of Job fits into and speaks into the grand narrative by standing apart from it. It stands apart from the "story" yet functions in a deep and critical way in relation to the worldview of Yahweh faith. The book of Job is vital to the missional story of the Bible, the *missio Dei*, because it asks the question only whispered previously: is the relationship to which God is restoring humanity genuine?

Although an uncomfortable, "theological irruption," the question of 1:9b is absolutely necessary.[137] At some point in the story of God's mission somebody, somewhere had to address this question. Yahweh's confidence in Job is so sure that he is willing to stake his name on his servant's response and, in so doing, enters into solidarity with him.[138] Though he did not choose to be so and was not aware of it, Job finds himself with the unique (dare we say privileged?) role of bearing the weight of the divine reputation. In his story a troubling doubt is raised about the very integrity of the mission of God. Ultimately vindication is achieved in and through Job on behalf of humanity, on behalf of God, and on behalf of God's mission.

The Book of Job Is Missional in the Way It Addresses the Potential and Cost of Character Formation

Although in a more concentrated and definitive way, it would therefore follow that the person of Job, and the book of Job, offer some kind of model for those experiencing unattributed suffering in the light of the

---

137. Ticciati, *Job*, 50.
138. Ticciati, "Does Job Fear God for Naught?," 363; *Job*, 74.

mission of God. As such the book of Job contributes to the formation of the people of God, who will process unattributed suffering "missionally."[139] By this I mean that, even though there may be no purpose behind a person's experience of suffering, it can still be purposeful.

The book of Job provides a model of a faithful believer in Yahweh who, in his mixed responses of acceptance, grief, confusion and fury, evidences a committed, honest engagement with his God. As such he witnesses to a genuine relationship that is more than just a "sham" arrangement of mutual benefit. Thus Job becomes a universalized or paradigmatic figure of the suffering believer, both in his experience of suffering, but also in how he processes it.

Writing on Jeremiah, Wright includes "The Missional Cost to the Messenger" as part of his missional reflections on the Prophet.[140] Although his points were made specifically with reference to the prophet it seems to me that this may also (perhaps especially) be applied fruitfully to Job. As explored in this chapter, Job occupied a unique and remarkable place in the questioning and vindication of the validity of the mission of God. But this privilege was, by definition, accompanied by terrible suffering. It is possible, therefore, to understand Job, paradigmatically, as someone who participated in God's mission through and because of unattributed suffering. As Bosch notes, mainly in the context of the servant of Yahweh in Isaiah 53 and the NT understanding of the cross, suffering is a key element of biblical mission.[141] While Job does not effect salvation through the suffering itself, God's mission is seen to be vindicated through Job's response to it. In clinging to God with all the honest, probing questions and struggle, does not the suffering believer witness to a genuine relationship with God?[142] Furthermore, if Bosch is correct in suggesting that, "True mission manifests itself only in a Church which agonizes with the victims of this world," Job provides the people of God with a compelling model.[143]

---

139. I do not make these points lightly but rather write as someone who has experienced some measure of intense grief, which inevitably will have influenced my reading of a text like Job.

140. See Wright, "Prophet to the Nations," 128.

141. Bosch, "Hermeneutical Principles," esp. 444–45, 450.

142. See Wright, *Mission of God*, 451–52.

143. Bosch, "Hermeneutical Principles," 450. Glaser speaks of suffering, or trauma, as "perhaps . . . a necessary equipment for mission" (Glaser, *Trauma*, 22).

It seems to me, therefore, that the view that Job's acceptance and submission are the only missionally valid response to his suffering is deeply inadequate as long as it fails to account for the missional legitimacy of his protest as well.[144]

The Book of Job Is Missional in the Way That It Encounters Other Cultures

Although the book was primarily for an Israelite audience it seems reasonable to me that, just as the author of Job consciously drew upon the wisdom ideas of other cultures, so he may have understood his own work as contributing to that international body of work. In that sense, then, perhaps this particularly Israelite text could then go on to have a "missional encounter" with non-Israelites as they heard and considered this particular take on the question of unattributed suffering. Among many other things, could the book of Job be described, therefore, as a "gift" to the nations?

As I have shown an important aspect of the missional nature of the Bible is the way in which biblical texts contribute to a rendering of reality based on Israel's faith in Yahweh, in contrast to alternative renderings offered by neighboring cultures. In chapter 5 I have shown how the book of Job may be seen as exhibiting such a missional encounter, particularly in relation to Babylonian religious beliefs.

I have suggested that it is not possible to establish definitively a direct relationship between Job and similar ANE texts, although I do not think this undermines the possibility of an implicit engagement with the ideas represented in both.

It seems reasonable (indeed, inevitable) that the author of Job was aware of at least some of the ways in which neighboring cultures sought to address the question of suffering. This may even be understood as adopting a known story (or stories) of a legendary suffering righteous person called Job and adapting it to suit his purposes, which certainly would have included giving it a more Yahweh-centered approach. The degree of consciousness with which the author did this is difficult to assess. Was the author deliberately "taking on" the neighboring worldviews, or did this happen indirectly? It is my assessment that there must have

---

144. This relates particularly to my treatment in chapter 2 of Waters's article, "*Missio Dei*."

been an element of the former going on in the book, although this is mixed in with a desire to tackle the mis-application of certain teachings found elsewhere in Israel's traditions. As such the book of Job does not deliver the only word in the Bible on suffering or Yahweh's governance; rather it contributes to a nuanced, canonical articulation of Israel's attempts to understand how they were to understand and live in the light of unattributed suffering while maintaining that Yahweh still ruled.

The book of Job's encounter with alternative explorations of unattributed suffering may be seen in both affirmation and contrast; that is, a stance of "critical openness." As noted above, it affirms the reality and significance of the vexing human problem of suffering. It also exhibits a cultural openness by employing a non-Israelite motif, thereby universalizing the significance of the biblical contribution, although such "openness" should not be over-interpreted as some have been prone to do.

While similarities of literary and thematic features may suggest a limited degree of affirmation or openness, I have shown that the distinctively Israelite perspectives offered by Job may be understood as evidencing a significant element of polemic. The driving contributory factor in Job's distinctiveness is Israel's monotheistic beliefs; that is, Yahweh's "transcendent uniqueness." Such a view of God intensified the central tension of the book of Job because, as creator and just ruler of the world, it is only to Yahweh that circumstances can be attributed. However, as well as intensifying the problem of unattributed suffering, I detect in Job an intensifying of the solution being offered, seen especially in the speeches of Yahweh which display a distinctive characteristic of the book.

Through the book of Job we see the articulation of Israel's monotheized and monotheizing worldview that sought to preserve the faith and identity of the people of God in contrast to idolatrous and false ideas. For the writer of Job, it was not enough to join the conversation; he had to present the truest word and, in doing so, expose the inadequacies of other attempts.[145] What seems particularly striking here is that the book of Job contains a strong polemic for Yahweh at the very moment when it is asking the most difficult questions of their God. Perhaps questions of the dissonance between the Wisdom Literature and other parts of the OT are not quite so stark when set against this ANE context.

On the assumption that the book of Job exhibits a degree of adoption and adaptation of a non-Israelite source, perhaps too this "transformed

---

145. Walton, *Job*, 38. See also Glaser, *Bible and Other Faiths*, 122.

borrowing" may serve as a type of model for communication of the gospel that may be carried out in contemporary mission contexts. There is a degree of acknowledgment of the wisdom of the nations, yet a critical engagement with it. There is an honest engagement with the questions of humanity, yet probed from Israel's unique and privileged position in relationship with Yahweh. Does this also encourage the people of God to search for elements of a culture that can be used as starting points or bridges for communication? I would suggest that there are indeed possibilities for missional practice exhibited in the book of Job which may be applied either in a local context or in a more cross-cultural setting.[146]

The Book of Job Is Missional Because It Articulates the Universality of the Pain of the World through the Means of the Particularity of Israel's Relationship with Yahweh

I have said that the book of Job encounters these other stories and (albeit with some affirmation) seeks to expose their inadequacies. However, in the context of a missional reading of the Bible, it is essential that this process of missional encounter is not seen as simply undermining the nations. If the book of Job critiques the worldviews of other cultures, it critiques falsehood within Israel's borders as well.[147]

It is not only natural and inevitable that the Bible contains a treatment on the universal theme of suffering. Missiologically speaking, it is *essential* that it does so. Suffering is a particularly stark example of the results of what has gone 'awry' in the world and if mission can be understood as "*getting at the something awry*" it seems evident that an honest examination of the question of suffering and divine justice is an essential part of biblical mission.[148] If Israel's faith in Yahweh really is the true rendering of reality then it is incumbent on them to have a "true word" on the subject, not to the detriment of the world but for the sake of the world.

While this is true of any part of the Bible, the book of Job presents a particularly striking aspect of this contention which is that this true

---

146. This builds on the thinking of several writers on wisdom and mission surveyed in chapter 2, although this had rarely been addressed specifically in relation to Job.

147. Again, the Van Zyl, "Missiological Dimensions," article makes this point clearly.

148. Seitz, *Figured Out*, 147.

word does not just mean a valid and clear answer to vexing human problems. In the book of Job, Israel's most sustained treatment of the theme of suffering exhibits a raw, honest, painful articulation of the problems, as well as probing its Yahwistic faith for possible answers.[149] Job plumbs the depths of suffering like no other work and so addresses human pain and suffering more profoundly and more truly than any other.

Israel must ask these questions on behalf of the world because, as Yahweh's chosen people, they are uniquely positioned to do so. In their particularity they are uniquely able to articulate universal pain and probe universal questions. In so doing they are able to speak "to and for all humanity" and it becomes incumbent on the church to do so as well as part of their participation in the mission of God.[150]

In chapters 4 and 5 I have used a missional hermeneutic to study the missional relevance of the book of Job. I have shown that Job may be understood as intensely missional, addressing crucial themes that connect with the mission of God in a variety of ways. In the next, final main chapter I continue my application to Job of a missional hermeneutic, by examining a particular theme that is of considerable importance, both in a holistic conception of mission and also in the book of Job itself: the treatment of the poor. Such a study builds on the groundwork laid in previous chapters and brings together some important elements of the universalizing impulse in Job. It is, therefore, a natural and, I would argue, compelling element of a missional reading of the book of Job.

---

149. "The core testimony of Israel, by appeal to the great transformative verbs of Yahweh and by the derivative adjectives and noun-metaphors of Israel's speech, made a case that Yahweh is competently sovereign and utterly faithful. And on most days that conclusion is adequate. It is a welcome conclusion because it issues in a coherent narrative account of reality. Israel, to be sure, affirms that conclusion of competent sovereignty and reliable fidelity. But Israel lives in the real world and notices what is going on around it. Israel is candid, refusing to deny what it notices. And so issues of competent sovereignty and reliable fidelity will remain in the Old Testament as Israel's belief-ful, candid, unfinished business. We know, moreover, that these two issues are paramount for all those who live in the world, whether they engage in God-talk or not. Thus these two points of cross-examination are not a safe intramural exercise for Israel. They are rather issues with which Israel struggles for the sake of the world" (Brueggemann, *Theology of the OT*, 324). See Wright, *Mission of God*, 450–52.

150. Pope, *Job*, xxxviii.

6

The Treatment of the Poor in Job

IN CHAPTER 1 I placed the idea of a missional reading of Job at the intersection of three converging trends: the increased acceptance of *missio Dei* and a holistic understanding of mission, the developing conversation of missional hermeneutics, and the surge of more general scholarly interest in the Wisdom Literature of the OT. In each of these cases the issue of the treatment of the poor features to some degree and, as such, provides an appropriate theme to which I may apply my missional reading of Job.

The theme of poverty also featured in chapter 2, where I highlighted social justice as a category of the use of Job in BMS. Here, writers such as Jesurathnam and Van Zyl sought to engage with the issue of poverty in relation to Job, finding important connections and demonstrating the relevance of the book for missional reflection.[1]

In the current chapter I seek to build on this work by examining the treatment of the poor in Job using my missional approach to the text. Following a brief expansion on the featuring of poverty in the spheres noted above I show how poverty may be identified as a significant motif in the book of Job itself. As well as providing further justification for my choice of this theme, this also sets an initial context for the Job texts under discussion later in the chapter. To do this I present, in tabular form, the frequency and distribution of key poverty terms in Job. After some preliminary remarks I give a synopsis of Job, summarizing the context, content and function of each pericope that addresses poverty to show how it fits into the flow of argument of the book.

1. Jesurathnam, "Dalit Interpretation"; Van Zyl, "Missiological Dimensions."

It is beyond the scope of the chapter to perform a detailed analysis of each reference to poverty and so I select three passages for in-depth examination: Job 24:1–17; 29:11–17; and 31:13–23. These texts are particularly worthy of attention because they contain the densest clusters of poverty terminology and the most sustained treatments of the poverty theme in the book. They can also be seen as important moments within the book as a whole, which will be demonstrated in the synopsis. For each of the three texts I offer an exegesis, which culminates in a missional reading of each one, based on the concluding reflections of chapter 5, but also drawing on broader missional questions identified in chapters 2 and 3.

In the final section of the chapter I conclude with a series of reflections based on the preceding discussion. In particular I set out how the book of Job speaks "to and for all humanity" about poverty, outlining a five-fold series of challenges that may be understood in relation to the church's mission.[2] In so doing I demonstrate how studying poverty in Job arises naturally out of a missional approach, and gives an enriched reading of the book. I also show how Job makes a significant and unique contribution to an understanding of the relationship between poverty and the mission of God.

Poverty as a Significant Theme

As noted in chapter 1, writing on holistic mission makes particular and consistent reference to the issue of poverty, which was one of the drivers behind its development.[3] Given this background, a missional reading of the Bible that is governed by a holistic view of mission would very naturally be sensitive to poverty issues.

Similarly, although in a less focused way, missional hermeneutics scholars have also addressed the significance of poverty as part of their approaches. As noted in chapter 3, for example, Wright devotes two chapters of *The Mission of God* to material on the themes of redemption and restoration, seeing these texts as closely related to a holistic view of mission and, as such, particularly relevant to issues of poverty and

---

2. Pope, *Job*, xxxviii.

3. This can be seen in the accounts of the development of holistic mission. See, for example, Tizon, *Transformation After Lausanne*, chapters 1–4; Padilla, "Holistic Mission," 157–58.

justice.[4] For Wright, poverty (alongside other social, economic and political concerns) is a most appropriate (indeed, necessary) topic of interest for a missional reading.

While Bauckham does not involve himself in technical discussions concerning the validity of holistic mission, he does note the importance of the theme of poverty, and integrates it as a core characteristic of the biblical narrative.[5] As part of his controlling motif for mission, which is the movement he discerns in the biblical story from the particular to the universal, Bauckham identifies the way in which God tends to facilitate the one-to-the-many movement through weakness: "God's way to his universal kingdom is through a movement of identification with the least."[6] For Bauckham this motif is profoundly important for how the people of God conduct themselves in the world and he is worth quoting at length:

> The church's mission cannot be indifferent to the inequalities and injustices of the world into which it is sent. The gospel does not come to each person only in terms of some abstracted generality of human nature, but in the realities and differences of their social and economic situations. It engages with the injustices of the world on its way to the kingdom of God. This means that as well as the outward movement of the church's mission in geographical extension and numerical increase, there must also be this (in the Bible's imagery) downward movement of solidarity with the people at the bottom of the social scale of importance and wealth. It is to these—the poorest, those with no power or influence, the wretched, the neglected—to whom God has given priority in the kingdom, not only for their own sake, but also for all the rest of us who can enter the kingdom only alongside *them*.[7]

Wright and Bauckham's contributions are different but complementary. Both see important connections between the missional nature of the Bible and issues of poverty, power and justice. They therefore give precedent for poverty to be a topic of interest in a missional reading of biblical texts.[8]

---

4. Wright, *Mission of God*, chapter 8–9. For other references to "poor" or "poverty," see 43–44, 216, 230, 245, 359, 398, 413, 418, 431, 426–37, 449, 451, 481, 505, 524, 549, 553.

5. Bauckham, *Bible and Mission*, 53–54.

6. Bauckham, *Bible and Mission*, 52.

7. Bauckham, *Bible and Mission*, 53–54.

8. See also Beeby, *Canon and Mission*, 56; Goheen, *Light to the Nations*, 93; Penner, *Missionale Hermeneutik*, chapter 2; Barram, "'Located' Questions."

As part of the increasing in interest in Wisdom Literature noted in the book's introduction scholars have paid greater attention to issues of wealth and poverty in these texts.[9] Similarly, the plethora of studies on poverty and social justice in the Bible often include treatments of the Wisdom books, albeit to varying degrees of depth.[10] Pleins, for example, surveys the book of Job as part of a wider project outlining the "social visions" of the OT.[11] He sees the book's use of both complaint and dialogue genres as creating a voice that is contrary to traditional wisdom reflections on social justice.[12]

In a similar work, albeit with a narrower focus on social justice, Houston, like Pleins, devotes several pages to the book of Job.[13] Despite the book of Job's "upper-class orientation" Houston considers social justice to be a highly significant issue, and one in whose light the broader issue of theodicy should be read.[14] For Houston, Job brings out for explicit examination certain implicit tensions embedded in the book of Proverbs, and it is Job 20–24 where the issue of social justice "comes to a head."[15] Of particular interest for Houston is Job's former status as a man of great wealth, power and honor, which meant that any talk of his own ethics revolved around the issue of how he treated those of lesser status.[16]

Another notable work on the theme is, *On Job*, in which liberation theologian Gustavo Gutiérrez reads the biblical book through the lens of his experience of suffering in Latin America.[17] While he shies away from "facile direct applications to the reality we face in Latin America" he does see as valuable a reading of the text that keeps his "attention on what it means to talk of God in the context of . . . the suffering of the poor— which is to say, the vast majority of the population."[18] At root Gutiérrez

---

9. See references in chapter 1 for examples of this trend.

10. See, for example, Pleins, *Social Visions*; "Poor, Poverty," 402–14; Malchow, *Social Justice*; Wright, *OT Ethics*; Houston, *Contending for Justice*; Weinfeld, *Social Justice*.

11. Pleins, *Social Visions*, 484–508.

12. Pleins, *Social Visions*, 484–85. Pleins's insights will be drawn upon in the synopsis below.

13. Houston, *Contending for Justice*, 126–31.

14. Houston, *Contending for Justice*, 127. On this question of the "elite" audience of the book of Job, Houston draws upon Brueggemann, "Theodicy"; Clines, "Why is There a Book of Job." See also Hamilton, "Elite Lives."

15. Houston, *Contending for Justice*, 127.

16. Houston, *Contending for Justice*, 128.

17. Gutiérrez, *On Job*.

18. Gutiérrez, *On Job*, xix, xviii.

sees Job as asking, "How are human beings to speak of God in the midst of poverty and suffering?"[19] He then traces this theme through the book including two chapters focusing on "The Suffering of Others" and "God and the Poor."[20]

It is evident, therefore, that the theme of poverty is a legitimate issue to examine in a study on the book of Job and that this is particularly (though not exclusively) relevant to a holistic missional approach. I now begin that study by looking at the language of poverty in the book.

An Overview of the Frequency, Distribution, and Function of Poverty Terms in Job

This section sets out a brief overview of the frequency, distribution, context and function of certain key poverty terms in Job, and is complemented by a discussion of poverty language within the flow of the whole book.[21] The frequency and distribution of אֶבְיוֹן (poor/destitute/needy),[22] דַּל (poor/weak),[23] עָנִי (poor/oppressed),[24] יָתוֹם (orphan/fatherless)[25] and אַלְמָנָה (widow)[26] are shown in the following table. The purpose is not to do a word study of poverty terms in the book of Job *per se*. Rather, these terms are viewed as a way of locating the poverty theme throughout the

---

19. Gutiérrez, *On Job*, 12.
20. Gutiérrez, *On Job*, chapters 5, 6, respectively.
21. For a helpful survey of the variety, meaning, and usage of poverty terms in the OT, see Pleins, "Poor, Poverty." While a discussion of the nuances of the different Hebrew terms would be instructive, for reasons of scope I refer the reader to relevant literature in each case. My focus in this chapter is the general theme of poverty and how it functions within Job; that is, what Job or his friends say about the poor. I have kept the survey focused on these five key terms as they best illustrate the poverty material, although I note that it could have been broadened to include less frequent terms such as רָעֵב "hungry" (Job 5:5; 22:7; 24:10) or עֲרוּמִּים "naked" (Job 22:6). It should also be noted that there is at points significant overlap between the terms, although this is not to deny that they have their own specific nuances (see the literature to explore this further).
22. Domeris, "אֶבְיוֹן," 228–32; Pleins, "Poor, Poverty," 403; Gerstenberger, "אבה" 15–19.
23. Pleins, "Poor, Poverty," 405; Carroll Rodas, "דלל," 951–54; Fabry, "דַּל," 208–30.
24. Pleins, "Poor, Poverty," 408; Gerstenberger, "ענה," 230–52; Martin-Achard, "ענה," 931–37; Dumbrell, "עָנִי," 454–64.
25. Ringgren, "יָתוֹם," 477–81; Bennett, *Injustice Made Legal*, 54.
26. Leeuwen, "אַלְמָנָה," 413–15; Hoffner, "אַלְמָנָה," 287–91.

book. The speaker is also noted in each case to illustrate how discussions of poverty fit within the overall flow of the book of Job.

Following a few preliminary remarks I will set out an account of the flow of the book, thereby locating the poverty texts within a broader context and showing how they function in each case to illustrate and accentuate the differing perspectives and strategies of the speakers.

Section	Speaker	אֶבְיוֹן	דַּל	עָנִי	יָתוֹם	אַלְמָנָה
		6x	6x	7x	7x (8x)	6x (7x)
1–2	Prologue					
3	Job					
4–5	Eliphaz	5:15	5:16			
6–7	Job				6:27	
8	Bildad					
9–10	Job					
11	Zophar					
12–14	Job					
15	Eliphaz					
16–17	Job					
18	Bildad					
19	Job					
20	Zophar			20:10 20:19		
21	Job					
22	Eliphaz				22:9	22:9
23–24	Job	24:4 24:14		24:4 24:9 24:14	24:3 24:9	24:3 24:21
25	Bildad					
26–27	Job					27:15
28	Job					
29–31	Job	29:16 30:25 31:19	31:16	29:12	29:12 31:17 (31:18) 31:21	29:13 31:16 (31:18)
32–37	Elihu		34:19 34:28	34:28 36:6 36:15		
38–41	Yahweh					
42	Epilogue					

Table 1: Frequency and Distribution of Key Poverty Terms in Job

Even a cursory glance at the above table is revealing. The poor are not mentioned at all in the frame narrative, although perhaps this is not surprising given the focus of the Prologue and Epilogue on events in heaven and on earth, specifically in relation to Job. Apart from three references early in the first speech cycle, and two in Zophar's second speech, poverty language is concentrated in the third speech cycle and Job's final defence, with five instances in Elihu's contribution. The terms tend to be clustered together, which is perhaps understandable given the frequent parallelism used in Hebrew poetry. With the exception of דַּל Job is the character who uses each poverty term the most.

When Yahweh answers Job in chapters 38 to 41 he makes no reference to the poor. Again, perhaps this is not surprising given the nature of the speeches, which focus on more general concerns of Yahweh's governance of the world, using language predominantly from the non-human spheres of the creation.

To complement these brief observations, a review of poverty language in the flow of the book of Job would be useful. Following the book's Prologue and Job's soliloquy in chapter 3, Eliphaz is the first of the friends to address Job. Speaking in relatively conciliatory terms Eliphaz attempts to draw Job back to orthodoxy and instil in him hope (4:1–6). Ultimately, it is the wicked that will perish, not the innocent (4:7–11). Drawing upon a revelation he was given, Eliphaz reminds Job that human beings are fragile and can't possibly withstand the moral attention of God (4:12–21). Even if the undeserving prosper for a short while, they are a short step from calamity (5:1–7). His main point is that, in the midst of his trouble, Job should seek God and commit his way to him, who is the great reverser of fortunes (5:8). God raises the lowly and the mourning (5:11), frustrates the scheming "wise" and hoists them on their own petard, leaving them groping about in the dark (5:13–5). Eliphaz's reference to the poor occurs in this section, which further illustrates an orthodox understanding of retribution. God saves the אֶבְיוֹן from the mouth of the sword of the schemers and from the hand of the mighty (5:15). Because of the vindicating and saving work of God against the wicked and on behalf of the poor, Eliphaz sees the דַּל (poor/weak) as having hope and injustice shutting its mouth (5:16). For Eliphaz Job has every reason to have hope. His present experiences can be reversed and Job should see it as divine discipline (5:17) (מוּסַר שַׁדַּי; cf. Prov. 3:11, מוּסַר יְהוָה). He should stand firm, commit his ways to God, and be assured that he will enjoy life, peace and blessing once more (5:17–27).

For Eliphaz, then, although the poor are victims of abuse, this is only a temporary situation and is part of the fleeting moment before the wicked are inevitably punished by God. The poor move from being objects of oppression to objects of rescue and, thus, instruments that confirm a theology of retribution.

In the following speech Job complains bitterly to his supposed comforters that they have not faced up to his situation. Indeed, they have withheld kindness and acted treacherously towards him (6:14–17). They distance themselves from him because they are threatened by his circumstances (6:21). To portray the depth of his sense of betrayal and abandonment by his friends (though it is curious that only Eliphaz has spoken thus far), Job characterizes them saying they would even cast lots for the יָתוֹם and bargain over their friend (6:27). In this context, then, the orphan is referenced in order to evoke abandonment and abuse.

The next use of poverty language is in two references in Zophar's second speech, which function as part of a lengthy poem on the fate of the wicked. In so doing he follows Eliphaz (15:17–35) and Bildad (18:5–21) who both discuss the fate of the wicked, a dominant motif in the second cycle, which paves the way for the third cycle.[27]

Any exultation and happiness enjoyed by the wicked, claims Zophar, is fleeting (20:5) and the godless person will soon be forgotten forever (20:6–9). Such will be his ignominious demise that his children will look to the poor (דַּל) for favor (20:10). Though initially sweet on his lips his evil will turn sour in his stomach and his ill-gotten gains will bring him no satisfaction and he will end up giving them back (20:12–18). In 20:19 Zophar reminds Job why such a dramatic fate awaits the wicked person:

כִּי־רִצַּץ עָזַב דַּלִּים בַּיִת גָּזַל וְלֹא יִבְנֵהוּ׃

For he crushed and abandoned the poor; he seized a house he did not build

The speech finishes with continued predictions of doom for the wicked at divine hands. Indeed, it is his portion and heritage from God (20:20–29).

For Zophar the poor function within the past and future of the wicked. They are both victims of his wicked schemes, but also beneficiaries of his downfall and a relative measure of how far the mighty fall.

---

27. Newsom, "Job," 446.

Behind the radical reversal of fortunes of the wicked is God himself, a guarantor of just order in the world.

Zophar's reintroduction of the poverty theme occurs at an important juncture in the development of the dialogue. Indeed, he seems to provide a new and potentially game-changing line of attack for Job.[28] It seems that the dialogue reaches a turning point at this stage. Following the intensification of the theme of the fate of the wicked by all three friends, it may appear as if they now have the clinching argument. Job responds by declaring in chapter 21 that the Emperor has no clothes. The wicked do indeed prosper and are not consigned to a miserable fate. Reversing the contentions of the friends, the wicked pass through life enjoying longevity, power, family, security, prosperity, joy, peace and a timely, contented end (21:7–13).[29] All this occurs despite rejecting God and his ways (21:14–16). The friends, Job declares, are naive and do not pay attention to what is observed far and wide: the wicked not only avoid retribution for their evil deeds; they prosper (21:29–33).

The dialogue, it seems, has now reached a tipping point for Job and his interlocutors, arriving at the heart of the issue.[30] In defending an orthodox view of retribution the friends have asserted that God punishes wrongdoing and vindicates the suffering. Job now directly repudiates that basic assumption of moral order. It is not that Job thinks this should not be how the world works. Rather, he claims that God is not consistent in, or faithful to his design of moral governance.

---

28. "Ironically, by raising the wealth issue, Zophar has unwittingly provided Job with the means to launch a frontal assault on the increasingly encircling arguments of the friends" (Pleins, *Social Visions*, 489). Pleins also speaks of the "wealth question" as a "catalyst" for Job's argument (Pleins, *Social Visions*, 488). He also detects in the book of Job a commitment to "solidarity with the poor," which is exemplified in this section of the book: "At the point where their success seems assured, where Job seems hopelessly trapped, the friends provide Job with a way of escape that deconstructs their entire system of thought. The friends are exposed as liars. If we fail to keenly observe the juxtaposition and movement of these speeches, we risk missing the question of wealth as a turning point. By introducing solidarity with the poor as a way out of the trap, the writer of the book of Job, as Gutiérrez so persuasively observes, has achieved a real breakthrough on the question of human suffering" (Pleins, *Social Visions*, 490).

29. Contrast the themes of strength (21:7; contra 15:29–34; 18:5–7; 20:6–11); the secure and fruitful household (21:8–11; contra 18:14–15, 19; 20:10, 28); multiplied wealth (21:10; contra 15:29; 20:10, 15); happiness, security, and a peaceful death (21:9–14; contra 15:21, 30; 18:13–14; 20:23–25); Newsom, *Contest*, 162.

30. See Houston, *Contending for Justice*, 127.

This is all too much for Eliphaz who, in the opening speech of the third cycle employs the treatment of the poor in a diatribe against Job. The gloves are now off. Job, he contends, must have behaved abominably in the past to be experiencing his current level of suffering (22:4-5). Job must have exerted his power with great cruelty towards the indebted, the naked, the weary and the hungry (22:6-8; cf. 29:11-17; 31:16-23) and must even have abused the widow and orphan:

אַלְמָנוֹת שִׁלַּחְתָּ רֵיקָם וּזְרֹעוֹת יְתֹמִים יְדֻכָּא

You have sent away widows empty, and the arms of orphans were crushed. (22:9)

As with Zophar in chapter 20, for Eliphaz the mistreatment of the poor and vulnerable seems particularly heinous, positioned as it is at the culmination of a list of crimes. While Zophar was describing the actions of the wicked in general that lead to their demise, Eliphaz speaks of these abuses as the assumed wicked deeds of Job. In the theme of wealth, poverty and injustice Eliphaz at last finds the explanation for Job's suffering.[31] They are the only explanation for the calamities he has experienced. God has done this to Job as punishment for his presumed wickedness (22:10-11). He then reasserts the clear moral governance of God in the world in relation to the wicked and the righteous and disapproves of Job's questioning of this (22:12-20). In keeping with his interest in hope for Job (cf. Job 5:17-21) Eliphaz reiterates that there is a way out for his suffering friend: submit to God and you will be restored (22:21-30).

Job opens the third speech cycle by yearning for an encounter with God for vindication, despite the terror of such a meeting (23:1-17). The second part of that speech has a dense concentration of poverty language (אֶבְיוֹן two times; עָנִי three times; יָתוֹם two times; אַלְמָנָה two times) and forms Job's most intense questioning of God's moral governance in the world. Why does God refrain from bringing timely, just judgments on the wicked? (24:1). His evidence for this is the plight of the poor and vulnerable, and the unanswered abuse of the wicked. His points are made concrete in a particularly poignant description of the poor and their abuse.[32] The wicked move landmarks and seize flocks, exploiting the

---

31. Pleins, *Social Visions*, 488.

32. It is difficult to disagree with Gutiérrez, who goes as far as to say this passage includes "the most radical and cruel description of the wretchedness of the poor that is to be found in the Bible" (Gutiérrez, *On Job*, 32). See also Grenzer, "Armenthematik," 229.

widow and orphan (24:2–3). The אֶבְיוֹן are thrust out of the way by the wicked and the עָנִי are forced to hide (24:4), thereby making them eke out a meagre existence on the margins of society, without even adequate clothing or shelter (24:4–8). In a parenthesis Job then declares that

יִגְזְלוּ מִשֹּׁד יָתוֹם וְעַל־עָנִי יַחְבֹּלוּ

There are those who seize the orphan from the breast, and take a pledge against the poor. (24:9)

How could God allow such a thing to go unpunished? These wretched people work for others for little return (24:10–11). God must hear their groaning but he does nothing (24:12). Alongside the terrible plight of the poor are the equally outrageous habits of the wicked. Job highlights the evil attitudes and actions of the wicked. They rebel against the light (24:12), kill the אֶבְיוֹן and עָנִי (24:14), and love the darkness (24:15–17). He also notes how the wicked do wrong to the childless woman and do no good to the אַלְמָנָה (24:21). The difficult passage 24:18–25 follows Job's train of thought in a series of imprecations against the wicked, accompanied by further complaint that God is not intervening in justice with enough consistency.[33] In chapters 3 and 31 Job curses his origins and his future; here, in chapter 24, he curses the wicked and, in so doing, appeals to God to act according to his own just character. The irony is that this should not be so. Why should Job need to remind God of his responsibilities?

For Job the poor in chapter 24 function as a case study in the inattentiveness of God to the moral order of the world. They are victims of oppressors who are not held to account by God. Job's focus at this point suggests that his experience of suffering has now developed his awareness of the plight of others in a more intense and personal way, giving him a solidarity with his "many counterparts in adversity."[34] Indeed, it may even be said that Job has a new perspective and a new sense of obligation to

---

33. The broader passage of 24:18–24 seems strange on the lips of Job in that it appears to express views closer to the friends. For a thorough survey of the issues, see, for example, Lo, *Job 28*, 104–26. No single view is without its complications. My own view on this complex issue is to read the passage with those who consider the passage to be including a series of curses on the wicked (though these authors differ on the precise occurrences of such curses); Newsom, "Job," 511–12; Hartley, *Job*, 350–51; Anderson, *Job*, 214; Wilson, *Job*, 275; Balentine, *Job*, 371. This seems to make the most sense of the flow of Job's thought and emotion in the context of the preceding passage.

34. Gutiérrez, *On Job*, 31.

speak out on behalf of the poor and despised, now that he relates more fully with them.³⁵

What becomes apparent is that Job and his friends are speaking of wholly different perceptions of reality. His offer of "counter-narratives" that expose the clichéd, iconic narratives of the friends with regards to the fate of the wicked suggest that the plight of the poor illustrates not just an exception to the rule, but a statement of a more universal truth that God does not seem to intervene as mechanically as was thought.³⁶

Bildad's final contribution is short and concentrates on the finitude and weakness of humanity in comparison with God (25:1–6). Job follows this with a speech on the unsearchable and powerful nature of God and his ways (26:1–14) and a restatement of his conviction that he is in the right (27:1–6). He concludes with a wish that the fate of his enemy be like that of the wicked (27:7). Addressing his friends once more he pre-empts anything Zophar might say by issuing a parody of a speech on the fate of the wicked, thereby demonstrating the breakdown in the dialogue.³⁷ Albeit a parody, as part of this final portrait Job declares that the אַלְמָנָה of the wicked man will not weep. In this case, the emphasis seems to be not on poverty, although he does predict that the wicked man (and thereby his widow) will become poor; rather it is on the lack of fond remembrance. Because of the satirical nature of the speech it is reasonable to assume that he does not mean what he says, especially in the light of 21:7–18.

Unlike the poem on wisdom in chapter 28, which contains no references to the poor, Job's final speech has two clear clusters of material on poverty, 29:11–17 and 31:13–23. In chapters 29 to 31 Job returns to the poverty theme reintroduced by Zophar and developed by Eliphaz and himself and casts it in the context of justice.³⁸

Job's final defence begins with recalling his life prior to the calamities. He was blessed by God and enjoyed much respect among his community

---

35. Míguez-Bonino, "Poverty as Curse, Blessing, and Challenge," 9. "Job now sees that the question being debated does not concern him alone. This realization gives new vigor to the protest of supposedly 'patient' Job" (Gutiérrez, *On Job*, 32). See Ceresko, "Option for the Poor," 185; Ruíz Pesce, "Dios del Pobre."

36. Houston, *Contending for Justice*, 127. See Newsom, *Contest*, 122–25. And, of course, this is what the friends find so threatening. See also Newsom, "Job," 382.

37. Newsom, "Job," 522. As with 24:18–25, the speaker of 27:13–23 has been widely debated. For the view that these are Job's words anticipating (rather sarcastically) those of the friends, and particularly Zophar, see Newsom, "Job," 522; Janzen, *Job*, 185.

38. Pleins, *Social Visions*, 489.

(29:1–11). The reason for his favored social standing was his treatment of the poor and vulnerable: he rescued the helpless עָנִי and יָתוֹם (29:12); received blessing from the one about to perish and caused the heart of the אַלְמָנָה to sing (29:13); he met the needs of the אֶבְיוֹן and vulnerable, whoever they were and whatever their needs (29:15–17). Indeed, he clothed himself in justice and righteousness, and righteousness clothed itself with Job (29:14). Because of his standing and character Job assumed his life of blessing was to continue uninterrupted (29:18–25). However, as the middle section of his final speech laments, his present condition is radically and tragically different. He is now the object of ridicule of people that formerly were far beneath him socially and economically (30:1–15).[39] In the final section of chapter 30 Job focuses on his turmoil in relation to God. He is in a wretched condition (30:16–19). He cries out to God but receives no answer; indeed he is persecuted by God rather than helped (30:20–23). What seems so unfair to Job is that he is being denied from God the compassion and help Job himself gave to the suffering, including the אֶבְיוֹן. His is a truly abject state, despite the solidarity he had with the poor and vulnerable (30:24–31).[40]

Job concludes his defence with a series of curses upon himself for crimes he denies committing, which (at least partially) deny Eliphaz's charges in 22:1–9.[41] He has not acted lustfully (31:1) or been deceitful (31:5). He has kept his heart and his ways pure (31:7–12). He has treated his slaves justly (31:13–15) and provided for all manner of poor and vulnerable people including the דַּל, the אַלְמָנָה, the יָתוֹם, and the אֶבְיוֹן (31:16–23). He has not placed his trust in wealth or fallen into idolatry (31:24–29). He refrained from gloating over or wishing for the misfortune of his enemies, and sought to offer hospitality to the stranger (31:29–32). He did not conceal his sin or misuse the land or its workers (31:33–34; 38–40). If only he could encounter God and gain an answer to his suffering! (31:35–37).

The poor and vulnerable feature significantly in these final parts of Job's main contribution to the book. On the surface their main function seems to be to illustrate Job's integrity: he has treated them well, defending them and providing for them. While the material on poverty in chapter 29 focuses on Job's "interfering with the relationship between client

---

39. See Houston, *Contending for Justice*, 129.
40. Gutiérrez, *On Job*, 40, 42.
41. Gutiérrez, *On Job*, 41.

and patron where that had descended into exploitation," in chapter 31 he concentrates on "his conduct of relationships with his own dependents."[42]

However, through this they function as a point of contention between Job and God, illustrating the deep ambiguity of his situation. Unlike in chapter 24 where their plight seems to evidence a lack of coherence in God's governance of the world, in chapters 29 to 31 Job's treatment of the poor and vulnerable demonstrate Job's plight. Job's perception of God's treatment of him is in marked contrast to his own treatment of the unfortunate. In setting it up this way Job aims to expose the mismatch between how God should treat Job, and how he does treat him.

With the words of Job ended, in the dialogue section at least, Elihu takes center stage and gives his own perspective on the situation in chapters 32 to 37. Having listened to the preceding debate out of deference to his superiors, Elihu can keep silent no longer (32:1–22). He considers Job to be at fault in the way he has spoken about God (33:8–13) and suggests that God uses suffering to rebuke mankind and bring him back to repentance and righteousness (33:15–33). In light of Job's challenges of God's moral governance, Elihu seeks to reassert the justice of God. God does not act wickedly or commit wrongdoing; rather he acts justly towards humanity (34:1–37). Indeed, he shows no partiality towards the rich over and against the דַּל because they are all created by him (34:19). Moreover, he punishes the wicked for their misdeeds and wrong attitudes: they caused the דַּל and the עָנִי to cry out, and so he hears them and takes action on their behalves (34:26–28). Elihu acknowledges that oppression happens, but looks on with praise as he sees God intervening; and even when God appears to be inactive, who are we to question him? (34:29–30).[43]

Following a dismissal of what he sees as Job's overly-inflated view of his own place before God (35:1–16) Elihu returns to a meditation on the greatness of God. In his might he brings the wicked to account and defends the עָנִי (36:5–6). While giving the wicked the chance to change their ways he will exact justice if they refuse to do so (36:9–12). Again, Elihu sees suffering as a potential method of communication from God,

---

42. Houston, *Contending for Justice*, 129.

43. "For the writer, the language of praise can reach into the world of suffering and social injustice. . . . The language of praise and creation permits crying out to God for justice, but it does not permit condemning God for inaction. . . . The language of worship does not supply an 'answer' or a 'reason' for suffering. Instead, worship molds a posture toward that suffering and toward God in the midst of suffering, the posture of anxious waiting" (Pleins, *Social Visions*, 495–96).

opening the ears of the עָנִי through their affliction (36:15). He then exhorts Job to respond correctly to his plight: he should choose the path of praise rather than the path of iniquity (36:17–24).

The remainder of Elihu's material focuses on the grandeur of God in relation to creation, which he feels should be the proper object of Job's attention (37:14). His final conclusion is that, because of the inviolability of God's justice, mankind should fear him and not think of their own wisdom too highly (37:23–24).

As noted above, poverty language does not occur in either the divine speeches or the book's Epilogue.[44] However, as I demonstrated in the previous chapter, Yahweh's speeches do shape how the book as a whole should be understood. Ultimately Job is led through his encounter with Yahweh to a place of acceptance that he is not equipped to tell God how he should govern the universe. However, this does not and should not negate the legitimacy of his complaints and questions. Yahweh still considers Job to have spoken "rightly" (42:7), which I take to mean that Job has spoken to God with honesty, even though he has also been presumptuous.[45]

Having painted in broad brushstrokes the ways in which the poverty theme occurs in the flow of the book of Job, I now pay particularly close attention to three passages that contain dense clusters of poverty language: Job 24:1–17; 29:11–17; and 31:13–23. In each case I offer an exegesis, leading to a missional reflection in the light of questions raised in chapter 3, and conclusions made in chapter 5.

Exegesis and Missional Reflection: Job 24:1-17

Job 24:1–17 forms part of a larger speech of Job's in chapters 23 to 24. While a treatment of the whole of this speech would be instructive, the concentration of poverty language in 24:1–17 commends this smaller unit for more focused analysis.

Following Job's initial question in verse 1, Job 24:1–17 focuses on the wicked actions and attitudes of those who oppress the poor, and the plight of the poor themselves. The theme of poverty is evident throughout, both in the evocative scenes depicted and in the frequency of poverty

---

44. Although, see the discussion above on the term מִשְׁפָּטִי in Job 40:8.
45. See Hartley, *Job*, 539; Lo, *Job 28*, 53; Brown, *Character*, 112.

terms used (אֶבְיוֹן in vv. 4, 14; עָנִי in vv. 4, 9, 14; יָתוֹם in vv. 3, 9; and אַלְמָנָה in v. 3).

The structure to be used in this exegesis reflects a palistrophe, which follows an opening complaint (v. 1) with themes of those who act against the poor (vv. 2–4, 13–17), the plight of the poor (vv. 5–8, 10–12), and a reprise (v. 9).[46]

Verse 1 is taken on its own, functioning as it does as an opening rhetorical question, although it could be absorbed into a larger opening section.

A key issue in discerning the overall flow of the passage is the identification of the subjects of verbs, which need to be worked out from the context.[47] The above structure reflects the changes in subject, and treats them as indicators of new units.

As in chapter 3, Job gives a speech that has no stated audience (whether God or his friends).[48] The overall genre of the passage seems to be a complaint in the form of a soliloquy and, although the extent to which it could be described as a disputation is debated, I take it to have an element of disputation in it as well.[49] Minor forms in the text include: lament, (v. 1)[50]; rhetorical questioning (v. 1); and a "*pathetic* description" of the poor (vv. 5–8, 10–12).[51]

The passage continues Job's speech, in which he had earlier expressed a yearning to meet with God so that Job could lay his case before him (23:3–4). Job is confident of the justice of his cause, but fearful of the prospect of such an encounter (23:7, 15–16). Yet despite his terror and the dark mystery he experiences, he refuses to be silenced (23:16–17).

The relationship between 24:1–17 and the rest of the chapter has been debated.[52] As indicated above, I have taken the view that 24:18–25

---

46. Though with different headings, this is the structure adopted, for example, by Wilson, *Job*, 264–73; Gordis, *Job*, 253.

47. As observed by Whybray, *Job*, 109.

48. Clines, *Job 21–37*, 591. See also Good, *Tempest*, 278–79.

49. Clines, *Job 21–37*, 591; Murphy, *Wisdom Literature*, 35; Habel, *Job*, 356; Janzen, *Job*, 164. For example, Gordis places chapter 24 in the ANE genre of complaint with reference to "the injustice of the world" (Gordis, *Job*, 253), while Hartley describes the chapter as "a complaint about unjust social conditions" (Hartley, *Job*, 336).

50. Gordis, *Job*, 253. Although this is disputed by Habel, *Job*, who sees verse 1 as the opening in a dispute rather than a lament.

51. Both suggested by Clines, *Job 21–37*, 591.

52. See the discussion in the synopsis of the whole book above.

develops the complaint against God's inaction, and also includes a series of curses that attempt to prompt God to intervene against the wicked.

Job 24:1 Opening Complaint

Building on chapter 23 in which he sees God (and his justice) as inaccessible, in chapter 24 Job explores the unjust, unvindicated suffering of others to illustrate that he is not alone in his plight, and to illustrate "God's abdication of responsibility for the world's moral governance."[53]

Neither Job, nor the exploited poor of this world receive appropriate justice or vindication, and so this depiction of the plight of the poor functions to develop Job's case as one who has been abused and abandoned. Given Yahweh's known commitment to the poor, it is also a challenge to God to say otherwise.

Rather than expecting an answer, Job's preliminary מַדּוּעַ functions as an opening to the complaint or lament.[54] While he may accept that God's punishment of the wicked may not be instantaneous, Job cannot understand why God does not intervene (at the very least!) at regular intervals.[55] Job's focus on "those who know him" וְיֹדְעָיו as the desired witnesses of these undelivered days emphasizes (un)vindicated piety.[56]

That the righteous do not see God's judgment on the wicked is doubly vexing; it allows the wicked to keep at their evil deeds, and also denies the upright hope and reward for their "faithful perseverance . . . Consequently, God's administration of justice seems sporadic, partial, and inconsistent."[57]

Job 24:2-4 Those Who Act against the Poor

Job now gives evidence for his initial complaint by offering some examples of unpunished wicked deeds, which would both discourage the

---

53. Clines, *Job 21–37*, 601. See also Balentine, *Job*, 358; Newsom, "Job," 514. "Where, then, is God in the midst of it all? Will God be deaf to the prayer of the poor? This time, Job's cry is not simply for himself" (Gutiérrez, *On Job*, 34).

54. For similar uses of מַדּוּעַ, see Job 3:12; 21:7. See also Balentine, *Job*, 366; Clines, *Job 21–37*, 601.

55. Clines, *Job 21–37*, 601. See Alden, *Job*, 244; Longman, *Job*, location 7698.

56. Clines, *Job 21–37*, 602.

57. Hartley, *Job*, 345.

pious and embolden the wicked, thus illustrating that "oppression and criminality flourish on the earth without any discernible sign of God's judgment."[58]

To remove someone's גְּבֻלוֹת was a serious offence and meant to assert one's power over a neighbor by absorbing their property into one's own.[59] Whether on the dubiously acquired land or elsewhere, the wicked also seize others' flocks and tend them as if they were their own.

While the victims of the deeds of verse 2 are not stated explicitly, in verse 3 it is the orphan and widow who receive unjust treatment. Without someone to protect them and their property, they have no means of recourse. It is likely in both cases that the animals are seized because of debt, either initially as a pledge or following a defaulting on payment.[60] In any case, to take them away from the orphan and widow was to remove a basic means of survival, and was considered to be an act of the worst kind of injustice.[61]

In verse 4 the poor (both אֶבְיוֹן and עָנִי) are denied the right to go freely about their business in public, being (perhaps violently) forced to leave the road.[62] Thus the attitude and acts of the wealthy wicked force

---

58. Newsom, "Job," 510; Clines, *Job 21–37*, 602. See also Good, *Tempest*, 279; Hartley, *Job*, 345–47; Balentine, *Job*, 367.

59. Describing it as "an assault on the social stability of the community," Newsom rightly sees a significance in the range of ways in which the issue is discussed, in "laws (Deut 19:14), covenant curses (Deut 27:17), prophetic denunciations (Hos 5:10), and wisdom teachings (Prov 22:28; 23:10)" (Newsom, "Job," 510). Clines notes that this would have been achieved with the "tacit approval" of the community, which adds a disquieting structural element to this case of abuse (Clines, *Job 21–37*, 602).

60. Hartley, *Job*, 346. He cites Deuteronomy 24:6 as a prohibition against this kind of activity. Clines suggests that verse 2 is also connected with peasant debt. See Clines, *Job 21–37*, 603; Wilson, *Job*, 267.

61. Habel, *Job*, 359; Newsom, "Job," 510; Longman, *Job*, location 7698; Whybray, *Job*, 109–10.

62. Gordis, *Job*, 265; Clines, *Job 21–37*, 604. Gordis detects either violence or the threat of violence here (cf. Habel, *Job*, 359). As with the previous verses, there is a subtle undercurrent of sanctioned, structural threat to the poor. Their fear is not for being set upon by opportunist criminals. Rather, they are afraid of the powerful in their midst who will (literally) add insult to injury by treating them with such callous contempt and, in this context, may cause great psychological damage as a result: "[It is as if] their very presence in society is a standing inducement to their oppressors to fasten upon them. It may also be a sign of self-effacement, as if they had internalized the scorn of their oppressors for them and had come to feel themselves unworthy members of society" (Clines, *Job 21–37*, 604).

the poor into hiding.[63] Their place in society is marginalized to make way for the greed and excesses of the wealthy. But who is challenging these abhorrent social structures that allow or even encourage this to happen?

Job 24:5–8 The Plight of the Poor

In rather stylized language, Job moves from the actions of the wicked against the poor to a more concentrated depiction of their resultant plight with a focus on survival.[64] Having been stripped of the means to generate their own income, the poor must forage for food in places usually associated with animals searching for food, thus capturing "the social and economic exclusion of the poor."[65] This image also seems apt as a metaphor for the meagre existence of the poor in the context of their work in the fields and vineyards of unscrupulous landowners.[66] Not only have the poor lost their property and must endure (at best) a negligible wage while they increase the wealth of the wicked, in verses 7 to 8 Job describes them as without clothing and shelter. While an initial reading may suggest they have literally no clothing and cling to a rock in the midst of a storm, a more likely meaning is that the poor lack an outer garment and find shelter amongst the rocks.[67] The use of the singular צוּר here may imply "an ironic allusion"[68] or "added sting"[69] to the tradition of God as a rock, a refuge and protector in difficult times and for the poor (Ps 18:3 [ET 2]; 62:3 [ET 2]; Deut 32:15; see also Isa 25:4).

---

63. Habel depicts them as being "compelled to leave the mainstream of society and eke out an existence in the hidden corners of their community" (*Job*, 359). See also Alden, *Job*, 246.

64. Clines, *Job 21–37*, 605. See also Habel, *Job*, 359; Wilson, *Job*, 268.

65. Newsom, "Job," 510. The wild ass, or "onager," seems like an apt metaphor, known as it was for its "ceaseless search for food" (Clines, *Job 21–37*, 605). See also Job 38:8; Habel, *Job*, 359.

66. Clines, *Job 21–37*, 605–6. See also Hartley, *Job*, 347; Wilson, *Job*, 268–69.

67. Clines, *Job 21–37*, 606–7; Wilson, *Job*, 269; Hartley, *Job*, 347; Alden, *Job*, 247. It is worth speculating whether the poor person has also lost this garment because of wicked creditor, contra Deut 23:10–13.

68. Habel, *Job*, 339

69. Newsom, "Job," 510–11. "If they expect God to be the 'Rock' . . . of their salvation . . . they will be sorely disappointed, for the 'rock' . . . they embrace provides neither companionship nor protection" (Balentine, *Job*, 368).

Job 24:9 Reprise: Those Who Act against the Poor

Changing the referent for "they" from the poor to the wicked, and returning to the theme of actions by the wicked against the poor, verse 9 seems to disrupt the flow of its surrounding verses. However, this need not mean that verse 9 is displaced.[70] Rather, as the focal point of the palistrophe, I choose to see it as a "reprise," breaking in with a former theme in an especially stark way. In this verse Job selects the worst instance of callousness to explain the extent of the wickedness in the world and, hence, the extent of God's supposed lack of proper governance.

As before, the language of exploitation seems tied to the abusive extremes of the debt system. The striking language of the nursing child being snatched seems hyperbolic, emphasizing once again the dismal plight and suffering of the poor alongside the wickedness of those who prey upon the vulnerable.[71]

Job 24:10–12 The Plight of the Poor

Echoing his similar complaint in verses 5 to 8, Job laments the pitiful working conditions and meagre existence of the poor laborers. In even sharper, ironic tones he portrays a certain societal evil by juxtaposing the hunger of the poor with the plenty that surrounds them; indeed, that they have a hand in producing.[72] Despite their hard work, they are denied a share in the staples of grain, oil and wine, which were representative of God's blessed provision of the land.[73] They are worse off than the oxen, alongside whom they work, or the visiting neighbor who does not

---

70. As suggested, for example, by Hartley, *Job*, 344; Pope, *Job*, 160, who both place it after verse 3.

71. Wilson, *Job*, 269–70; Habel, *Job*, 359–60; Hartley, *Job*, 347; Newsom, "Job," 511. It should also be noted that, as in verse 2, Job is complaining about the community or system that legitimates and facilitates this practice, rather than just unscrupulous individuals. See Clines, *Job 21–37*, 608.

72. Habel, *Job*, 360. "That some people should be able to starve in the midst of plenty is an especial injustice in the social structure" (Clines, *Job 21–37*, 608). "The injustice is even more scandalous because the poor who lack everything and suffer hunger and thirst are the very ones who work to produce for others the food they cannot have for themselves. There is no respect for their basic right to life, though this is the foundation of all justice" (Gutiérrez, *On Job*, 34).

73. Hartley, *Job*, 348. See Clines, *Job 21–37*, 608–9, for the significance of the harvests.

work on the land but may still benefit from it (Deut 25:4; 23:25–26 [ET 24–25]).[74]

Job's sweeping generalisations about the plight of the poor laborer should be seen in the context of his original contention in verse 1. His complaint is not that every landowner is oppressive but that, in general, society and (much more significantly for Job) God himself look on while the poor are exploited and denied the proper means for survival.[75] Job's current argument could be summed up in verse 12. The poor are as good as dead. They groan (נאק) and cry out (שׁבע).[76] Yet despite the pitiful conditions of the poor and the violation of justice as seen in the exploitation of the poor, Job contends that God does not act. In answer to his question in verse 1, Job suggests that God does not act because he does not perceive that there is anything wrong with the world.[77] For Job, God seems complicit in the social wickedness he has reflected upon, because by refusing to punish its perpetrators as committing wrongdoing, he is saying that these things do not matter. But, says Job, they matter intensely.

Although his subject echoes certain prophetic texts (for example, Isa 58) Job does not call on society to mend its ways, but on God to mend his: "This is the way the world is, says Job, and the real injustice is that God does nothing about it, neither avenging the oppressed nor punishing their oppressors."[78] In an ironic echo of 1:22, in which Job refuses to charge God with תִּפְלָה (wrongdoing), Job now questions God on the basis of God's apparent refusal to charge the wicked with תִּפְלָה.[79]

Having moved from his own experience to the suffering he sees more widely in the world, it seems likely that Job identifies in some way with those he is depicting in this passage.[80] As Gutiérrez so poignantly puts it:

---

74. Clines, *Job 21–37*, 609; Newsom, "Job," 511.

75. Clines, *Job 21–37*, 609; Hartley, *Job*, 349; Wilson, *Job*, 271.

76. See the groaning of the oppressed in Exodus 2:24; 6:5, and of the poor in Psalms 12:6, ET 5. See also Job crying out in 19:7. See Clines, *Job 21–37*, 610; Newsom, "Job," 511.

77. Newsom, "Job," 511; Balentine, *Job*, 368–69.

78. Clines, *Job 21–37*, 609. For connections here with Exodus, see Balentine, *Job*, 369, and, especially, Janzen, who sees a critique of the Exodus tradition of God hearing the cries of the oppressed: "In contrast to Exodus 3, however, God does not think anything is wrong (24:12c). Where is the God of the Exodus? Where is the God of the burning bush? Where is *Yahweh*?" (Janzen, *Job*, 170).

79. Newsom, "Job," 511; Clines, *Job 21–37*, 610.

80. Longman, *Job*, location 7773–74.

Job realizes that his own situation is that of the poor. Where, then, is God in the midst of it all? Will God be deaf to the prayer of the poor? This time, Job's cry is not simply for himself, for he knows that he is part of the world of the poor. It is in that setting that he asks his question, and it carries with it the questions of all those whom he has just recognized as his fellows in misfortune.[81]

Job 24:13–17 Those Who Act against the Poor

Continuing his assessment of the corrupt world in which he lives, Job turns to "the moral chaos of criminality" in which the values of light and darkness are reversed by the corrupt.[82] These particular evildoing enemies of the light break the sixth, seventh and eighth commandments and tend to do so under the cover of darkness.[83]

In previous verses the wicked have committed their moral wrongdoing largely through the legitimating social systems. In verses 13 to 17, however, Job places the wicked in the company of undeniable lawbreakers, thus portraying their legitimated acts of exploitation as no better than the kind of crimes that are acknowledged by all.[84]

In the context of the present discussion verse 14b is particularly important, continuing as it does the theme of the (mis)treatment of the poor. Clines questions the need to identify the wealth or social standing of the murder victim prior to their death; their victimisation has made them oppressed.[85] While he is right to conclude that the verse places the wicked of verses 2 to 12 in the company of outright lawbreakers, to dilute the identity of the poor and needy in verse 14 seems unnecessary. Verses 2 to 12 give many and varied ways in which the poor are oppressed; adding their murder to this disturbing list gives Job's rhetoric a final flourish.

To murder the poor and needy is the ultimate act of power over them. Perhaps it might also be said that the various injustices depicted in verses 2 to 12 become a slow form of murder. The wicked squeeze the

---

81. Gutiérrez, *On Job*, 34.
82. Newsom, "Job," 511; Habel, *Job*, 361; Balentine, *Job*, 361.
83. Clines, *Job 21–37*, 610; Balentine, *Job*, 370.
84. Clines, *Job 21–37*, 611. See Newsom, "Job," 511, who sees continuity in the passage through the continued victimization of the vulnerable.
85. Clines, *Job 21–37*, 612.

life out of the poor, which ultimately results in murder: "The daily life of the poor is a dying."[86]

The point is that these victims are, "innocent citizens who are unable to muster any resistance" and whose murder will go unnoticed and unpunished.[87] And yet God seems to do nothing.

The intense and poignant portrait of the plight of the poor is particularly strong in Job 24:1–17 and exhibits Job's paradigmatic function well. The mistreatment of the poor is a generally observed phenomenon to which Job can appeal, and so his argument has a universal resonance. Job's point is that these things matter and so, I would argue, they matter in mission. As he meditates on the general abuse of the poor, Job himself embodies the movement from the particular to the universal. He now speaks, not only about the injustice of his own situation, but also the injustice of God's apparent inactivity concerning the universally observed mistreatment of the poor. Here is a prime example of Job speaking "to and for all humanity" concerning the clear disconnect between how things are and how things should be.[88] In so doing it seems that in Job the book provides a model of advocacy before humanity and, ultimately, before God on behalf of the poor. The suffering of the poor should be named and brought to the attention of those who would choose to ignore it.[89] Even in the midst of pain the church's participation in the mission of God should include an element of such speech. Moreover, it seems precisely because Job's complaints concerning the abuse of the poor arise out of the context of his own wrestling with unattributed suffering, that they have such intensity and power. The text may, therefore, function in formative ways to shape the people of God in and through unattributed suffering in ways that may not occur without these experiences. The missional potential of such costly vulnerability speaks not only to the missional potential of submission, but also to the missional potential of complaint.[90]

---

86. Gutiérrez, *On Job*, 33.
87. Hartley, *Job*, 350.
88. Pope, *Job*, xxxviii.
89. See Ruíz Pesce, "Dios del Pobre."
90. Contra Waters, "*Missio Dei*," who only sees the former.

Exegesis and Missional Reflection: Job 29:11–17

Job's concluding speech, in which he makes a final assertion of his innocence, divides into three clear sections. Chapter 29 focuses on Job's past and portrays his life before the calamities in idealistic imagery. His yearning for former days sets up the stark contrast of chapter 30 which concentrates on his present dire straits. This contrast is regularly alluded to by means of the repeated phrase, "and now" (וְעַתָּה) in 30:1, 9, and 16.[91] While Job evokes his past in chapter 31, this passage has more to do with the future, both as the time when the curses he calls upon himself would occur, but also in anticipation of the long-awaited encounter with God.[92]

In broad terms the speech as a whole can be understood as a soliloquy, although this description should be nuanced to allow for the oddity, for example, of Job's direct address to God in 30:20–23.[93] As with chapter 3, however, Job's soliloquy in chapters 29 to 31 has a purpose and an implied audience. Job is intent on eliciting a response from God and in his closing speech he seeks to do just that. The speech moves from a poignant remembrance of his past (chapter 29) to a lament (chapter 30), and finally to an oath of innocence or purification (chapter 31).[94]

In chapter 29 Job looks back to his past, remembering better times. This recollecting is done using a *"description of an experience,"* an unusual form with possible connections to texts such as Song 3:1–4; 5:2–7, certain Psalms that reflect on Israel's historical experiences (Ps 105; 106), or even Proverbs 8.[95]

Job 29:11–17 seems to function as the focal point of the chapter as a whole, as reflected, for example, by Habel who sees Job 29 as a palistrophe with verses 11 to 17 at its center.[96] The framing of the speech with an introduction and summation sets the themes of the chapter in context. The structure as a whole picks up on the key themes of blessing

---

91. Clines, *Job 21–37*, 976; Newsom, "Job," 544; Balentine, *Job*, 453; Habel, *Job*, 417.

92. Clines, *Job 21–37*, 976.

93. Clines, *Job 21–37*, 976.

94. Designations of the genres of these sub-units vary slightly but exhibit a large degree of commonality. See Murphy, *Wisdom Literature*, 39; Hartley, *Job*, 385; Habel, *Job*, 405.

95. Clines, *Job 21–37*, 978; Habel, *Job*, 406. Clines dismisses the Psalms connection as the remembrance there is of God's deeds, whereas Job concentrates mainly on his own acts.

96. Habel, *Job*, 406–7. See Alden, *Job*, 282. See also Murphy, *Wisdom Literature*, 38, who opts for similar units though without identifying the passage as a palistrophe.

and honor, two grievous losses in Job's life, and these in turn surround the central passage in which he describes the reason for his good standing. This core set of verses can be more fully outlined to demonstrate the focal point still further with Job "Acclaimed as Good" (verse 11); "Savior of the Oppressed" (verses 12–13); "Pivot: The Righteous One" (verse 14); "Savior of the Oppressed" (verses 15–16); and "Ruler Over Evil" (verse 17).[97]

The exegesis below treats the passage as one unit rather than breaking it down into small subunits. However, the outline above informs the overall message of the text and should therefore play a part in its interpretation. In particular, special attention should be paid to the central verse, 29:14.[98]

In 29:11–17 Job reflects upon his past efforts to administer justice in his community. Judging by the previous verses, he was held in high esteem by all those around him. This is in part explained as an acknowledgment of his high social standing, which he used to great effect on the behalf of the poor.

Verse 11 opens the section by claiming that Job was resoundingly approved of by those who witnessed him. The honor ascribed to Job, that he is blessed and approved, suggest that he "embodies the values of the community."[99]

This sign of communal respect was important enough to Job that he uses it to headline his acts of righteousness and justice.[100] In the following verses he gives a number of examples of the kind of acts that have earned this respect, even awe. In so doing, they give a window into the values Job and his community held as particularly worthy.

The first beneficiaries of Job's dispensations of justice are the עָנִי and יָתוֹם, who are said to have cried out (שׁוע) and been without help (וְלֹא־עֹזֵר לוֹ), respectively. Job claims to have rescued (מלט) them, which seems to function both as a denial of Eliphaz's charge in Job 22:6–9, while simultaneously exposing what he perceives as God's refusal to do the same for

---

97. Habel, *Job*, 407. The phrases are Habel's, although he replicates the text below each one.

98. "At the center of Job's memory is the conviction that his blessed life was built on relationships cemented by righteousness and justice (v. 14)" (Balentine, *Job*, 441).

99. Newsom, "Job," 539. See also Houston, *Contending for Justice*, 129; Balentine, *Job*, 441–42.

100. Clines, *Job 21–37*, 988. Indeed, it appears that "Job presents his justice as his sole claim for honor in the community, in preference to his wealth or his ancestry" (Houston, *Contending for Justice*, 129).

him or the "wounded" (19:7; 24:12; 30:20).[101] Thus Job has acted like an ideal ruler, reversing the fortunes of the vulnerable.[102]

In verse 13 Job recalls how the one about to perish blessed him.[103] This could mean that he prevented them from dying (as may have been the case with the poor in verse 12), or that he made their impending death more comfortable, or that just before they died these people thanked Job for all he had done for them.[104] All three options seem plausible and it is attractive to consider all three as being true. In any case, what is clear is that, with all his power and status, Job was in that privileged place of engaging with people at their most finite and vulnerable. Yet he acknowledges that he too gained from the encounter; indeed, there is a sense in which he was the ultimate recipient from the exchange, receiving the blessing of the one whom he helped.[105]

Paralleled with the blessing of the one about to perish is the joyful song of the widow. The likely tone of this song is not clear, although it was probably more than her heart being inspired "to hum a tune joyfully"[106] and seems more likely to be referring to "a metaphorical 'cry' of the heart, greeting a relief from a situation of despair" thanks to Job's provision of food, clothing or protection from creditors.[107]

At the heart of the passage is a movement from the concrete to the abstract as Job reflects on his intimate acquaintance with righteousness and justice.[108] Thus, "I put on righteousness and it clothed itself with me (v. 14a)."[109] The clothing oneself with righteousness metaphor is

---

101. Pope, *Job*, 188; Clines, *Job 21–37*, 988; Habel, *Job*, 410; Anderson, *Job*, 232. See also Gutiérrez, *On Job*, 41, who sees the complaint to God as added in a related passage in 30:24–25.

102. See Ps 72:1–4, 12–17; Habel, *Job*, 410; Hartley, *Job*, 391; Gordis, *Job*, 320; Newsom, "Job," 538; Houston, *Contending for Justice*, 128.

103. Perhaps there is a faint, ironic echo here of Job's wife's charge to him to ברך God and die (2:9).

104. Clines, *Job 21–37*, 988. See also Alden, *Job*, 283; Wilson, *Job*, 317.

105. Newsom, "Job," 538. See also Hartley, *Job*, 391.

106. Hartley, *Job*, 391.

107. Clines, *Job 21–37*, 988.

108. Habel, *Job*, 408, notes this change at this "pivotal" verse. See also Houston, *Contending for Justice*, 129.

109. Many (for example, ESV; NRSV; Hartley, *Job*, 390; Gordis, *Job*, 314) take וַיִּלְבָּשֵׁנִי as repeating the idea of the first verb; hence, "I put on righteousness, and it clothed me." Others, however, understand it as referring to righteousness clothing *itself* with Job, which is the rendering taken here. See Driver and Gray, *Job*, 1:249; 2:201;

used elsewhere (for example, Isa 59:17; Ps 132:9) and suggests that Job "adorned himself with this quality, and it brought honor to him, as a costly garment would."[110] Righteousness became, as it were, Job's "public skin" and, combined with the מְעִיל and צָנִיף of his justice, were to communicate the persona appropriate for office.[111] Verse 14b functions as a "rhetorical flourish" to the already lofty claim that Job adorned himself in righteousness and justice.[112]

The first part of the verse, however, demands further attention. Job contends that righteousness actually clothed itself with him. Given the oddness of this phrase, it is perhaps unsurprising that commentators and translators have often tended to render this in a way that makes a similar point to the first half of the stich.[113]

Explanations for the phrasing are provided by a few, older scholars. Driver and Gray, for example, expand on their translation with, "it filled or possessed me."[114] Gesenius explains, "I am covered without with righteousness as a garment, and within it wholly fills me."[115] Strahan calls it a "fine expression, meaning that righteousness made itself visible in me—one might almost say, embodied or incarnated itself in me," a concept suggested by Peake as well.[116]

Clines is not convinced by most of these explanations, concluding that, "it is rather that righteousness itself became more glorious, more

---

Balentine, *Job*, 442; Clines, *Job 21–37*, 929; Pope, *Job*, 185; Janzen, *Job*, 203. Note the developing discussion in the main text.

110. Clines, *Job 21–37*, 988.

111. Newsom, "Job," 538; Clines, *Job 21–37*, 989. The robe and turban were thought to symbolize "one's status, e.g., that of a king (Isa 62:3) or a high priest (Zech 3:5). While Job presided as elder his clothes witnessed to his complete commitment to justice. Indeed, Job implanted these qualities deep within himself so that they controlled his words and decisions" (Hartley, *Job*, 391).

112. Clines, *Job 21–37*, 989.

113. See textual note above.

114. Driver and Gray, *Job*, 1:249. They further elaborate, "I wore righteousness and righteousness wore me."

115. Gesenius, *Lexicon*, 430.

116. Strahan, *Job*, 246. "As we might say, became incarnate in me" (Peake, *Job*, 256). Reference is often made in the discussion to Judges 6:34, in which the Spirit of Yahweh is said to clothe itself with Gideon (וְרוּחַ יְהוָה לָבְשָׁה אֶת־גִּדְעוֹן). As cited, for example, in Clines, *Job 21–37*, 989.

noticeable and acclaimed, through adopting Job as its outward form, making itself visible in Job (Strahan)."[117]

In my view Clines dismisses too readily the suggestions of others, which all contribute to the overall idea being put across by Job. It is not just that Job "put on" his ethical values; rather, they penetrated, saturated and possessed him. To see Job was to see righteousness. His claim, hyperbole though it may have been, was that righteousness was incarnated or embodied in him.

In the final three verses of the section (vv. 15–17) Job highlights further case studies in his implementation of righteousness and justice. It is perhaps notable that, having talked in incarnational terms for the way righteousness has clothed itself with him, Job now incarnates or contextualizes himself according to the needs he perceives. He himself embodies what is lacking. His language is "personal and intimate," taking on the form of need in each case (eyes for the blind and feet to the lame), and evoking the parental metaphor to conceptualize his assistance to the poor.[118]

However, the language of verses 15 to 17 is not simply "pious sentiment . . . but rather a forceful expression of Job's capacity to protect the interests of such people in the court and the community at large."[119] As the father was the economic and legal linchpin of the family unit, by taking on this persona, Job was stepping into the essential power role that ensured the protection and survival of those who in effect became his dependents.[120] This was economic reality, not just literary artistry.

Job's ethics, suggests verse 16b, also went well beyond the call of duty in that he took up the cause of the stranger or outsider.[121] Again, Job embodies Israel's ethics in his distribution of righteousness and justice. The גֵּר (who is presumably in view here) was often set alongside other marginal groups in Israel, and so it fits that Job mentions dealing with them, especially as they were vulnerable in comparable ways to the orphan and widow.

The incarnation of righteousness and justice in Job could manifest itself as "a protective rage" against the victimisation of the weak, as

117. Clines, *Job 21–37*, 989.
118. Newsom, "Job," 538.
119. Habel, *Job*, 411.
120. Clines, *Job 21–37*, 989–90.
121. Clines, *Job 21–37*, 990.

depicted, for example, in verse 17 where Job took on the wicked "beasts" by establishing justice and nullifying their power.[122]

The missional significance of Job 29:11–17 follows two related themes. First, the passage continues Job's complaint to God, which I have depicted as functioning paradigmatically for universal questions. The imagery that Job employs in verses 11–17 resembles that used of Yahweh in his dealing with the vulnerable and their oppressors. Indeed, "The values and identity that Job articulates for himself are very similar to those Israel attributed to God."[123] This seems particularly prescient in 40:10–13 when Yahweh challenges Job to take on a more cosmic, divine role and clothe himself in majesty, dignity, glory and splendour (ESV), and crush the wicked.[124]

As well as defending his integrity, therefore, Job is making the point that he is intimately acquainted with righteousness and justice. In the context of the book, this seems deeply ironic, adding both power and poignancy to his complaints that God has abandoned these indispensable values in the world (24:1–17), and more specifically, in Job's life (19:7–9).[125] While Job went out of his way for justice by championing the cause of the one he did not know, God, who knew him most intimately neglected Job's cause and persecuted him (chapter 10).

Secondly, Job 29:11–17 has the effect of setting out examples of a model of ideal ethical behavior, which relates closely to the missional shaping function of the Bible. Job's actions in 29:11–17 exhibit his attempt to bring about the blessing and שָׁלוֹם of Yahweh into a society marked by

---

122. Newsom, "Job," 539; Habel, *Job*, 411. It should be noticed that the passage begins and ends with Job's rescuing, at times with force. See Houston, *Contending for Justice*, 129. Gutiérrez suggests that Job's reflections on the poor in recent speeches now come to his mind and enrich his final monologue: "He continues to defend his integrity, as he had promised. But because he now has in mind other innocent persons besides himself, his argument is enriched, and his voice changes pitch, as it were. As he recalls his past and the demands made by his God, he shows a clear understanding of the religious meaning of service to the poor" (Gutiérrez, *On Job*, 39).

123. Newsom, "Job," 539. She elaborates: "God, too, is a champion of the oppressed (Deut 24:17–22; Prov 23:10–11), a father to the orphan and protector of widows (Ps 68:5[6]), closely identified with righteousness and justice (Ps 89:14[15]), a shepherd (23:1) who delivers victims from the jaws of the wicked (Ps 3:7[8])." See also Gutiérrez, *On Job*, 40.

124. Habel, *Job*, 411.

125. Habel, *Job*, 410. See also Good, *Tempest*, 300, who sees Job's claims as surpassing the justice not only of other people but also God himself.

the results of a world gone "awry."[126] Of particular significance, in my view, is the role verse 14 plays in this portrait. Job does not simply carry out acts of justice and righteousness; he is their very embodiment. Such an intimate expression of the relationship between Job and these characteristics speaks of an intense and holistic expression of Yahweh's ethics. As such, the passage acts as a profound challenge to the church as it seeks to exhibit the values of the Kingdom of God.

Exegesis and Missional Reflection: Job 31:13–23

The climax of Job's final speech is an extended oath of innocence in which he attempts to force God's hand. It is structured around a series of curses relating to sins he claims not to have committed. Notably, the sins under examination are more to do with Job's "attitudes and motives" than specific acts outlawed, for example, in the Decalogue.[127]

Scholars differ over exactly how many sins (and therefore sub-units) are present in the chapter, although it tends to be between ten and sixteen.[128] The placement of verses 35 to 37 is also contested as it seems out of place, appearing to be more appropriate at the very end of the chapter. However, Habel's structure allows for their existing location and is adopted here: A Covenant and Curse Motif (vv. 1–3); B Challenge (vv. 4–6); C Catalogue of Crimes (vv. 7–34); B1 Challenge (vv. 35–37); A1 Covenant Witness and Curse (vv. 38–40).[129]

Having set the passage in context, the focus of this exegesis now turns to verses 13 to 23, which concentrate on Job's treatment of the poor and vulnerable in a particularly sustained way. The passage is divided into two parts, reflecting its two main thematic units.

Job 31:13–15

In this opening section Job rejects the notion that he has mistreated his slaves, and builds on his assertion in 29:11–17 that he has been a

---

126. See Seitz, *Figured Out*, 147, 157.

127. Hartley, *Job*, 407; Newsom, "Job," 551.

128. For a discussion on this, see Hartley, *Job*, 408. See also Gordis, *Job*, 542–46; Newsom, "Job," 553–54; Clines, *Job 21–37*, 1013.

129. Habel, *Job*, 427–28 (his headings). For the inner inclusio, Habel notes the repeated use of the key terms of counting ספר and steps צעד in verses 4 and 37.

champion of justice. Although slaves had few legal rights (for example, Exod 21:1–11; Jer 34:8–22) Job was committed to justice to such an extent that he was prepared to acknowledge their just complaints when they arose, even when they were about him.[130] By not rejecting their cause Job was agreeing to recognize it and take it seriously and, in effect, claim to have gone far beyond what was required of him, acknowledging that both male and female slaves had rights and that they could question his treatment of them.[131]

His motivation for such righteous behavior related, claims Job, to his sense of the potential for God to intervene and call him to account for his treatment of his servants. Given their lack of access to normal civil legal proceedings, Job seems to be suggesting that the slave's cause would go to a hearing with God.[132]

Verse 15 adds a further motivation for Job's ethics towards his slaves, although it has broader implications as well. As well as a sober acknowledgement that God is on the side of the slaves and will hold Job to account for any mistreatment, Job's behavior towards them is driven by a belief that he and they share the same origins.

The imagery of the womb (בֶּטֶן and רֶחֶם) has already been a motif of the book.[133] In the present context it functions to highlight a certain degree of equality amongst people. It is important to establish what Job is, and is not saying in this verse. Gordis, for example, suggests that these verses offer "a ringing affirmation of Job's conviction that all men, the lowest and the highest alike, are equal in rights because they have been created by God in the identical manner."[134] Similarly, for Habel:

> Job's rationale for regarding his slaves as equals with other citizens is his common humanity with them (v. 15). The belief

---

130. Habel, *Job*, 434.

131. Longman, *Job*, location 9330–33; Balentine, *Job*, 487; Clines, *Job 21–37*, 1020.

132. Clines, *Job 21–37*, 1020, citing, though building upon a point made by Rowley, *Job*, 255. See also Hartley, *Job*, 414.

133. See Job 1:21; 3:1–19; 10:8–22; 24:20; 31:13–23; 38:8, 29. Both terms are found more frequently in Job than in any other biblical book: בֶּטֶן sixteen times in Job (seventy-two in OT); רֶחֶם five times in Job (thirty-one in OT). Of particular note on this theme are Janzen, *Job*; Perdue, *Wisdom in Revolt*. See also Balentine, *Job*, 488.

134. Gordis, *Job*, 348. As a chilling aside, he also observes that Hölscher, *Hiob*, deleted verse 15 on linguistic grounds, but Gordis speculates, "Is it possible that in publishing his commentary in Germany in 1937, in the heyday of Nazism, this statement of human solidarity was not palatable and that its deletion represents a tribute which virtue paid to vice?" (Gordis, *Job*, 348).

that a common Creator and a common human origin justifies regarding all mortals as equals with common rights before God and the court is consistent with the creation theology elsewhere in wisdom literature (Prov 17:5a; 22:2).[135]

Clines, however, is more circumspect: Job "says nothing of human equality, which he does not believe in: he only says that he and slaves have also been created by the one God, and implies that that fact gives them some basic human rights, not that all humans should be treated alike or that they are 'equal in rights' (Gordis)."[136]

Clines's caveat is instructive but Job does seem to be saying something about human equality. At the very least he is suggesting, as Clines admits, that there is a degree of equality inherent among humankind, even if Job is not advocating a total equality in legal or social status.[137]

A further comment needs to be made about the justice and slavery theme and how it connects to Job's broader agenda. One image that the book employs to depict the relationship between God and Job, or humanity more broadly is that of a master and עֶבֶד (Job 1:8; 2:3; 7:2). In 7:1–2 Job likens humanity to a slave who longs for relief. Perhaps Job 31:15 is Job's way of claiming a more righteous understanding and execution of the slave-owner's commitment to justice than God.[138] While Job has not rejected his servant's just cause, he feels that God has rejected his (Job 19:1–12).

Job 31:16–23

In echoes of Eliphaz's accusations of 22:6–9 and Job's claims of 29:11–17, this section focuses on Job's righteous treatment of the poor and vulnerable in society.[139] In a series of five "if" statements Job highlights a number of actions that would deserve punishment. Implicit in these, of course, is the right way to live and act.

---

135. Habel, *Job*, 435.

136. Clines, *Job 21–37*, 1021, citing Gordis, *Job*, 348.

137. As suggested above, he was still assuming that the slaves would not have access to the legal process. See Houston, *Contending for Justice*, 130; Newsom, "Job," 553.

138. Habel, *Job*, 434.

139. Gutiérrez, *On Job*, 42; Anderson, *Job*, 242; Habel, *Job*, 435; Pope, *Job*, 204. See also Clines, *Job 21–37*, 1021.

In verses 16 to 23 Job reflects upon his treatment of the דַּל, the אַלְמָנָה, the יָתוֹם, the אֹבֵד, and the אֶבְיוֹן. The greatest desire (חֵפֶץ) of the poor must be the basic means of survival, which would include food (18), clothing (19–20), and legal protection (21).[140] Perhaps other necessities of a whole life are hinted at as well, such as hope (16) and fellowship or belonging (17, 18).

Failing eyes may refer to the physical symptoms of hunger and impending death.[141] More likely it refers to a loss of hope. Figuratively, the widow has strained her eyes looking desperately for help, only to be denied or ignored and, so, to have lost hope of deliverance.[142]

It is not quite clear whether Job intends verse 17 as a general metaphor for his generosity towards the orphan, or whether he actually did sit down with the marginalized around his table.[143] Likewise, it is not evident why Job would be eating a morsel or crust (פַּת) in the first place. It may be a (rather dubious) claim to humble eating habits.[144] Alternatively, it could be that Job is arguing from the extreme to make a point. To deny the poor a mere crust would be rather callous; what would Job be losing by doing so?

Regardless of the exact significance of what is being eaten, sharing his food with the marginalized (cf. Prov 22:9; Isa 58:7) is another way of illustrating "that he is a hero of the oppressed."[145]

---

140. Without the capacity for legal "survival," a person was vulnerable and risked losing their capacity for physical "survival."

141. "Death is not far away, since the eyes lose their light and focus as life slips away. Lackluster eyes can also be the result of suffering and hunger, with consequent loss of vitality" (Wilson, *Job*, 343).

142. See Job 11:20; Ps 69:4 ET 3; Clines, *Job 21–37*, 1021; Balentine, *Job*, 488. Hartley, *Job*, 416, sees it more as a sense of worthlessness, gained by the degradation of being turned away despite one's begging. While this is possible, the issue of hope seems more appropriate as the dominant motif.

143. A tension brought out by Clines, *Job 21–37*, 1022.

144. Clines, *Job 21–37*, 1022; Strahan, *Job*, 260–61.

145. Habel, *Job*, 435.

Verse 18 has been much discussed by scholars, which I translate as: "For from my youth the orphan grew up with me[146] as with[147] a father, and from my mother's womb I guided the widow."[148] Job's claim in the first part of the verse could be understood in two main ways. First, it could simply be an expression of hyperbole, suggesting that it has been Job's lifelong habit to act as a father figure for the orphan. Related to this, the second way of reading the verse is to see it as also explaining Job's extraordinary compassion for the orphan. Could it be, as proposed by Hartley[149] and Davidson[150], that Job learned his ethics towards the marginalized because his own father modelled it to him?

While it is most likely that the former reading is the correct one, Clines is unnecessarily harsh to dismiss Hartley and Davidson's

---

146. Several issues are at play in translating the term גְּדֵלַנִי, as reflected in the attention given to it by scholars. Driver and Gray, *Job*, 2:225, for example, amend the text to גִּדְּלַנִי (he raised me) with the subject as God. This leads them to the attractive idea that "Job's care for the needy . . . rested on another . . . principle of religion, viz. gratitude for God's fatherly care of himself from his earliest days . . . and the consequent desire to be like God in his conduct towards his needy fellow-men" (Driver and Gray, *Job*, 1:267). Habel, *Job*, 426, considers a reference to God at this point as "intrusive" and rejects their emendation. However, it does not seem too out of place in what Job is trying to achieve. It could be, for example, a further ironic point made by Job to both defend his righteousness, and also accuse God of abandoning such a close relationship. Drawing a connection between an interpretation like this and the meaning of Job's name, "Where is the father?" is tempting. See Janzen, *Job*, 214.

Pope, *Job*, 426; Clines, *Job 21–37*, 965, prefer to alter גְּדֵלַנִי to a piel first person form, אֲגַדְּלֶנּוּ (I brought him up). However, while this simplifies matters in one sense, the text as it stands can be understood as suggesting this meaning without the need for alteration. Gordis, *Job*, 349; Habel, *Job*, 426, understand the MT as an intransitive qal form ("he grew up with me"), which Clines, *Job 21–37*, 965, (accounting for their rendering) describes as having a "datival suffix." My preference is to retain the MT, although Clines and Pope's rendering produces the same idea. Although not explicit in the Hebrew, the "he" must be referring to the orphan of verse 17.

147. בְּאָב could either be seen as (with Gordis, *Job*, 349) "a contraction of two prepositions" or (with Clines, *Job 21–37*, 966) an omission. Either way, it can be taken as meaning "as with a father."

148. The object is not identified but presumably refers to the widow of verse 16. See Gordis, *Job*, 349; Pope, *Job*, 204; Longman, *Job*, location 9369–70. See also Clines, *Job 21–37*, 966, for a review of the discussion.

149. Hartley, *Job*, 416.

150. "Job probably did not achieve his greatness, he was born to it. And possibly he inherited the traditions of a great and benevolent house. And thus even from his youth he took the place toward the poor of a patron and father" (Davidson, *Job*, 18).

suggestion as "gratuitous supposition."[151] At the very least they raise the issue of whether Job's ethics were shaped by his family context, in addition to his own thinking and sense of righteousness and justice. It seems at least possible that, in the communal culture in which Job lived, his own upbringing shaped him. He himself sought to shape and guide his own children (Job 1:1–5) and so it does not seem unreasonable that Job's father would have sought to do the same with him.[152]

In parallel with verse 18a is an even more extreme hyperbole that Job guided (נחה) the widow from the time he was in his mother's womb.[153] The repeated idea is that Job acted towards the vulnerable in ways that they needed. Gordis explains the use of נחה with reference to the imagery of Isaiah 51:18, suggesting that he treated the widow "with filial loyalty."[154]

In verses 19 to 20 Job turns to the theme of clothing the poor and the perishing. He claims to have ensured their survival through the gift of a fleece from his flock. If the fleece was tied around the waist the loins (חלצים) would have been particularly warmed.[155] There must also be an echo here of Job 29:13, where Job similarly received a blessing from the perishing one.

In verse 21 Job returns to the judicial scene. It is not certain what Job means by raising (נוף) his hand against the orphan but the sentiment is clear.[156] Despite his legal power and status, and all the implied support available to him, Job refused to take the easy path and protect the interests of the powerful (himself included) at the expense of the vulnerable, who had no such support. Were this to have been the case, Job calls on God to exact poetic justice on his body. Mirroring the raised arm, to

---

151. Clines, *Job 21–37*, 1022.

152. Otherwise, is the reader to suppose that Job came to economic, social, and political prominence from nowhere? To push the speculation one step further, perhaps it is notable that both Hartley and Davidson assume that Job was a natural child of his father. Is it at all possible that he himself was an orphan, and that this, too, drives his sense of obligation to the poor?

153. Although נחה usually connotes divine guidance, there are several instances of people as the subject, leading or guiding, e.g., Num 23:27; Ps 78:72; Prov 6:22; 11:3; Merrill, "נחה," in *NIDOTTE* 3:76.

154. Gordis, *Job*, 349. Although the verb used in Isa 51:18 is נהל.

155. Clines, *Job 21–37*, 1023. See also Pope, *Job*, 204.

156. Suggestions vary amongst scholars. See, for example, Hartley, *Job*, 417; Pope, *Job*, 205; Alden, *Job*, 304.

have one's shoulder or arm dislocated or broken was to have one's power compromised.¹⁵⁷

Job completes this unit with a related yet widening reflection on his motivation for avoiding unrighteousness and injustice. As in verse 14 he is fully aware that his deeds do not go unnoticed by God, although this seems a little ironic in view of his claims in, for example, chapter 24. His sense of God here is more disturbed than the foundational wisdom value of the fear of Yahweh, and is reminiscent of Bildad's idea that dominion and dread are with God (הַמְשֵׁל וָפַחַד עִמּוֹ).¹⁵⁸ The thought of encountering God and being condemned for wickedness terrified him and, therefore, acted as a guiding motivation for correct behavior.¹⁵⁹ Specific to the preceding denials, Job stood in the middle of the power spectrum. However great and powerful, the man with power will answer to the God with ultimate power for the way he treats those without power.

Job 31:13–23 continues the missional elements observed in the previous passages in that it both contributes to the articulation of Job's (and hence, humanity's) struggles in relation to God, while also exhibiting an implicit ethical challenge to its audience. In defending his own justice and righteousness, Job intensifies the seeming incongruity between his past actions and present experience, thereby defending himself and attacking Yahweh. Job knows what justice should look like, as he demonstrates with a range of examples from his past. As well as laudable action he also exhibited an attitude of integrity, thereby eschewing any sense of hidden sin or hypocrisy.

As in 29:11–17 Job describes an idealized picture of his correct use of power, bringing blessing and שָׁלוֹם to a broken world. His commitment to human equality (albeit with the caveats noted above) and action on

---

157. Hartley notes the common OT motif which "indicates that one's power has been decisively broken," and comments that God is often the one who does the breaking (referring to Ps 10:15; 37:17; Jer 48:25; Ezek 30:21–22. In Job 29:12 the יָתוֹם is said to be without help (וְלֹא־עֹזֵר לוֹ). If Job, who had help (וְאֶזְרֹעִי), had abused the יָתוֹם he himself would end up, figuratively at least, without help. Hartley notes that the curse would leave his strength broken, "leaving him helpless" although he does not pick up explicitly on the irony noted above. See Hartley, *Job*, 417.

158. Job 25:2; Clines, *Job 21–37*, 1023.

159. Hartley, *Job*, 417. See also Newsom: "he knows that he would have to answer to one wielding even greater power (v. 22). Once again, the relation between Job and a more vulnerable member of the community is mirrored by Job's relation to God" (Newsom, "Job," 554).

behalf of the marginalized, add further scope to the formative function of the text, in relation to the participation of the church in God's mission. These elements will be drawn out in greater detail in the final section of this chapter.

The Treatment of the Poor, the Book of Job, and the Mission of God

The connection between mission and the poverty theme in Job is predicated on the assumption that the people of God are to be engaged in significant ways in the issues of poverty and justice and that this engagement is understood as being a profoundly missional activity.

It has also been shown in this chapter that the poverty motif, particularly seen in descriptions of the plight and (mis-)treatment of the poor, plays an important role in the development of the book of Job, and especially from Job's perspective as he seeks to question his circumstances and achieve vindication.

This concluding section to the chapter offers some reflection on the theme of poverty in the book of Job as it might relate to the participation of the people of God in the mission of God. Of particular interest is how the book of Job contributes uniquely in this way; that is, not just what Job affirms about broadly held views on poverty, but what the book teaches that is additional to, or even in tension with these.

Michael Barram asks, "In what ways does this text proclaim good news to the poor and release to the captives?"[160] Perhaps a prior question the book of Job poses is whether in fact there *is* good news to be preached to the poor in this particular text. More than any other part of the Bible, Job confronts the reader with the desperate plight of the poor and the brutal reality of oppression. But it also brings these issues into a broader framework exploring the question of God's governance of the world, and how human beings are supposed to live in the light of this.

It is commonplace to think of the book of Job as the literature of struggle and protest. I would propose that as part of this description we might consider the ways in which the book struggles and protests on behalf of the poor. This protest can be conceptualized as challenging five different parties concerning their engagement with the poor: God, the

160. Barram, "'Located' Questions."

friends, the wicked, the self, and the world. How the book does this will shape the content and structure of this concluding reflection.

The Depiction of the Poor in the Book of Job[161]

The book of Job does not flinch in the face of poverty. In various texts the plight of the poor is acknowledged and investigated leading to the identification of several characteristic motifs, which I have summarized as: victimhood, dispossession, hopelessness and advocacy. Before moving to the main missional reflection, a brief review of the motifs connected with the poor would be useful.

Victimhood

In a broad sense, the poor are often understood as victims of oppression and exploitation. Eliphaz recognized that the poor were vulnerably weak and could be exploited by the might of the wicked and, more abstractly, a personified injustice (5:15–16). He also acknowledged that they could be the victim of callous disregard and that their strength and power (such as it was) could easily be crushed (22:9). The poor are seen as victims of the exploitation, overly zealous application and perversion of the debt system (24:2–3, 9). They are the victims of marginalisation (24:4), unscrupulous working conditions (24:10–11), and even murder (24:14).

Often on the receiving end of the attitudes and acts of the wicked, the poor are wronged (24:21), crushed and abandoned (20:19), and trapped like prey in the teeth of the unrighteous (29:17). Clearly the poor were often the victims of exploitation in the legal setting, which relates to the debt system noted above, as well as being implied by texts such as 22:9; 29:11–12, 17; 31:21. To an extent the poor are also seen as victims of the harsh realities of nature, to which they are vulnerable following other aspects of their victimhood (24:7–8).

Finally, Job sees the poor as victims of God. While Elihu considers affliction and adversity to be instruments of God's deliverance and

---

161. I am well aware of the complexities of delineating sociological terms and identities such as "the poor" and "justice." Though sociologically informed, my primary purpose here is not to provide a sociological examination of "the poor" in the time of Job or the supposed setting in Uz. Rather, I am examining the literary and theological personalities as they are presented in Job.

teaching of the poor (34:15), Job focuses instead on the way in which the poor are exploited precisely because God does not hold the wicked to account. Thus, he suggests, the poor are both the victims of the wicked and of God's negligence (24:1).

Dispossession

Related to their victimhood, the poor are described in the book of Job as being dispossessed in a variety of ways. The emphasis with this motif is on what they lose and are deprived of.

Job's terrible new world (or, rather, the world he feels he knows in new and profoundly intensified ways) is one in which widows have their children taken away (6:27; 24:9) and the poor are dispossessed of much needed property (20:19; 24:2-4, 9). Their vulnerability is seen in part in their loss of help and hope (29:12-13; 31:16). The exploitation of others and the more general hostile circumstances of life can lead to the poor being without basic commodities necessary for survival such as food, clothing and shelter (24:5-8, 10-12; 31:16-20). In the extreme case the poor are dispossessed of life itself (24:14).

In the court setting the poor are easily exploited, meaning they are often dispossessed of their legal voice either because they have lost the protection of a patriarchal figure or because their voice carries little weight compared with wealthy opponents (29:12, 16-17; 31:21). Thus, because of the close ties between economic wealth and legal influence, the poor are disempowered to such an extent that they are dispossessed of justice.

As well as these more obvious forms of dispossession other forms of loss and degradation should be noted. These may be categorized into two related areas. First, the poor are to some extent dispossessed of their identity, humanity and dignity. They are treated as objects to be gambled over (6:27); they are marginalized and terrified (24:4); they become like animals in their struggle to survive and in how they are treated by the wicked (24:5-6; 29:17); they experience the ignominy of not being able to provide the basic necessities of life for themselves and their families (24:4-8) and the humiliation of having to work amongst great wealth without the recourse to enjoy it (24:10-11).

The second category may refer to the ways in which the poor are dispossessed of fellowship, community and social standing. The marginalisation they experience at the hands of the wicked (24:4) forces them outside of the normal societal context, as does their need to roam around the wastelands for food rather than in the bosom of the community (24:5–6). How could the poor enjoy the fellowship of a communal meal if they had no food (31:17)? Easily ignored and oppressed, theirs is a shadow existence, moving in and out of society yet maintaining little substance in the community.

Hopelessness

The result of this exploitation and loss is the wretched, desperate plight of the poor. This motif emphasizes the more subjective, though no less real, experience of those trapped in poverty.

The pathetic conditions in which the poor (fail to) eke out an existence exercise Job's mind considerably. Their impotence in the economic and legal spheres (24:2–14) suggests little hope of reversal. They are trapped in a downward spiral of poverty, debt and exploitation. They are hardly able to survive, let alone build for a sustained future. Although Eliphaz sees the intervention of God as giving the poor hope (5:15–16), Job sees no such reason for optimism, unless someone like him is able to get involved (29:12–17; 31:16; cf. 22:9).

Advocacy

Because of their desperate plight and powerlessness, the poor are depicted as being in dire need of advocacy by those in a position to give them help and hope. Being unable to stand up for themselves, they need individuals and communities to act with righteousness and justice and intervene on their behalves.

For Eliphaz and Elihu it is God himself who intervenes by punishing the wicked and rescuing the poor (5:15–16; 36:6).[162] Job, however, focuses on God's lack of intervention, most notably when complaining that God does not keep adequate account of the oppressive deeds of the wicked (24:1–17). Therefore, when one is in a position to intervene effectively, passivity in the face of oppression seems as bad as oppression itself. Eliphaz seems to recognize this when challenging Job about his

---

162. Indeed, for Eliphaz in particular, God is the one who intervenes and Job is the one who has oppressed (22:9). Job reverses this contention.

ethical behavior: Job, he believes, has allowed the orphan's arms to be crushed, presumably when he could have championed his cause (22:9). By contrast, Job maintains that if he had not intervened on their behalf, the poor would still have not been heard or had help (29:12); would have perished or done so more miserably (29:13); would have had no joyful song to sing (29:13); would have starved and been isolated (31:17); and would have been perpetual victims in legal proceedings (31:21).

The plight of the poor is seen to be closely tied to a cycle, or downward spiral of poverty leading to vulnerability and oppression, which in turn leads to further and deeper experiences of poverty. Without intervention the cycle cannot be broken.

Job and Solidarity with the Poor

It seems evident that Job saw himself as occupying a place of solidarity with the poor, thus exhibiting Bauckham's call for the church to mirror the Bible's "downward movement of solidarity with the people at the bottom of the social scale of importance and wealth."[163]

One repeated theme in the book of Job is the way in which Job seems to draw inspiration from the reality and plight of the poor in relation to his own circumstances, and how he uses this motif of poverty to explore his own predicament. Building on the previous section it could be suggested that in some way the motifs of the plight of the poor could also offer ways in which Job understands himself and his relationship with God. Although his mood and beliefs change and develop there are times where Job certainly does struggle with feelings of victimization (for example, 30:16–23), dispossession (29:2–10), hopelessness (17:1–16) and a need for advocacy (19:23–29).[164]

Job seems to have had some sense of solidarity with the poor prior to the catastrophes of the Prologue, as evidenced in the way he engaged with the poor in his former days, mainly through his speeches in chapters 29 to 31. Although there is a degree of power distance between him and the poor in these passages, with Job as the powerful one acting on their behalf, in places the language suggests a degree of mutuality (29:13; 30:25; 31:15).[165] However, following the calamities and the following grief and

---

163. Bauckham, *Bible and Mission*, 54.

164. This could be pressed too far, but it is a suggestive thought nevertheless.

165. "Job, then, sees himself as a father to the poor and enemy of those who seek

vexation, Job experiences an invigorated sense of identity with those who are suffering, as if their plight is now more vivid, intense and personal to him than it had been before. Suddenly he now has

> many counterparts in adversity.... The question he asks of God ceases to be a purely personal one and takes concrete form in the suffering of the poor of this world. The answer he seeks will not come except through commitment to them and by following the road—which God alone knows—that leads to wisdom.[166]

Nothing else has changed in the world yet everything has changed for Job and it is with this new perspective that he looks on the familiar and finds new vexation. In chapter 24, for example, Job articulates the elephant in the room that he seems to have been content to ignore in his former life.

Indeed, it may even be said that Job has a new sense of obligation to speak out on behalf of the poor and despised, now that he relates more fully with them.[167] Suddenly his questions are not just for himself but for the poor as well.[168] And in so doing he is also asking the questions for all humanity, thereby further demonstrating the paradigmatic function I have discussed as part of my missional reading. Job is representative of humanity, embodying the pain and vexation of the human experience and struggling to understand how this relates to a God who assures us that he is governing the world with righteousness and justice. Job asks honest questions on behalf of a hurting world.[169] He is able to because he is uniquely positioned to do so, both in his relationship with God but also through his experiences.

In some way Job seems to provide a model for the people of God to ask these hard questions of God in the midst of our own pain, yet in the context of relationship. Who else can ask these questions? When else do we face up to these questions? Perhaps the crucible of suffering and solidarity, then, provides the necessary context in which to confront what

---

to devour them. He regards himself as upright because he has cultivated a neighborly solidarity with the oppressed and dispossessed" (Gutiérrez, *On Job*, 42). Perhaps Gutiérrez is slightly overstating the case, but it still seems a valid point.

166. Gutiérrez, *On Job*, 31.
167. Gutiérrez, *On Job*, 32. See also Ceresko, "Option for the Poor," 185.
168. Gutiérrez, *On Job*, 34.
169. Brueggemann, *Theology of the OT*, 324; Wright, *Mission of God*, 450–52.

the world needs the people of God to wrestle with. It is to the nature of these confrontations that I now turn.

Ways in Which the Book of Job Challenges on Behalf of the Poor

The theme of the treatment of the poor in Job opens the way to a series of challenges envisioned by the book of Job, and relates closely to the shaping of the church for its participation in God's mission. These challenges relate to God himself, to the false theology of the friends, to the wicked in society, to the self, and to the world at large.

Challenging God

As part of his overall effort to challenge God about his own experience and the seeming lack of God's moral governance in the world, Job questions God about the existence of poverty and injustice. In his former days Job's advocacy on behalf of the poor was seen, among other places, in the court of law. He used his power for their benefit. Now that Job has no power and influence, and is himself in need, his advocacy takes a different form. Now he is advocating for himself, but in doing so he advocates for the poor as well. Out of a place of suffering rather than power, he is able to bring his complaint (and hence the complaint of the whole world) to God.

Perhaps it is precisely because of his (former) close relationship with God, and because of his current circumstances, that Job was uniquely positioned to ask such questions of God. He does so not only for himself and for the poor but, in a sense, for humanity as a whole.

Job's deep pathos with the poor occurs because he has been confronted personally with injustice in a way that has opened his eyes to a much more troubled perspective on what was there all along. Why does God allow oppression, abuse, corruption, suffering and poverty to go unpunished?

Job 24 is a crucial text in this regard, depicting as it does the desperate plight of the poor and the wickedness that so often causes and exploits this poverty.[170] While I would not claim that Job is right in his

---

170. Job's speeches in chapters 21 and 24 seem to be crucial in the debate because they name the obvious flaws in the cause-consequence theology. In echoes of so-called prosperity theology, Job points out that the emperor has no clothes: the tight

assertions at all times, he is surely correct to bring the issue to bear. This form of lament and questioning is an essential part of relating to God in that it maintains a *"genuine covenant interaction"* that enables humanity to engage with God in all experiences of life, rather than just the joyful ones.[171] It also guards against a *"stifling of the question of theodicy,"* which could have dangerous repercussions for public discourse on questions of justice.[172]

In challenging God, Job tries to provoke him into action on behalf of himself but also, in the broader scheme, on behalf of the poor, as exemplified in the movement between pathetic description and calls for retribution in chapter 24. It is not, as will be shown, that Job is uninterested in the culpability of the wicked in the sins of oppression. Rather, Job sees the ultimate moral arbiter as not carrying out his responsibilities thoroughly enough.[173] In confronting God (or trying to at least) with the plight of the poor, Job is giving their cries a voice.[174]

Later in the book Job will repent of the presumptuous claims he has made in the dialogue (42:1–6). However, this does not delegitimize the questions he has brought to bear.[175]

Challenging the Friends

Throughout the dialogue Job contends with his comforters (though he never interacts with Elihu) and challenges their simplistic assumptions about the nature of the causes and consequences of sin and suffering. It has been shown that the question of social injustice became a pivotal theme in the developing dialogue, especially in chapters 20 to 24.

---

relationship between cause and consequence plainly does match reality.

171. Brueggemann, "Costly Loss," 60. My thinking on the church's responsibility to lament before God on behalf of the world was crystalized by a devotional talk given by Sheryl Haw, Micah Network's International Director, at Redcliffe College some years ago. See also the recent work of Ross, "Lament and Hope."

172. Brueggemann, "Costly Loss," 61.

173. "For the sake of the dying wounded, and for the sake of a world that should be more than an open grave, Job believes that covenantal fidelity requires a courageous indictment of injustice, even if it means rebelling against the Creator who sees nothing wrong" (Balentine, *Job*, 370).

174. See also the connection with the exodus in Job 24, discussed above.

175. See my final reflection on the Yahweh speeches below.

Job's experience has left him deeply dissatisfied with the attempts of his friends to make sense of his life and, consequently, the governance of God in the world. By challenging the friends, Job confronts what he perceives as simplistic and inadequate talk about God. Instead he advocates for an honest assessment of the dissonance between what is believed and what is experienced. Through his suffering Job has undergone a paradigm shift in how he views the relationship between his deeds and their inevitable reward; trying to convince his friends of his new perspective, which now seems so obvious, is a task that he must undertake, but ultimately fails to do.[176] Nevertheless, the book of Job calls on the people of God to challenge false assumptions about God's dealings with the world when they are exposed as inadequate, even if in doing so cherished beliefs are questioned.[177]

On behalf of himself and the poor, Job confronts the friends with the inadequacy of their theology. In so doing he gives a voice and a dignity to their suffering, and forces those with over-simplistic theology to face the limitations of their views.[178]

Challenging the Wicked

Although Job's primary focus is on the God who seems to let the wicked get away with all manner of social injustices, the book of Job nevertheless includes a theme of challenge to the wicked. This can be seen in two ways. First, through his defence of his former life, Job sets out elements of what he considered to be an appropriate response to seeing social injustice for a person in a position of power (cf. 29:11–17; 31:13–23). One of Job's commendable actions was to confront the wicked, sometimes with force, to free those being exploited (29:12, 17).

Secondly, and less directly, since the calamities Job also opens up a new challenge to the wicked by protesting against their success and injustice (21:7–34; 24:1–17) and calling on God to bring vindication and justice (24:18–25).

---

176. See Newsom, *Contest*, for an exploration of the enormity of the gap between Job's perspective and theirs.

177. See Newsom, "Job," 382.

178. One issue which has some contemporary resonances with the friends' misapplication of cause and consequence is that of the "prosperity teaching" roundly criticized, for example, in Wright, *Cape Town Commitment*, 63, 65.

Challenging the Self

Three challenges can be detected in the book of Job concerning the self in relation to poverty and injustice. The first can be seen in Job's review of his past life and his defence of his righteousness and justice. In such a review there is an implicit challenge to the self to examine one's own actions and attitudes towards the poor and marginalized. From his own perspective he passes the test of self-examination. Both in what he has done (for example, 29:11–17) and in what he has refrained from doing (chapter 31) Job is satisfied, although it is not until chapter 42 that Job reaches some kind of resolution in his own mind concerning Yahweh's actions.

But what of the reader? With its vision of social ethics the one encountering the book of Job must ask themselves the same questions, and prepare to be challenged as to their own ethical standards.[179]

A second challenge that could be evoked is a more implicit, even anachronous one. For all his empathy with the poor and efforts to address their circumstances, Job never seems to question either the effect of his wealth on them or the societal system in which he played a formidable part. These seem to me to be anachronistic questions that have the potential to lead the reader away from the core message of the book.[180] However, while not the primary issue within the book's overt dealings with injustice, the suspicions of some as to the motives and presuppositions of Job do raise important questions about the systemic nature of the poverty and oppression cycle.

While it may be unfair and anachronous to question Job's unquestioning complicity in the social structures of his world it would seem appropriate for the reader to consider their own complicity in unjust structures.[181] To what extent are we complicit in, as well as working against injustices?

A third challenge is for the church to walk alongside the poor and participate in their suffering as a means of solidarity, eschewing a purely arm's length engagement with social justice issues.[182]

---

179. For an example of what this might look like, see Ellen Davis's discussion on complicity and the cursing Psalms in Davis, *Getting Involved with God*, 28–29.

180. See, for example, Wilson's discussion on this question, in Wilson, *Job*, 344–46.

181. See Van Zyl, "Missiological Dimensions," 29–30.

182. Míguez-Bonino, "Poverty as Curse, Blessing, and Challenge," 11.

Challenging the World

In what ways (implicitly or explicitly) does the book of Job contribute towards an engagement with issues of poverty? How is the individual or community to respond when confronted with the sometimes brutal realities of poverty in the world? A number of themes can be discerned from the Joban material under discussion, which I present as: acknowledgement; lament; telling the story of poverty; and interventional ethics.

Acknowledgement

One response to poverty, of course, is to ignore it. This has never been an option for Job who claims to have engaged with the issue from an early age (31:18). There seems to be an inherent tension in chapters 29 to 31 in that Job was able to work for the poor without feeling the need to question why God allowed them to be oppressed in the first place. Following the calamities of chapters 1 and 2 he now views the world differently, and the issue of poverty becomes a fundamentally troubling question (24:1). For Job, the phenomenon of poverty, suffering and oppression had become heavily loaded and needed to be acknowledged by his interlocutors, as well as by God himself.

For Elihu God is the one who hears the cry of the poor and afflicted (34:28), yet Job dares to suggest that God fails to do so (24:1, 12). The first step to tackling poverty and injustice is to acknowledge that it exists and needs addressing.

Lament

At one point in his reflection on his former life Job says that he wept and grieved for the poor (30:25). This is a rare insight into how Job felt about the poor. Most of the material reflects on his actions on their behalf and we are left to infer his emotional connection to them. This particular text seems designed to shame God: Job responded rightly to the unfortunate, yet when Job was in trouble, God refused to meet him in comfort and rescue (30:20). Moreover, Job accuses God of cruelty and persecution (30:21–22).

As well as this explicit comment, Job's heartfelt response to poverty can be discerned through his descriptions of the plight of the poor in the main texts examined above. There seems to be genuine pathos in his language, especially chapter 24. Job now sits with the poor and sees his unjust treatment echoed and exposed in more general injustice.

To push the boundaries of the language, Job might say that to truly understand and engage with brokenness one must be broken oneself.

Telling the Story of Poverty

It is not enough for Job to face up to poverty himself. Albeit in the context of proving his argument, Job tells the story of the poor to force recognition in his interlocutors (24:1–17). Should not his comforters be similarly grieved and vexed by the phenomenon of poverty, suffering and oppression in the world?

While Job advocates for the poor in formal settings (see discussion below) it should be noted that Job's response to the plight of the poor is in part to voice their plight, with great eloquence and pathos. How else will they be heard?

Interventional Ethics: Protection, Provision and Restoration

As well as acknowledging and grieving over the cries of the poor, Job describes ways in which he intervened on their behalf. Largely in his final speech of chapters 29 to 31, Job sets out his ethic. Through direct claim and implication Job outlines what actions could and should be taken on behalf of the poor including: rescue (29:12, 17); relief and provision (29:13, 15; 31:16–20); a meeting of need (29:15); a pursuit of legal justice (29:15–16; 31:21); and the giving of hope (31:16).

In these deeds Job shows some of the ways in which he sought to bring transformation to the lives of the poor and vulnerable. With reference to his description of the realities of poverty above, Job addressed their sense of victimhood, dispossession, hopelessness and need for advocacy. As such he is instrumental in breaking the cycle of poverty and oppression, for some at least.

The key idea driving his ethics is 29:14 in which he talks of the intimate relationship (embodiment, even) between himself and the concept of righteousness and justice. He did not do his ethics purely out of duty or at a distance. His attitude and actions towards the poor and vulnerable flowed out of his identity, as he sought to live out kingly and divine values.

A missional reading of Job, as I have conceived it, therefore places the suffering of the believer within the hopeful context of transformational encounter with Yahweh. We articulate our pain and the pain of the world before God, as only the people of God are able to do. The book of Job suggests that facing up to the experience of unattributed suffering, with all the attendant vexation, weakness and confusion, is an inevitable, indeed, necessary part of our participation in God's mission. It is this pain that leads us into a more meaningful solidarity with and advocacy on behalf of the suffering. Yet even while the lament goes on, we also find ourselves as dust and ashes, committing ourselves and others to the wisdom of Yahweh and, therefore, to Yahweh himself.

7

Summary and Conclusions

THIS FINAL CHAPTER HAS three aims. First, I provide a brief summary of the overall aim and content of the study. Secondly, I revisit the three aspects of the missional nature of the Bible outlined in chapter 1: the Bible as a product, record and means of mission. However, I now apply the categories specifically to Job in order to draw out my findings. Thirdly, I discuss the contribution of this study to scholarship, and consider the missional hermeneutics conversation in particular.

Summary

The aim of this study has been to develop and apply a missional hermeneutic to the book of Job; that is, to offer a reading of Job in the light of the missional nature of the Bible. Chapters 1 to 3 set out to approach a missional hermeneutic for Job. In the introductory chapter I set the initial context for this reading by clarifying my understanding of Christian mission to include the concepts of *missio Dei* and holistic mission. Drawing on the emerging conversation on missional hermeneutics, I then set out how different dimensions of biblical texts might be understood as missional, addressing the concepts of the Bible as a product, record and means of mission.

In chapter 2 I gave a detailed analysis of the ways in which the book of Job has featured in previous scholarship that has sought to bring together the Bible and mission, especially those works aiming to set out a biblical theology of mission. A significant proportion of such works either did not engage with Job at all or did so in rather peripheral and underdeveloped ways. However, a good number of studies did make at least some mention of Job and I was able to isolate a number of themes on which scholars concentrated when addressing the book. For each theme I assessed scholars' use of Job and pointed to ways in which my study differed from them, either through a development of the theme or because I chose not to incorporate it significantly within the scope of my work.

Through this survey I discerned significant room left by scholarship and concluded that the time is ripe for a more intentional, substantial, sustained and nuanced treatment of Job in the light of the missional nature of the Bible. I also suggested that missional hermeneutics provides a promising approach for just such a project.

But precisely how should a more intentional, substantial, sustained and nuanced treatment of Job and mission proceed? This was the purpose of chapter 3 in which I provided a framework for a missional reading of Job developed through an engagement with the emerging conversation on missional hermeneutics. This chapter, therefore, examined the different approaches taken by advocates of missional hermeneutics, focusing on two main categories in particular: the relationship between the text and the *missio Dei*; and the way the text forms the people of God for participating in the *missio Dei*. Although overlapping at some important points (especially in their use of the *missio Dei* concept), these approaches are somewhat varied and, in my view, uneven in places. My treatment in chapter 3 led me to develop my own approach to Job that adopted and adapted certain elements of the missional hermeneutics conversation, in a way that made them most appropriate for a reading of the book of Job, within the scope of this book. I therefore concluded the chapter with several lines of inquiry for a missional reading of Job, which were followed through in the rest of the study. These lines included the relationship between Job and the *missio Dei*; the function of a universalizing impulse within Job; the way in which Job contributes to an articulation of a Yahweh-shaped rendering of reality (over and against other renderings) in relation to the question of unattributed suffering; and the way in which the treatment of the poor functions within Job. At several points these issues also connected with the idea of Job as a text that shapes and equips its audience for their participation in the mission of God.

Taking on these themes, chapters 4 to 6 sought to apply a missional hermeneutic to the book of Job. In chapter 4 I paid particular attention to the universalizing impulse evident in Job. This involved a detailed treatment of the significance of the non-Israelite theme in the book, and the way in which this motif, along with others, sets up the book as of universal (and therefore missional) significance. This tied my discussion particularly closely to the way in which the book of Job relates to the *missio Dei*. Of special note was the question of the accuser in 1:9b ("Is it for nothing חִנָּם that Job fears God?") which, in my view, challenged the very legitimacy of the *missio Dei*. In the book of Job, I concluded, the very mission of God is questioned and vindicated.

In chapter 5 I then moved the discussion in a different, though related direction, which was to consider how the book of Job related to similar texts in the ANE. While this demonstrated that Job was in a long-established tradition of reflections on unattributed suffering, I also showed, crucially, that the book exhibits some important Israelite distinctives. This is evident especially in the monotheistic assumptions driving the book, seen especially in the Yahweh speeches in chapters 38 to 41.

Chapter 6 continued my missional reading of Job in an important direction. Given my holistic understanding of mission, the treatment of the poor became a clearly appropriate subject of study. While continuing some of the themes evident in chapters 4 and 5 (for example, Job as a universalized figure) it also set them in the context of a particular thematic study. While others have noted the theme of poverty in Job, my framing of it in the context of mission enabled me to tie the ethical teaching on poverty in the book to the shaping of the Christian Church's participation in the *missio Dei*. In this regard, I concluded the chapter by setting out a series of challenges made by the book: challenges to God, to Job's friends, to the wicked, to the self, and to the world.

The Missional Dimensions of the Book of Job

In chapter 1 I defined a missional hermeneutic as an approach to biblical interpretation that seeks to read texts in the light of the missional nature of the Bible. The result of my application of a missional hermeneutic to Job is that I am able to articulate more fully than has hitherto been achieved some of the ways in which the book might be described as missional. To show this I will return to the three aspects of the missional nature of the Bible outlined in chapter 1, but now with specific reference to the book of Job. Although there are some elements of overlap between the three categories, I prefer to keep them distinct for the purposes of clarity.

Job as a Product of God's Mission

That such a sustained and probing examination of unattributed suffering is part of Scripture says something profoundly important for the mission of God. In my view the inclusion of the book of Job acknowledges such vexing and intense human experiences, and legitimizes serious attempts to engage with them in a constructive manner. As such, Israelite sages are seen to be contributing to an established international conversation on suffering, and offering a probing of the issue that is shaped by faith in Yahweh. The very existence of the book of Job declares that Yahweh takes the universal experience of human suffering seriously. This would suggest that the book similarly obligates the Church to engage with this issue with honesty and integrity as part of our participation in the mission of God.

The way in which the book of Job sets itself up as being universally relevant is also significant. Israel's perspective on unattributed suffering is not to be understood as applicable only within the borders of Israel, even if this is assumed to be the book's primary audience. The universalizing motif present in the book appears to make a claim that the book "speaks to and for all humanity"; that is, Israel's answers are the world's answers.[1]

Implicit in this universal appeal of the book, however, is a critique of explanations for unattributed suffering that are not governed by a belief in Israelite monotheism. As such the book of Job exhibits a missional encounter with alternative belief systems. While affirming certain aspects of alternative treatments (in literary form and certain thematic elements) the book of Job offers a contrasting and distinctive understanding of the issues in line with Israel's faith in Yahweh. Ultimately it offers a deeper probing of the question of unattributed suffering, while also pointing forward to hope in Yahweh himself. As such it exhibits the way in which the Bible may be understood as a monotheizing or Yahwizing literature, contributing to an articulation of a rendering of reality shaped by Yahweh faith, which is voiced over and against competing renderings.

Job and the Story of God's Mission

How does the book of Job relate to the *missio Dei*? An important qualification I have articulated in my treatment of this theme is that, contrary

---

1. Pope, *Job*, xxxviii.

to how it is often understood, it is not sufficient to ask simply how a text fits into and progresses the chronological storyline of God's mission. For a book like Job this line of questioning will be of limited value, not least because of the complexities of its compositional origins, but also because it does not record events that progress the "plot" of the biblical story. Instead I have preferred to ask the question, in what ways does this text relate to the story of God's mission? A distinctive contribution of the book of Job to thinking about the biblical story is, I have concluded, to ask how the book stands apart from, and speaks into that story. The book of Job is vital to the missional story of the Bible, the *missio Dei*, because it probes a necessary yet uncomfortable question: is the relationship to which God is restoring humanity genuine?

As the book of Job reaches its climax it responds to the essential question by vindicating both Job and Yahweh and, in doing so, vindicates the *missio Dei* itself.

Job as a Means of God's Mission

In what ways did the book of Job seek to shape and equip the people of God for their participation in the *missio Dei*? Moreover, how might Job be continuing "to confront, to convert, and to transform the [church] for faithful witness?"[2] Within the scope of this study I have identified a number of ways in which the book of Job functions formatively for mission.

While Job occupied a unique place in the questioning and vindication of the validity of the mission of God, his representative or paradigmatic function identified particularly in chapters 4 and 5 contributes to formative ways in which the people of God may process unattributed suffering "missionally." That is, though suffering may appear purposeless it may be faced purposefully. Unlike the approach of Waters, I do not restrict the missional potential of such experience solely to submission and acceptance, missionally appropriate though these responses may be. Rather, I understand the book of Job to be providing a model of a faithful believer in Yahweh who, in his mixed responses of acceptance, grief, confusion and fury, witnesses to a genuine, committed, honest engagement with his God. Ultimately, this seems to me to witness to a more complete

---

2. Guder, "Biblical Formation," 62.

picture of faith and, as such, offers to a watching world a more compelling vision of life with God.

The suffering people of God, then, may understand themselves to be in a painfully privileged space. With the rest of the world we experience the ambiguities and pain of human experience, yet we do so as conscious participants in the *missio Dei*. Moreover we are uniquely placed to articulate our pain to God and, following Job, to do so on behalf of the world. This is one way in which the church may carry out its missional mandate to agonize with the world's victims.[3] Protest and complaint in all its particularities before God, therefore, may be understood as being just as missionally significant as acceptance and submission. However, the book of Job also suggests that God is more than a sounding board for the world's pain. Job's way of understanding his experiences is transformed through his encounter with Yahweh, which leads him to reframe his view of the world from a principle of retribution to that of wisdom, and the fear of Yahweh.

This dismantling of the retribution principle has significant missional implications, not least through the church's engagement with poverty. In chapter 6 I rooted the discussion in the poverty theme in Job. Acknowledging the importance of poverty issues in a holistic conception of mission, the book of Job may be understood as seeking to shape the church by issuing a series of challenges. In the light of the book of Job the church must consider how we enter into solidarity with the poor and advocate alongside them concerning unjust structures and practices. Job issues a call to the church to acknowledge poverty, to lament over it, to articulate it, and to practice interventional ethics in terms of protection, provision and restoration. Crucially it requires the church to critique false beliefs and assumptions concerning the poor, whether this is observed in society in general or within Christian theology and practice. As such the church should examine itself to consider possible ways in which we are complicit in the exploitation of the poor.

This outline of the different missional dimensions of the book of Job demonstrates how my work has brought the missional nature of Job into sharper focus. As such my conviction expressed in chapter 1 that Job warrants greater missional attention seems vindicated. Related to this, I will now set out the contribution of this study to scholarship.

---

3. Bosch, "Hermeneutical Principles," 450.

The Contribution of This Study to Scholarship

I hope that this volume will encourage deeper reflection on the book of Job and mission, as well as helping to develop the missional hermeneutics conversation. As is evident, my study owes a great debt to scholars engaging in missional hermeneutics, and I hope it provides a useful case study in applying this very fruitful approach to biblical interpretation. Through my application of a missional hermeneutic to the book of Job, I have demonstrated that it is not only possible, but also beneficial and important for biblical scholars and missiologists to read Job missionally. By bringing the missional significance of Job into sharper focus, the approach has shown how Job can and should be considered more intentionally and more substantially when relating the Bible and mission, and that missional hermeneutics can be usefully employed to provide an appropriate framework.

More specifically, it seems to me that my study points the missional hermeneutics conversation forward in a number of important ways. First, while the approach of missional hermeneutics as a whole has been shown to be effective, this study has also highlighted some limitations in the conversation. Although still emerging, it seems that the conversation has not yet paid sufficient attention to texts that do not fit neatly within and progress the chronological storyline of the *missio Dei*. Perhaps one reason for this is the way in which the question concerning the *missio Dei* has been framed, implying that a text must be shown to fit into the missional narrative of the Bible. By asking the question, "How does this text stand apart from, and speak into the grand narrative?" my treatment of Job has shown how framing the question slightly differently can prove very effective in understanding the relationship between a text and the *missio Dei*. Put simply, different texts may require different types of questions to bring out their missional significance most fully.

Secondly, more consistent and detailed work should be carried out on the ANE background of texts. As I demonstrated in chapter 5, such insights enable the monotheizing process of the text to be seen much more clearly and aid the articulation of Yahweh's transcendent uniqueness. In so doing, we are able to gain greater insights into the text's missional origins and context, and, therefore, its contemporary missional relevance.

Thirdly, building on the discussion in chapter 3, scholars should probe more deeply the question of how Old Testament texts feature and engage with non-Israelites. As I have sought to do with Job, more nuanced questions should be asked about the significance of their non-Israelite status and how we are to think of them in relation to the *missio Dei*.

The final and, in my view, most significant challenge to those working in the field of missional hermeneutics encompasses both an affirmation of the approach and a call to action. That missional hermeneutics facilitates a fruitful reading of a text like Job should be a significant encouragement to missional hermeneutics scholars. However, I would also argue that its emergence has profound implications for BMS because it gives scholars the tools actively to seek out texts that cannot be fitted into the chronological storyline of the *missio Dei* as simply as those often treated. It is therefore the responsibility of missional hermeneutics scholars to actively pursue readings of texts that have hitherto been marginalized or neglected. If we take up this challenge, I am convinced that many new insights will be gained for the academy and the church.

Although my concentration has been on the contribution of my study to BMS, such a missional reading also has implications for more general Job scholarship. By bringing into sharper focus the ways in which the book of Job may be considered as missional, I have provided a fresh perspective from which to read the book. If this study has made it more likely that missional questions will be on the agenda of more general biblical scholarship, then it has served its purpose well.

Bibliography

Albright, William F. "Northwest-Semitic Names in a List of Egyptian Slaves from the Eighteenth Century BC." *Journal of the American Oriental Society* 74 (1954) 223–33.
Alden, Robert L. *Job*. Nashville: B&H, 1993.
Allen, Joel S. "Job 3: History of Interpretation." In *DOTWPW* 361–71.
Allen, Roland. *Missionary Methods: St. Paul's or Ours?* London: Robert Scott, 1912.
Allen, Wayne W. "The Missionary Message of Job: God's Universal Concern For Healing." *Caribbean Journal of Evangelical Theology* 6 (2002) 18–31.
Alter, Robert. *The Wisdom Books: Job, Proverbs, and Ecclesiastes: A Translation with Commentary*. New York: Norton, 2010.
Anderson, Francis I. *Job: An Introduction and Commentary*. Leicester: InterVarsity, 1976.
Balentine, Samuel E. *Job*. Macon: Smyth & Helwys, 2006.
Barr, James. *The Concept of Biblical Theology: An Old Testament Perspective*. London: SCM, 1999.
Barram, Michael. "The Bible, Mission, and Social Location: Toward a Missional Hermeneutic." *Interpretation* 61 (2007) 42–58.
———. "'Located' Questions for a Missional Hermeneutic." *Gospel and Our Culture Network*, November 1, 2006. Online. https://gocn.org/library/95.
———. *Missional Economics: Biblical Justice and Christian Formation*. Grand Rapids: Eerdmans, 2018.
———. "A Response at AAR to Hunsberger's 'Proposals' Essay." Paper presented at the Annual Meeting of the American Academy of Religion, Chicago, IL, November 1, 2008. Online. https://gocn.org/library/a-response-at-aar-to-hunsbergers-proposals-essay.
Bartholomew, Craig G., and Michael W. Goheen. "Story and Biblical Theology." In *Out of Egypt: Biblical Theology and Biblical Interpretation*, edited by Craig G. Bartholomew et al., 144–71. Grand Rapids: Zondervan, 2004.
Bashford, James. *God's Missionary Plan for the World*. London: Robert Culley, 1907.
Bauckham, Richard. *Bible and Mission: Christian Witness in a Postmodern World*. Carlisle: Paternoster, 2003.
———. "Biblical Theology and the Problems of Monotheism." In *Out of Egypt: Biblical Theology and Biblical Interpretation*, edited by Craig G. Bartholomew et al., 187–232. Grand Rapids: Zondervan, 2004.

———. *Mission as Hermeneutic for Scriptural Interpretation*. Currents in World Christianity Position Paper 106. Cambridge: Cambridge Centre for Worldwide Christianity, 1999.

Bavinck, Johan H. *An Introduction to the Science of Missions*. Translated by David H. Freeman. Philadelphia: Presbyterian and Reformed, 1960.

Beeby, H. Daniel. *Canon and Mission*. Harrisburg, PA: Trinity, 1999.

———. *Mission and Missions*. London: Christian Education Movement, 1979.

———. "A Missional Approach to Renewed Interpretation." In *Renewing Biblical Interpretation*, edited by Craig G. Bartholomew et al., 268–83. Carlisle: Paternoster, 2000.

Bekele, Girma. "The Biblical Narrative of the *Missio Dei*: Analysis of the Interpretive Framework of David Bosch's Missional Hermeneutic." *International Bulletin of Missionary Research* 35.3 (2011) 153–58.

Bennett, Harold V. *Injustice Made Legal: Deuteronomic Law and the Plight of Widows, Strangers, and Orphans in Ancient Israel*. Grand Rapids: Eerdmans, 2002.

Bevans, Stephen B., and Roger P. Schroeder. *Constants in Context: A Theology of Mission for Today*. Maryknoll, NY: Orbis, 2004.

Blackburn, W. Ross. *The God Who Makes Himself Known: The Missionary Heart of the Book of Exodus*. Nottingham: Apollos, 2012.

Blauw, Johannes. *The Missionary Nature of the Church: A Survey of the Biblical Theology of Mission*. London: Lutterworth, 1962.

Block, Daniel I. *Ezekiel 1–20*. Grand Rapids: Eerdmans, 1997.

Booth, Wayne C. *The Rhetoric of Fiction*. Chicago: University of Chicago Press, 1961.

Bosch, David J. "Hermeneutical Principles in the Biblical Foundation for Mission." *Evangelical Review of Theology* 17.4 (1993) 437–51.

———. "Mission in Biblical Perspective." *International Review of Mission* 74.296 (1985) 531–38.

———. "Reflections on Biblical Models of Mission." In *Toward the Twenty-First Century in Christian Mission*, edited by James M. Phillips and Robert T. Coote, 175–92. Grand Rapids: Eerdmans, 1993.

———. "The Scope of the 'BISAM' Project." *Mission Studies* 6.1 (1989) 61–68.

———. "The Scope of Mission." *International Review of Mission* 73.289 (1984) 17–32.

———. "Towards a Hermeneutic of 'Biblical Studies and Mission.'" *Mission Studies* 3.2 (1986) 65–79.

———. *Transforming Mission: Paradigm Shifts in Theology of Mission*. Maryknoll, NY: Orbis, 1991.

———. "The Vulnerability of Mission." *The Baptist Quarterly* 34.8 (1992) 351–63.

———. "The Why and the How of a True Biblical Foundation for Mission." In *Zending Op Weg Naar De Toekomst*, edited by Johannes Verkuyl, 33–45. Kampen: J. H. Kok, 1978.

———. *Witness to the World: The Christian Mission in Theological Perspective*. London: Marshall, Morgan & Scott, 1980.

Botterweck, G. Johannes, and Helmer Ringgren, eds. *Theological Dictionary of the Old Testament*. 14 vols. Translated by Geoffrey W. Bromiley et al. Grand Rapids: Eerdmans, 1974–2004.

Brenner, Athalya. "Job the Pious? The Characterization of Job in the Narrative Framework of the Book." *JSOT* 43 (1989) 37–52.

Bricker, Daniel P. "Innocent Suffering in Egypt." *TB* 52.1 (2001) 83–100.

———. "Innocent Suffering in Mesopotamia." *TB* 51.2 (2000) 193–214.
Brown, Francis, et al. *The Brown-Driver-Briggs Hebrew and English Lexicon*. Peabody: Hendrickson, 2007.
Brown, William P. *Character in Crisis: A Fresh Approach to the Wisdom Literature of the Old Testament*. Grand Rapids: Eerdmans, 1996.
Brownson, James V. "A Response at SBL to Hunsberger's 'Proposals' Essay." Paper presented at the Annual Meeting of the Society of Biblical Literature, Boston, MA, November 22, 2008. Online. https://gocn.org/library/a-response-at-sbl-to-hunsbergers-proposals-essay.
———. *Speaking the Truth in Love: New Testament Resources for a Missional Hermeneutic*. Harrisburg: Trinity, 1998.
Brueggemann, Walter. "The Costly Loss of Lament." *JSOT* 36 (1986) 57–71.
———. "Theodicy in a Social Dimension." *JSOT* 33 (1985) 3–25.
———. *Theology of the Old Testament: Testimony, Dispute, Advocacy*. Minneapolis: Augsburg Fortress, 1997.
Burnett, David. *The Healing of the Nations: The Biblical Basis of the Mission of God*. 2nd ed. Carlisle: Paternoster, 1996.
Campbell, Evvy H., ed. *Holistic Mission*. Lausanne Occasional Paper 33. Pattaya, Thailand: Lausanne Committee for World Evangelization, 2004. Online. http://www.lausanne.org/docs/2004forum/LOP33_IG4.pdf.
Carroll Rodas, M. Daniel, "דלל." In *NIDOTTE* 1:951–54.
Carter, Charles W. "The Book of Job." In vol. 2 of *Wesleyan Bible Commentary*, edited by Charles W. Carter, 1–176. Grand Rapids: Eerdmans, 1968.
Carver, William O. *The Bible a Missionary Message: A Study of Activities and Methods*. New York: Fleming H. Revell, 1921.
———. *Missions in the Plan of the Ages: Bible Studies in Missions*. New York: Fleming H. H. Revell, 1909.
Ceresko, Anthony R. *Psalmists and Sages: Studies in Old Testament Poetry and Religion*. Bangalore: St. Peter's Pontifical Institute, 1994.
Chisholm, Robert B. "The Polemic Against Baalism in Israel's Early History and Literature." *Bibliotheca Sacra* 150 (1994) 267–83.
Clarke, Benjamin. "Misery Loves Company: A Comparative Analysis of Theodicy Literature in Ancient Mesopotamia and Israel." *Intermountain West Journal of Religious Studies* 2.1 (2010) 78–92.
Claydon, David. "Holistic Mission." In *Global Dictionary of Theology*, edited by William A. Dyrness and Veli-Matti Kärkkäinen, 402–4. Nottingham: InterVarsity, 2008.
Clements, Ronald E. *Wisdom in Theology*. Carlisle: Paternoster, 1992.
Clifford, Richard J. *The Wisdom Literature*. Nashville: Abingdon, 1998.
Clines, David J. A. "False Naivety in the Prologue to Job." In vol. 2 of *On the Way to Postmodern: Old Testament Essays, 1967–1998*, 735–44. Sheffield: Sheffield Academic, 1998.
———. *Job 1–20*. Nashville: Thomas Nelson, 1989.
———. *Job 21–37*. Nashville: Thomas Nelson, 2006.
———. *Job 38–42*. Nashville: Thomas Nelson, 2011.
———. "Job's Fifth Friend: An Ethical Critique of the Book of Job." *Biblical Interpretation* 12.3 (2004) 233–50.

———. "Why Is There a Book of Job, and What Does It Do to You If You Read It?" In *The Book of Job*, edited by Wim A. M. Beuken, 1–20. Leuven: Leuven University Press.

Cornhill, C. H. *Einleitung in das Alte Testament mit Einschluss der Apokryphen und Pseudepigraphen*. 2nd ed. Freiburg: Mohr, 1896.

Corrie, John, ed. *Dictionary of Mission Theology: Evangelical Foundations*. Nottingham: InterVarsity, 2007.

Crenshaw, James L. "Job, Book of." In *ABD* 3:858–68.

———. *Old Testament Wisdom: An Introduction*. 3rd ed. Louisville: Westminster John Knox, 2010.

———. *Reading Job: A Literary and Theological Commentary*. Macon: Smyth & Helwys, 2011.

Davidson, Andrew B. *The Book of Job*. Cambridge: Cambridge University Press, 1889.

Davies, Ellen F. *Getting Involved with God: Rediscovering the Old Testament*. Plymouth: Cowley, 2001.

Davy, Tim J., and Michael W. Goheen. "Missional Hermeneutics Bibliography." In *Reading the Bible Missionally*, edited by Michael W. Goheen, 330–38. Grand Rapids: Eerdmans, 2016.

Day, John. "Baal (Deity)." In *ABD* 1:545–49.

———. "How Could Job Be an Edomite?" In *The Book of Job*, edited by Wim A. M. Beuken, 392–99.

Dell, Katherine. *"Get Wisdom, Get Insight": An Introduction to Israel's Wisdom Literature*. Macon: Smyth & Helwys, 2000.

Dhorme, Édouard. *A Commentary on the Book of Job*. Translated by Harold Knight. London: Thomas Nelson, 1967.

Domeris, W. R. "אֶבְיוֹן." In *NIDOTTE* 1:228–32.

Driver, Samuel R., and George B. Gray. *A Critical and Exegetical Commentary on the Book of Job*. 2 vols. Edinburgh: T & T Clark, 1921.

Duguid, Ian M. *Ezekiel*. Grand Rapids: Zondervan, 1999.

Dumbrell, William J. "עָנִי." In *NIDOTTE* 3:454–64.

Duquoc, Christian. "Demonism and the Unexpectedness of God." *Concilium* 169 (1983) 81–87.

Eakin, Frank E. "Wisdom, Creation and Covenant." *Perspectives in Religious Studies* 4 (1977) 226–39.

Eaton, John H. *Job*. Sheffield: Sheffield Academic, 1985.

Endris, Vince. "Yahweh versus Baal: A Narrative-Critical Reading of the Gideon/Abimelech Narrative." *JSOT* 33.2 (2008) 173–95.

Enns, Peter E. *Exodus*. Grand Rapids: Zondervan, 2000.

Estes, Daniel J. *Handbook on the Wisdom Books and Psalms*. Grand Rapids: Baker Academic, 2005.

Fabry, Heinz-Joseph. "דַּל *dal*." In *TDOT* 3:208–30.

Filbeck, David. *Yes, God of the Gentiles, Too: The Missionary Message of the Old Testament*. Wheaton: Billy Graham Center, 1994.

Flemming, Dean. "Revelation and the *Missio Dei*: Toward a Missional Reading of the Apocalypse." *Journal of Theological Interpretation* 6.2 (2012) 161–78.

Flett, John G. *The Witness of God: The Trinity, "Missio Dei," Karl Barth, and the Nature of Christian Community*. Grand Rapids: Eerdmans, 2010.

Freedman, David Noel, ed. *Anchor Bible Dictionary*. 6 vols. New York: Doubleday, 1992.

Fretheim, Terence E. "חנן." In *NIDOTTE* 2:203–6.
Gerstenberger, Erhart S. "אבה *'bh* to want." In *TLOT* 1:15–19.
———. "עָנָה II *'ānâ*." In *TDOT* 11:230–52.
Gesenius, Wilhelm. *Gesenius's Hebrew and Chaldee Lexicon to the Old Testament Scriptures*. Translated by Samuel P. Tregelles. London: S. Bagster and Sons, 1857.
Glaser, Ida. *The Bible and Other Faiths: What Does the Lord Require of Us?* Leicester: InterVarsity, 2005.
———. *Trauma, Migration, and Mission: Biblical Reflections from a Traumatized Hebrew*. Oxford: Church Mission Society, 2008.
Glasser, Arthur F., et al. *Announcing the Kingdom: The Story of God's Mission in the Bible*. Grand Rapids: Baker, 2003.
Glover, Robert H. *The Bible Basis of Missions*. Chicago: Moody, 1946.
Goheen, Michael W. "Bible and Mission: Missiology and Biblical Scholarship in Dialogue." In *Christian Mission: Old Testament Foundations and New Testament Developments*, edited by Stanley E. Porter and Cynthia Long Westfall, 208–32. Eugene, OR: Pickwick, 2010.
———. "Continuing Steps Toward a Missional Hermeneutic." *Fideles* 3 (2008) 49–99.
———. "A Critical Examination of David Bosch's Missional Reading of Luke." In *Reading Luke: Interpretation, Reflection, Formation*, edited by Craig G. Bartholomew et al., 229–64. Grand Rapids: Zondervan, 2005.
———. "A History and Introduction to a Missional Reading of the Bible." In *Reading the Bible Missionally*, edited by Michael W. Goheen, 3–27. Grand Rapids: Eerdmans, 2016.
———. *A Light to the Nations: The Missional Church and the Biblical Story*. Grand Rapids: Baker Academic, 2011.
———. "Notes Toward a Framework for a Missional Hermeneutic." *Gospel and our Culture Network*, 2006. Online. https://gocn.org/library/notes-toward-a-framework-for-a-missional-hermeneutic.
———. "The Urgency of Reading the Bible as One Story." *Theology Today* 64 (2008) 469–83.
Goheen, Michael W., and Craig Bartholomew. *Living at the Crossroads: An Introduction to Christian Worldview*. London: SPCK, 2008.
Goldingay, John. *Israel's Gospel*. Vol. 1 of *Old Testament Theology*. Milton Keynes: Paternoster, 2003.
———. *Job for Everyone*. London: SPCK, 2013.
Good, Edwin M. *In Turns of Tempest: A Reading of Job with a Translation*. Stanford: Stanford University Press, 1990.
Goppelt, Leonhard. *The Variety and Unity of the Apostolic Witness to Christ*. Translated by John Alsup. Vol. 2 of *Theology of the New Testament*. Grand Rapids: Eerdmans, 1982.
Gordis, Robert. *The Book of God and Man: A Study of Job*. Chicago: University of Chicago Press, 1965.
———. *The Book of Job: Commentary, New Translation, and Special Studies*. New York: Jewish Theological Seminary of America, 1978.
Gorman, Michael J. *Becoming the Gospel: Paul, Participation, and Mission*. Grand Rapids: Eerdmans, 2015.
Gospel and Our Culture Network (GOCN). "Forum on Missional Hermeneutics: Call for Papers, 2012 Annual Meeting (Chicago, IL)." *Society of Biblical Literature*.

Online. https://www.sbl-site.org/meetings/Congresses_CallForPaperDetails.aspx?MeetingId=21&VolunteerUnitId=491.
Gottwald, Norman K. *The Hebrew Bible: A Socio-Literary Introduction*. Philadelphia: Fortress, 1985.
Gray, John. "The Book of Job in the Context of Near Eastern Literature." *ZAW* 82.2 (1970) 251–69.
Greenberg, Moshe. *Ezekiel 1–20*. Garden City: Doubleday, 1983.
Grenzer, Matthias. "Die Armenthematik in Ijob 24." In *Das Buch Ijob: Gesamtdeutungen—Einzeltexte—Zentrale Themen*, edited by Theodor Seidl and Stephanie Ernst, 229–78. Frankfurt am Main: Peter Lang, 2007.
Guder, Darrell L. "Biblical Formation and Discipleship." In *Treasure in Clay Jars: Patterns in Missional Faithfulness*, edited by Lois Y. Barrett, 59–73. Grand Rapids: Eerdmans, 2004.
———, ed. *Missional Church: A Vision for the Sending of the Church in North America*. Grand Rapids: Eerdmans, 1998.
———. "Missional Hermeneutics: The Missional Authority of Scripture—Interpreting Scripture as Missional Formation." *Mission Focus: Annual Review* 15 (2007) 106–21.
———. "Missional Pastors in Maintenance Churches." *Catalyst: Contemporary Evangelical Perspectives for United Methodist Seminarians*, March 1, 2005. Online. http://www.catalystresources.org/missional-pastors-in-maintenance-churches.
Gutiérrez, Gustavo. *On Job: God-Talk and the Suffering of the Innocent*. Translated by Matthew J. O'Connell. Maryknoll, NY: Orbis, 1987.
Habel, Norman C. *The Book of Job*. London: SCM, 1985.
Hallo, William W., and K. Lawson Younger, eds. *The Context of Scripture*. 3 vols. Leiden: Brill, 1997–2003.
Hamilton, Mark. "Elite Lives: Job 29–31 and Traditional Authority." *JSOT* 21.1 (2007) 69–89.
Hartley, John E. *The Book of Job*. Grand Rapids: Eerdmans, 1988.
———. "Job: Theology of." In *NIDOTTE* 5:780–96.
———. "Job 2: Ancient Near Eastern Background." In *DOTWPW* 346–61.
Hedlund, Roger E. *The Mission of the Church in the World: A Biblical Theology*. Grand Rapids: Baker, 1991.
Hesselgrave, Ronald P. *I Know That My Redeemer Lives: Suffering and Redemption in the Book of Job*. Eugene, OR: Wipf & Stock, 2016.
Hoffman, Yair. *A Blemished Perfection: The Book of Job in Context*. Sheffield: Sheffield Academic, 1996.
Hoffner, H. A. "אַלְמָנָה' *almānāh*." In *TDOT* 1:287–91.
Hölscher, Gustav. *Das Buch Hiob*. Tübingen: J. C. B. Mohr, 1937.
Horton, Robert F. *The Bible, a Missionary Book*. 2nd ed. Edinburgh: Oliphant, Anderson & Ferrier, 1908.
Houston, Walter J. *Contending for Justice: Ideologies and Theologies of Social Justice in the Old Testament*. London: T & T Clark, 2006.
Hunsberger, George R. "Mapping the Missional Hermeneutics Conversation." In *Reading the Bible Missionally*, edited by Michael W. Goheen, 45–67. Grand Rapids: Eerdmans, 2016.
———. "Proposals for a Missional Hermeneutic: Mapping a Conversation." *Missiology* 39.3 (2011) 309–21.

Janzen, J. Gerald. *Job*. Louisville: John Knox, 1985.
Jenni, Ernst, and Claus Westermann, eds. *Theological Lexicon of the Old Testament*. 3 vols. Translated by Mark Biddle. Peabody: Hendrickson, 1997.
Jesurathnam, K. "A Dalit Interpretation of Wisdom Literature with Special Reference to the Underprivileged Groups in the Hebrew Society: A Mission Perspective." *Asia Journal of Theology* 25.2 (2011) 334–57.
Jones, Hywel R. *Job*. Darlington: Evangelical, 2007.
Joyce, Paul M. "'Even If Noah, Daniel, and Job Were in It . . .' (Ezekiel 14:14): The Case of Job and Ezekiel." In *Reading Job Intertextually*, edited by Katherine Dell and Will Keynes, 118–28. London: Bloomsbury T & T Clark, 2013.
Kaiser, Walter C. *Mission in the Old Testament: Israel as a Light to the Nations*. Grand Rapids: Baker, 2000.
Kane, J. Herbert. *Christian Missions in Biblical Perspective*. Grand Rapids: Baker, 1976.
Kelly, Michael B. "Biblical Theology and Missional Hermeneutics: A Match Made *for* Heaven . . . on Earth?" In *Eyes to See, Ears to Hear: Essays in Memory of J. Alan Groves*, edited by Peter Enns et al., 61–76. Phillipsburg: P & R, 2010.
Kitchen, Kenneth A. "Proverbs 2: Ancient Near Eastern Background." In *DOTWPW* 552–66.
Knauf, E. Axel. "Uz." In *ABD* 770–71.
Konkel, August H. "Job." In *Job, Ecclesiastes, Song of Songs*, by August H. Konkel and Tremper Longman, 1–249. Carol Stream: Tyndale, 2006.
Köstenberger, Andreas J., and Peter T. O'Brien, *Salvation to the Ends of the Earth: A Biblical Theology of Mission*. Downers Grove, IL: InterVarsity, 2001.
Krüger, Thomas. "Did Job Repent?" In *Das Buch Hiob und seine Interpretationen*, edited by Thomas Krüger et al., 217–29. Zürich: Theologischer, 2007.
Kynes, Will. "Job and Isaiah 40–55: Intertextualities in Dialogue." In *Reading Job Intertextually*, edited by Katherine Dell and Will Keynes, 94–105. London: Bloomsbury T & T Clark, 2013.
Lambert, Wilfred G. *Babylonian Wisdom Literature*. Oxford: Oxford University Press, 1960.
Lapham, Henry A. *The Bible as Missionary Handbook*. Cambridge: W. Heffer & Sons, 1925.
LaSor, William S. "Uz." In vol. 4 of *The International Standard Bible Encyclopedia*, edited by Geoffrey W. Bromiley, 959. 2nd ed. Grand Rapids: Eerdmans, 1988.
Lausanne Movement. "The Manila Manifesto." 1989. Online. http://www.lausanne.org/en/documents/manila-manifesto.html.
Legrand, Lucien. *Unity and Plurality: Mission in the Bible*. Translated by Robert R. Barr. Maryknoll, NY: Orbis, 1990.
Leeuwen, Cornelis van. "אַלְמָנָה." In *NIDOTTE* 1:413–15.
Leeuwen, Raymond C. van. "Wealth and Poverty: System and Contradiction in Proverbs." *Hebrew Studies* 33 (1992) 25–36.
Lo, Alison. *Job 28 As Rhetoric: An Analysis of Job 28 in the Context of Job 22–31*. Leiden: Brill, 2003.
Long, Thomas G. *What Shall We Say? Evil, Suffering, and the Crisis of Faith*. Grand Rapids: Eerdmans, 2011.
Longman, Tremper. *Job*. Grand Rapids: Baker Academic, 2012.
———. "Job 4: Person." In *DOTWPW* 371–74.

Longman, Tremper, and Peter Enns, eds. *Dictionary of the Old Testament: Wisdom, Poetry & Writings*. Nottingham: InterVarsity, 2008.
Loughlin, Gerard. *Telling God's Story: Bible, Church, and Narrative Theology*. Cambridge: Cambridge University Press, 1996.
Macintosh, A. A. *Hosea*. Edinburgh: T & T Clark, 1997.
Malchow, Bruce V. *Social Justice in the Hebrew Bible*. Collegeville: Liturgical, 1996.
Marshall, I. Howard, *New Testament Theology: Many Witnesses, One Gospel*. Nottingham: Apollos, 2004.
Martin-Achard, Robert. *A Light to the Nations: A Study of the Old Testament Conception of Israel's Mission to the World*. Translated by John P. Smith. Edinburgh: Oliver and Boyd, 1962.
———. "ענה 'nh to be destitute." In *TLOT* 2:931–37.
Matthey, Jacques. "Serving God's Mission Together in Christ's Way: Reflections on the Way to Edinburgh 2010." *IRM* 99.1 (2010) 21–38.
McConville, J. Gordon. *God and Earthly Power: An Old Testament Political Theology*. London: T & T Clark, 2006.
McKane, William. *Jeremiah I–XXV*. Edinburgh: T & T Clark, 1986.
Merrill, Eugene H. "נחה." In *NIDOTTE* 3:76.
Micah Network. "The *Micah Declaration* on Integral Mission." In *Justice, Mercy and Humility: The Papers of the Micah Network International Consultation on Integral Mission and the Poor (2001)*, edited by Tim Chester, 17–23. Carlisle: Paternoster, 2002.
Míguez-Bonino, José. "Poverty as Curse, Blessing and Challenge." *Iliff Review* 34.3 (1977) 3–13.
Mitchell, Stephen. *The Book of Job*. Rev. ed. New York: Harper Perennial, 1992.
Moberly, R. Walter L. *The Bible, Theology, and Faith: A Study of Abraham and Jesus*. Cambridge: Cambridge University Press, 2000.
———. "Solomon and Job: Divine Wisdom in Human Life." In *Where Shall Wisdom Be Found?*, edited by Stephen C. Barton, 3–17. Edinburgh: T & T Clark, 1999.
Montgomery, Helen B. *The Bible and Missions*. West Medford: Central Committee on the United Study of Foreign Missions, 1920.
Moran, William L. "The Babylonian Job." In *The Most Magic Word: Essays on Babylonian and Biblical Literature*, edited by Ronald S. Hendel, 182–200. Washington, DC: Catholic Biblical Association of America, 1992.
Murphy, Roland E. *Wisdom Literature: Job, Proverbs, Ruth, Canticles, Ecclesiastes, and Esther*. Grand Rapids: Eerdmans, 1981.
Myers, Bryant L. *Walking With the Poor: Principles and Practices of Transformational Development*. Maryknoll, NY: Orbis, 1999.
Nel, Philip J. "שלם." In *NIDOTTE* 4:130–35.
Newbigin, Lesslie. *Truth to Tell: The Gospel as Public Truth*. London: SPCK, 1991.
Newsom, Carol A. *The Book of Job: A Contest of Moral Imaginations*. Oxford: Oxford University Press, 2003.
———. "Job." In *The First Book of Maccabees, the Second Book of Maccabees, Introduction to Hebrew Poetry, the Book of Job, the Book of Psalms*, edited by Leander E. Keck, 317–637. Vol. 4 of *The New Interpreter's Bible*. Nashville: Abingdon, 1996.
———. "Re-considering Job." *Currents in Biblical Research* 5.2 (2007) 155–82.
O'Collins, Gerald. *Salvation for All: God's Other Peoples*. Oxford: Oxford University Press, 2008.

Okoye, James C. *Israel and the Nations: A Mission Theology of the Old Testament*. Maryknoll, NY: Orbis, 2006.
Opperwall-Galluch, N. J., and William S. LaSor. "Uz." In vol. 4 of *The International Standard Bible Encyclopedia*, edited by Geoffrey W. Bromiley, 959. 2nd ed. Grand Rapids: Eerdmans, 1988.
Pachuau, Lalsangkima. "*Missio Dei.*" In *DMT* 232–34.
Padilla, C. René. "Holistic Mission." In *DMT* 157–62.
Peake, Arthur S. *Job*. Rev. ed. Edinburgh: T. C. & E. C. Jack, 1905.
Penchansky, David. *The Betrayal of God: Ideological Conflict in Job*. Louisville: Westminster John Knox, 1990.
Penner, Peter F. *Missionale Hermeneutik: Biblische Texte Kontextuell und Relevant Lesen*. Schwarzenfeld: Neufeld Verlag, 2012.
Perdue, Leo G. *Wisdom in Revolt: Metaphorical Theology in the Book of Job*. Sheffield: Almond, 1991.
———. *Wisdom Literature: A Theological History*. Louisville: Westminster John Knox, 2007.
Perlstein, David. *God's Others: Non-Israelites' Encounters With God in the Hebrew Bible*. Bloomington: iUniverse, 2010.
Perriman, Andrew. *Re: Mission: Biblical Mission for a Post-biblical Church*. Milton Keynes: Authentic Media, 2007.
Peskett, Howard, and Vinoth Ramachandra. *The Message of Mission: The Glory of Christ in All Time and Space*. Leicester: InterVarsity, 2003.
Peters, George W. *A Biblical Theology of Missions*. Chicago: Moody, 1972.
Pinker, Aron. "The Core Story in the Prologue-Epilogue of the Book of Job." *Journal of Hebrew Scriptures* 6 (2006) 1–27.
Pinnock, Clark H. *A Wideness in God's Mercy: The Finality of Jesus Christ in a World of Religions*. Grand Rapids: Zondervan, 1992.
Piper, John. *Let the Nations be Glad! The Supremacy of God in Missions*. 2nd ed. Leicester: InterVarsity, 1993.
Pleins, J. David. "Poor, Poverty (Old Testament)." In *ABD* 5:402–14.
———. "Poverty in the Social World of the Wise." *JSOT* 37 (1987) 61–78.
———. *The Social Visions of the Hebrew Bible*. Louisville: Westminster John Knox, 2001.
Plummer, Robert L., and John Mark Terry, eds. *Paul's Missionary Methods: In His Time and Ours*. Nottingham: InterVarsity, 2012.
Pope, Marvin H. *Job: Introduction, Translation, and Notes*. Garden City: New York, 1965.
Preuss, Horst D. *Old Testament Theology*. Vol. 2. Translated by Leo G. Perdue. Louisville: Westminster John Knox, 1996.
Pritchard, James B., ed. *Ancient Near Eastern Texts Relating to the Old Testament*. 3rd ed. Princeton: Princeton University Press, 1969.
Reitman, James. *Unlocking Wisdom: Forming Agents of God in the House of Mourning*. Springfield: Twenty-First Century, 2008.
Rétif, André, and Paul Lamarche. *The Salvation of the Gentiles and the Prophets*. Baltimore: Helicon, 1966.
Ringgren, Helmer. "יָתוֹם *yāṯôm*." In *TDOT* 6:477–81.
Rogers, Cleon L. "קָדִים." In *NIDOTTE* 3:871–73.
Ross, Cathy. "Lament and Hope." *Anvil* 34.1 (2019) 21–26.

Rowe, Ignacio M. "Scribes, Sages, and Seers in Ugarit." In *Scribes, Sages, and Seers: The Sage in the Eastern Mediterranean World*, edited by Leo G. Perdue, 96–108. Göttingen: Vandenhoeck & Ruprecht, 2008.

Rowley, Harold H. *Job*. London: Thomas Nelson and Sons, 1970.

———. *The Missionary Message of the Old Testament*. London: Carey, 1945.

Ruiter, Bert de. *A Single Hand Cannot Applaud: The Value of Using the Book of Proverbs in Sharing the Gospel with Muslims*. Nurnberg: VTR, 2011.

Ruíz Pesce, Ramón E. "Dios del Pobre: Amor Gratuito y Sufrimiento del Inocente— Leer el Libro de Job desde San Juan de la Cruz a Gustavo Gutiérrez." *Studium: filosofía y tealogía* 5 (2002) 207–20.

Russell, Brian D. *(re)Aligning with God: Reading Scripture for Church and World*. Eugene, OR: Cascade, 2016.

———. "What is a Missional Hermeneutic?" *Catalyst: Contemporary Evangelical Perspectives for United Methodist Seminarians*, April 1, 2010. Online. http://www.catalystresources.org/what-is-a-missional-hermeneutic.

Saayman, Willem, and Klippies Kritzinger, eds. *Mission in Bold Humility: David Bosch's Work Considered*. Maryknoll, NY: Orbis, 1996.

Salter, Martin C. *Mission in Action: A Biblical Description of Missional Ethics*. London: Apollos, 2019.

Sanders, James A. *Canon and Community: A Guide to Canonical Criticism*. Philadelphia: Fortress, 1984.

Sandoval, Timothy J. *The Discourse of Wealth and Poverty in the Book of Proverbs*. Leiden: Brill, 2006.

Sanneh, Lamin O. *Whose Religion is Christianity?: The Gospel Beyond the West*. Grand Rapids: Eerdmans, 2003.

Sarna, Nahum M. "Epic Substratum in the Prose of Job." *JBL* 76 (1957) 13–25.

Schertz, Mary. "Response." *Mission Focus: Annual Review* 15 (2007) 122–24.

Schnabel, Eckhard J. *Jesus and the Twelve*. Vol. 1 of *Early Christian Mission*. Leicester: Apollos, 2004.

Schultz, Richard L. "Nationalism and Universalism in Isaiah." In *Interpreting Isaiah: Issues and Approaches*, edited by David G. Firth and Hugh G. M. Williamson, 122–44. Nottingham: Apollos, 2009.

———. "'Und sie verkünden meine Herrlichkeit unter den Nationen' Mission im Alten Testament unter besonderer Berücksichtigung von Jesaja." In *Werdet meine Zeugen! Weltmission im Horizont von Theologie und Geschichte*, edited by Hans Kasdorf and Friedemann Walldorf, 33–53. Neuhausen-Stuttgart: Hänssler, 1996.

Scriptural Reasoning. "FAQs." Online. http://www.scripturalreasoning.org/faqs.html.

Sedlmeier, Franz. "Ijob und die Auseinandersetzungsliteratur im alten Mesopotamien." In *Das Buch Ijob: Gesamtdeutungen—Einzeltexte—Zentrale Themen*, edited by Theodor Seidl and Stephanie Ernst, 85–136. Frankfurt am Main: Peter Lang, 2007.

Segal, Alan F. *Life After Death: A History of the Afterlife in Western Religion*. New York: Doubleday, 2004.

Seitz, Christopher R. *Figured Out: Typology and Providence in Christian Scripture*. Louisville: Westminster John Knox, 2001.

Selms, Adrianus van. *Job: A Practical Commentary*. Translated by John Vriend. Grand Rapids: Eerdmans, 1985.

Senior, Donald, and Carroll Stuhlmueller. *The Biblical Foundations for Mission*. London: SCM, 1983.

Seow, Choon L. *Job 1–21: Interpretation and Commentary*. Grand Rapids: Eerdmans, 2013.

Skreslet, Stanley H. *Comprehending Mission: The Questions, Methods, Themes, and Prospects of Missiology*. Maryknoll, NY: Orbis, 2012.

Sparks, Kenton L. *Ancient Texts for the Study of the Hebrew Bible: A Guide to the Background Literature*. Peabody: Hendrickson, 2005.

Stott, John R. W. *Christian Mission in the Modern World*. 2nd ed. Downers Grove, IL: InterVarsity, 2008.

Strahan, James. *The Book of Job Interpreted*. Edinburgh: T & T Clark, 1914.

Strange, Daniel. *The Possibility of Salvation among the Unevangelized: An Analysis of Inclusivism in Recent Evangelical Theology*. Carlisle: Paternoster, 2002.

Stroope, Michael W. *Transcending Mission: The Eclipse of a Modern Tradition*. London: Apollos, 2017.

Sugden, Chris. "Mission as Transformation—Its Journey among Evangelicals since Lausanne I." In *Holistic Mission: God's Plan for God's People*, edited by Brian Woolnough and Wonsuk Ma, 31–36. Oxford: Regnum, 2010.

———. "What is Good about Good News to the Poor?" In *Mission as Transformation: A Theology of the Whole Gospel*, edited by Vinay Samuel and Chris Sugden, 236–60. Oxford: Regnum, 1999.

Sunquist, Scott W. *Understanding Christian Mission: Participating in God's Mission*. Grand Rapids: Baker Academic, 2013.

Susaimanickam, Jebamalai. "An Indian Problem of Evil: The Caste System: A Dalit Reading of the Book of Job." In *Indian Interpretation of the Bible: Festschrift in Honor of Prof. Dr. Joseph Pathrapankal, CMI*, edited by Augustine Thottakara, 181–200. Bangalore: Dharmaram, 2000.

Taber, Charles R. "Missiology and the Bible." *Missiology* 11.2 (1983) 229–45.

Taylor, William, et al. *Sorrow and Blood: Christian Mission in Contexts of Suffering, Persecution, and Martyrdom*. Pasadena: William Carey, 2012.

Thampu, Valson. *Rediscovering Mission: Towards a Non-Western Missiological Paradigm*. New Delhi: TRACI, 1995.

Tiessen, Terrance L. *Who Can Be Saved? Reassessing Salvation in Christ and World Religions*. Leicester: InterVarsity, 2004.

Ticciati, Susannah. "Does Job Fear God for Naught?" *Modern Theology* 21.3 (2005) 353–66.

———. *Job and the Disruption of Identity: Reading Beyond Barth*. London: T & T Clark, 2005.

———, ed. "The Wisdom of Job." Special issue, *The Journal of Scriptural Reasoning* 4.1 (2004).

Tizon, Al. *Transformation After Lausanne: Radical Evangelical Mission in Global-Local Perspective*. Oxford: Regnum, 2008.

Toorn, Karel van der. "Theodicy in Akkadian Literature." In *Theodicy in the World of the Bible*, edited by Antii Laato and Johannes C. de Moor, 57–89. Leiden: Brill, 2003.

Tur-Sinai, Naphtali H. *The Book of Job: A New Commentary*. 2nd ed. Jerusalem: Kiryat-Sefer, 1967.

Van Zyl, Danie C. "Missiological Dimensions in the Book of Job." *IRM* 91.360 (2002) 24–30.

VanGemeren, Willem A., ed. *New International Dictionary of Old Testament Theology and Exegesis*. 5 vols. Carlisle: Paternoster, 1996.

Verkuyl, Johannes. "The Biblical Notion of Kingdom: Test of Validity for Theology of Religion." In *The Good News of the Kingdom: Mission Theology for the Third Millenium*, edited by Charles van Engen et al., 71–95. Maryknoll, NY: Orbis, 1993.

———. *Contemporary Missiology: An Introduction*. Translated by Dale Cooper. Grand Rapids: Eerdmans, 1978.

Vialle, Catherine, et al. *Sagesse Biblique et Mission*. Paris: Les Édition du Cerf, 2016.

Vicchio, Stephen J. *Job in the Ancient World*. Eugene, OR: Wipf & Stock, 2006.

Vicedom, Georg F. *The Mission of God: An Introduction to a Theology of Mission*. Translated by Gilbert A. Thiele and Dennis Hilgendorf. Saint Louis: Concordia, 1965.

Walls, Andrew. *The Missionary Movement in Christian History: Studies in the Transmission of Faith*. Maryknoll, NY: Orbis, 1996.

Walton, John H. *Genesis*. Grand Rapids: Zondervan, 2001.

———. *Job*. Grand Rapids: Zondervan, 2012.

———. "Job 1: Book of." In *DOTWPW* 333–46.

Washington, Harold C. *Wealth and Poverty in the Instruction of Amenemope and the Hebrew Proverbs*. Atlanta: Scholars, 1996.

Waters, Larry J. "*Missio Dei* in the Book of Job." *Bibliotheca Sacra*, 166 (2009) 19–34.

Weinfeld, Moshe. "Job and its Mesopotamian Parallels—A Typological Analysis." In *Text and Context: Old Testament and Semitic Studies for F. C. Fensham*, edited by Walter Claassen, 217–26. Sheffield: JSOT, 1988.

———. *Social Justice in Ancient Israel and in the Ancient Near East*. Minneapolis: Fortress, 1995.

Weiss, Meir. *The Story of Job's Beginning*. Jerusalem: Magness, 1983.

Wenham, Gordon J. *Genesis 1–15*. Waco: Word, 1987.

Whybray, R. Norman. *Job*. Sheffield: Sheffield Academic, 1998.

———. *Wealth and Poverty in the Book of Proverbs*. Sheffield: JSOT, 1990.

Widbin, R. Bryan. "Salvation for People Outside Israel's Covenant?" In *Through No Fault of their Own? The Fate of Those Who Have Never Heard*, edited by William V. Crockett and James G. Sigountos, 73–83. Grand Rapids: Baker, 1991.

Wilson, Gerald H. *Job*. Milton Keynes: Paternoster, 2007.

Wilson, Lindsay. *Job*. Grand Rapids: Eerdmans, 2015.

———. "Job as Problematic Book." In *Exploring Old Testament Wisdom: Literature and Themes*, edited by David G. Firth and Lindsay Wilson. London: Apollos, 2016. Kindle.

Wittenberg, G. H. "The Lexical Context of the Terminology for 'Poor' in the Book of Proverbs." *Scriptura* 2 (1986) 40–85.

Wolde, Ellen van. *Mr and Mrs Job*. London: SCM, 1997.

Wolterstorff, Nicholas. *Lament for a Son*. Grand Rapids: Eerdmans, 1987.

Woolnough, Brian. "Good News for the Poor—Setting the Scene." In *Holistic Mission: God's Plan for God's People*, edited by Brian Woolnough and Wonsuk Ma, 3–14. Oxford: Regnum, 2010.

Wright, Christopher J. H. "'According to the Scriptures': The Whole Gospel in Biblical Revelation." *ERT* 33.1 (2009) 4–18.

———, ed. *The Cape Town Commitment: A Confession of Faith and a Call to Action (Didasko Files)*. Peabody, MA: Hendrickson, 2011.

———. "Mission and Old Testament Interpretation." In *Hearing the Old Testament: Listening for God's Address*, edited by Craig G. Bartholomew and David J. H. Beldman, 180–203. Grand Rapids: Eerdmans, 2012.

———. *The Mission of God: Unlocking the Bible's Grand Narrative*. Nottingham: InterVarsity, 2006.

———. "The Old Testament and Christian Mission." *Evangel* 14.2 (1996) 37–43.

———. *Old Testament Ethics for the People of God*. Leicester: InterVarsity, 2004.

———. "Old Testament Theology of Mission." In *Evangelical Dictionary of World Missions*, edited by A. Scott Moreau, 706–9. Grand Rapids: Baker, 2000.

———. "'Prophet to the Nations': Missional Reflections on the Book of Jeremiah." In *God of Faithfulness: Essays in Honor of J. Gordon McConville on his 60th Birthday*, edited by Jamie A. Grant et al., 112–29. London: T & T Clark, 2011.

———. *Salvation Belongs to Our God: Celebrating the Bible's Central Story*. Nottingham: InterVarsity, 2008.

———. *Thinking Clearly about the Uniqueness of Jesus*. Crowborough: Monarch, 1997.

Wright, G. Ernest. "The Old Testament Basis for the Christian Mission." In *The Theology of the Christian Mission*, edited by Gerald H. Anderson, 17–30. London: SCM, 1961.

Wright, N. T. *The New Testament and the People of God*. London: SPCK, 1992.

———. *Scripture and the Authority of God*. London: SPCK, 2005.

Yancey, Philip. *The Bible Jesus Read*. Grand Rapids: Zondervan, 1999.

Yong, Amos. *Mission After Pentecost: The Witness of the Spirit from Genesis to Revelation*. Grand Rapids: Baker Academic, 2019.

www.ingramcontent.com/pod-product-compliance
Lightning Source LLC
Chambersburg PA
CBHW050439240426
43661CB00055B/2442